THE EXPANSION OF CHRISTIANITY

CHRISTIANITY AND THE CELTS

THE EXPANSION OF CHRISTIANITY

Timothy Yates

CHRISTIANITY AND THE CELTS

Ted Olsen

LION
SCHOLAR

Published by
Lion Hudson Limited
Wilkinson House, Jordan Hill Business Park
Banbury Road, Oxford OX2 8DR, England
www.lionhudson.com

ISBN 978 1 9125 5222 1

e-ISBN 978 1 9125 5223 8

'The Expansion of Christianity': first paperback edition 2004
'Christianity and the Celts': first paperback edition 2003

Acknowledgments

See p. 269 for text acknowledgements.

All maps and diagrams copyright Lion Hudson IP Limited

Cover image: © PetarPaunchev / istockphoto.com

A catalogue record for this book is available from the British Library

CONTENTS

PART 1

THE EXPANSION
OF CHRISTIANITY

INTRODUCTION

This account attempts to describe how Christianity expanded across
the world. It does not claim to be a complete history of the church
from AD 1 to AD 2000. It concentrates on pioneers, Peter and Paul in
the 1st century, Columba and Aidan in the Celtic period, and on great
missionary figures such as Willibrord and Boniface, Francis Xavier and
Robert de Nobili, John Eliot and David Brainerd, William Carey, Robert
Moffatt and David Livingstone, Mary Slessor and Florence Young to
name a selection. The approach taken is geographical, chapters after the
first dealing with continents; and chronological, so that some sense of
development in each area of the world is presented in a time sequence.

One of the many deficiencies of such a treatment is that, with the
concentration on expansion, those considerable reverses experienced
by the Christian world, most particularly from Islam in the 7th and
8th centuries, have received little coverage. Something that should not
be forgotten is that Christian expansion has not been a continual success
story. The great historian of Christian expansion, Kenneth Latourette,
put forward the so-called wave theory, by which, despite retreat in
periods of its history, to his eye each wave of Christianity reached further
than the last.

Certainly in the 20th century Christianity became worldwide in the
sense that churches were planted in every major ethnic group in the
world, leading one archbishop of Canterbury, William Temple, in
the 1940s to call this 'the great new fact of our time'. According to the
figures in the *World Christian Encyclopedia*, the statistician David Barrett
estimates that there are now some 2,000 million Christians in the world,
some 33 per cent of the whole world population. Whereas decline has
been experienced in Europe, there has been remarkable growth in the
continent of Africa in the 20th century, from some 10 million in 1900 to
over 200 million in 2000.

For centuries Christianity was quite as much an Asian religion as it
was European. The existence of churches in Egypt and in Ethiopia from
the earliest times until today is a reminder also that Christianity retained

a foothold in Africa even after the collapse of the North African church of Tertullian, Cyprian and Augustine before the assaults of tribes from Europe and the forces of Islam. For our age it is important to describe the roots of Asian and African Christianity in the early centuries before the age of the explorers led to the expansion of Europeanized Christianity after 1500.

CHAPTER 1
THE MEDITERRANEAN WORLD

Christianity begins with Jesus of Nazareth. In regard to expansion, the Gospels suggest that Jesus himself put strict limits on his own mission. To a non-Jewish woman, he said, 'I was sent only to the lost sheep of the house of Israel' (Matthew 15:24). There are signs, however, that he envisaged wider effects from his mission. For example, in response to the faith of a Roman soldier he was prompted to say, 'people will come from east and west, from north and south, and will eat in the kingdom of God', while Jews may not. This suggests that non-Jews, Romans and others would become members of God's 'kingdom', even to the exclusion of the chosen race of the Old Testament.

Nevertheless, it was not until after the crucifixion and the preaching of the resurrection that Christianity began to grow beyond Jesus' personal following of the 12 apostles, the 72 disciples of his mission and the rest of the movement's adherents of his lifetime. His execution fell in the time of Pontius Pilate's governorship, whom we know from extra-biblical sources to have been governor of Judea during AD 26–36. We do not know the precise date of the crucifixion but AD 30 or 33 have been advanced as likely. Figures such as Jesus' forerunner, John the Baptist, and Pilate himself appear in non-biblical histories like those of Josephus (AD c. 37–c. 100) or Tacitus (AD c. 55–c. 113).

For the expansion of the church in its early years we are, however, heavily dependent on Luke, who wrote two volumes, possibly aimed at a representative Roman enquirer given the name of Theophilus (God-beloved), known to us as the Gospel of Luke and the Acts of the Apostles. The second volume took the story of the Christian movement from the mid-30s to the mid-60s of the 1st century, a crucial period of its development.

Whatever subsequent generations have accepted or rejected, the early Christians believed that the crucified Jesus had been raised from death by an act of God. Luke gives us sample speeches, rather in the manner of the great Greek historian, Thucydides, which seek to convey the basic Christian message as he believed it to have been presented. Peter,

Two early historians

John surnamed the Baptist . . . was a good man and exhorted the Jews to lead righteous lives, to practise justice towards their fellows and piety towards God and so doing to join in baptism . . . a consecration of the body implying that the soul was cleansed by right behaviour.

Josephus, *Antiquities,* **18.117–118**

Nero fastened the guilt [for the fire of Rome] and inflicted the most exquisite tortures on a class hated for their abominations, called Christians by the populace. Christus, from whom the name had its origin, suffered the extreme penalty during the reign of Tiberius at the hands of one of our procurators, Pontius Pilate, and a deadly superstition, thus choked for a moment, again broke out not only in Judea, the first source of the evil but also in the City.

Tacitus, *Annals,* **XV.44.2–8**

leader of the apostolic band, in the first account we have of a Christian sermon given to an audience of Jews, emphasized that God had raised the crucified Jesus: 'This Jesus God raised up, and of that all of us are witnesses.' Jesus was the Messiah of Jewish expectation: 'God has made him both Lord and Messiah, this Jesus whom you crucified' (Acts 2:36). Offensive as this message must have been to devout Jews, assembled in Jerusalem to celebrate the Jewish festival of Pentecost, in Luke's account 3,000 people became Christians on that day and were baptized. The emphasis on the resurrection was to remain central as the movement spread, so that it featured equally in addressing a sophisticated audience of Greeks in Athens. The early preachers saw themselves as 'witnesses', people who had firsthand evidence of an act of God and, in Peter's case, experience of eating and drinking with the risen Jesus (Acts 10:41).

Luke's programme

For some time in the 30s Christianity remained a sub-sect of Judaism. Luke recorded that a number of Jewish priests joined the movement. Nevertheless, in Luke's own understanding there was to be a programme of expansion. The risen Christ had told his followers that their witness to him was to extend from Jerusalem to wider Judea and Samaria and to the ends of the earth (Acts 1:8). By far the largest leap for the young movement was from Jew to non-Jew or Gentile. Luke showed the intermediate step to the Samaritans, regarded as heretics by orthodox Jews; and to a Jewish proselyte (convert) and Ethiopian African, who was a fringe adherent of Judaism (Acts 8). The main emphasis in Acts was to be on the Gentile mission. Luke himself was a Gentile, probably a Syrian. He developed his theme by way of the conversion of Saul of Tarsus, who became Paul, the apostle to the Gentiles, a story told three times in the book as a form of emphasis (Acts 9; 22; 26); and also through the story of Peter and Cornelius, a Roman soldier and centurion, told twice (Acts 10; 11). In this story Luke provided a beginning for Gentiles that was equivalent to what the day of Pentecost had been for Jews – Gentiles too experienced the Holy Spirit as a result of Peter's preaching about Jesus and joined the church by baptism.

'[Luke] first saw that the new Israel like the old was destined to have its history and recognized that sacred history must be related to the history of the world. The life of the church is not to be a frenzied proclamation . . . but a steady programme of expansion throughout the world.'

Stephen Neill, *A History of Christian Missions*

If the early part of Acts can be called the acts of Peter, the later chapters are the acts of Paul. Paul's dramatic conversion has been dated as early as AD 34. The story itself reveals that there were already Christians in Syria and Damascus.

There was also a strong enough church in Antioch in Syria for Christians there to be called by that name for the first time (up to then they may have been called only those of 'the Way', as a sub-sect of Judaism [Acts 24:14]). Saul himself, as a former persecutor of Christians, faced the danger that he would still be regarded as an agent provocateur. It took the generosity of spirit of Barnabas, whom Luke tells us was a Jewish Cypriot, to recruit him as a Christian teacher for the growing church. It was from Antioch that

'I was travelling to Damascus with the authority and commission of the chief priests, when at midday along the road . . . I saw a light from heaven, brighter than the sun, shining around me and my companions. When we had all fallen to the ground, I heard a voice saying to me in the Hebrew language, "Saul, Saul, why are you persecuting me? It hurts you to kick against the goads." I asked, "Who are you, Lord?" The Lord answered, "I am Jesus whom you are persecuting."'

Paul before King Agrippa, Acts 26:12–15

what could be called the first 'overseas' mission took place, when Saul and Barnabas were sent by the local church to Cyprus and conducted a preaching tour across the island from Salamis to Paphos.

Paul the missionary

Gradually, Saul, by now 'Paul', replaced Barnabas as the missionary leader: 'Barnabas and Saul' became 'Paul and Barnabas'. Paul appeared to have a definite strategy as he moved around the Mediterranean world. Many upright Gentiles, represented in Luke's writings by the Ethiopian treasurer and the Roman centurion Cornelius, were attracted by the high moral standards and teaching of the Jewish synagogues and religion. This Gentile fringe, already instructed in the Jewish scriptures of the Old Testament, provided Paul with a natural platform for the Christian gospel. Paul would visit the synagogues of the Jewish dispersion as a first point of entry, as at the other Antioch in Pisidia in modern Turkey and nearby Iconium. Luke showed that this resulted ultimately in hostility from the Jewish communities but also that, as at Iconium, 'a great number of both Jews and Greeks' became Christians.

Through the 40s and 50s, Paul spent much time as an itinerant Christian preacher, teacher and leader. An important point of departure was his decision, which Luke attributes to the Holy Spirit and a dream or vision of a Greek man from Macedonia, to cross over to mainland Europe rather than pursue his mission to northern Turkey. In Greece he went from Philippi, the town named after Alexander the Great's father, to Thessalonica and then to Athens and Corinth. We know from his first letter to the Thessalonian Christians (which vies with Galatians as his earliest letter), written probably in AD 49, that his preaching to these Greeks called on them to give up the worship of idols in order to serve instead 'the living and true God' and his Son Jesus 'whom he raised from the dead' (1 Thessalonians 1:9–10). Christianity challenged the polytheism of the ancient world, whether Zeus (Jupiter) and Hermes (Mercury) at Lystra or the goddess Artemis (Diana) at Ephesus.

In Corinth Paul appeared before the Roman proconsul, Gallio, which enables us to date his visit through the evidence of an inscription to AD 51. His work in the Mediterranean world, which included lengthy spells in Corinth of 18 months and in Ephesus of two years, ended with imprisonment in Caesarea and an appeal to Rome, the result both of Jewish hostility and his preference for Roman justice.

By then, however, the emperor was Nero, who was to blame the fire of Rome on Christians in AD 64. By tradition, both Peter and Paul were executed in Rome in the 60s although Acts leaves Paul under house arrest in Rome over a two-year period, apparently free to receive visitors and 'teaching about the Lord Jesus with all boldness and without hindrance' (Acts 28:31). His own letter to the Roman Christians, written in the mid-50s, had given evidence of the size of the Roman church by that time and set out his most comprehensive version of Christianity, as also his hope (probably unrealized) of visiting Spain to preach the gospel as the culminating point of his Mediterranean mission (Romans 15:23).

Rome and persecution

Between Luke's account, which effectively takes the spread of Christianity from Jerusalem to Rome in 30 years, and the writings of the Christian historian Eusebius of Caesarea, friend and admirer of the emperor Constantine, there is a period of over 200 years (AD 60–300) with little formal writing of history but considerable development. Persecution and martyrdom became increasingly a sign of the strength of Christianity as a movement, which aroused the fears of the authorities of the Roman empire. The letters of the early bishop of Antioch, Ignatius (c. 35–c. 107), on his way to martyrdom in Rome, have survived. They show that like many Christians of the early period he appeared to welcome his destiny.

The aged bishop of Smyrna (today's Izmir), Polycarp, who had heard the apostle John preach in his youth, was invited to abjure Christ to save his life. He replied, 'Eighty-six years have I served him and he has never done me wrong: how can I blaspheme my King and Saviour?' He was burned to death, probably in AD 155. A correspondence between the governor of Pontus in Asia Minor, Pliny the younger, and the emperor Trajan,

'May I have joy of the beasts that are prepared for me . . . I will even entice them to devour me promptly . . . now I am beginning to be a disciple. May nothing of things visible or invisible seek to allure me, that I may attain to Jesus Christ.'

Ignatius, *Letter to the Romans*, V

Pliny and Trajan in correspondence

It is my custom, lord emperor, to refer to you all questions where I am in doubt . . . this is the course I have taken with those who are accused before me as Christians. I asked them whether they were Christians and if they confess I asked them a second and third time with threats of punishment. If they kept to it, I ordered them for execution; for I held no question that whatever it was they admitted in any case obstinacy and unbending perversity deserved to be punished.

Pliny to Trajan

You have adopted the proper course, my dear Secundus, in your examination of the cases of those who are accused to you as Christians, for indeed nothing can be laid down as a general ruling . . . they are not to be sought out: but if they are accused and convicted, they must be punished – yet on this condition, that whoever declares himself to be a Christian . . . shall obtain pardon on his repentance however suspicious his past conduct may be.

Trajan to Pliny c. AD 112

written around AD 112, has survived, showing some attempt at leniency but also willingness to execute any intransigent Christians.

Emperors after Trajan, such as Decius (emperor 249–51) and Diocletian (emperor 284–305), instituted severe persecutions. There were sufficient Christians in North Africa for memorable martyrdoms to take place in Carthage of a young married woman called Perpetua and her slave girl Felicity, who were thrown to wild beasts after trial. It was also in North Africa that great problems were to be raised for church leaders by those who sought certificates (*libelli*) from the Roman authorities in time of persecution and then wished to reunite with the church. Cyprian, a great bishop of Carthage, grappled with this problem between 248 and 258. It was the North African, Tertullian (c. 160–c. 225), with his arresting style, who wrote that 'the blood of Christians is seed', often misquoted as 'the blood of the martyrs is the seed of the church'.

As well as North African Carthage, Egypt had become an important centre of Christianity. Alexandria, one of the great cities and centres of civilization in the ancient world, became also a centre of Christian learning. Three leading theologians and apologists (advocates) for the faith were connected with the school of theology there: Pantaenus, who died around 190 and who will appear in the next chapter as an early missionary to Asia, Clement of Alexandria (c. 150–215), and one of the great speculative minds of Christian history, Origen (c. 185–254). The ancient Egyptian church, the Coptic church, has existed until today, and it was Egypt that provided the seeds of monasticism, a movement of great importance for the church of the future, through pioneering ascetic saints such as Antony (c. 251–356) and Pachomios (c. 290–346). The latter emphasized community for monks. Egypt also produced one of the most influential Christians of all time in Athanasius (c. 296–373), bishop of Alexandria from 328, to whom we shall return.

Christian writings

The spread of Christianity also involved Christian writings. Paul's letters, written between AD 45 and AD 65, were addressed to Christian communities for the most part and to their problems of belief and behaviour. The Gospels, however, were aimed at persuading the unconvinced also. It is thought that Mark's was the first Gospel, probably dating AD 64, and by AD 100 the others were in circulation. As a form of literature they were unlike any other in the ancient world. They were not biographies or 'lives of Jesus', nor philosophical writings, nor histories. Perhaps the best description of them can be found in John: 'these are written so that you may come to believe that Jesus is the Christ, the Son of God, and that through believing you may have life in his name' (John 20:31). In our terms they might be thought of as extended tracts, inviting belief in Christ as the life-giver. Luke expressed his purpose to his unknown enquirer, Theophilus, as 'to write an orderly account for you, most excellent Theophilus, so that you may know the truth concerning the things about which you have been instructed' (Luke 1:3–4).

> 'Those who lived with reason, even though they were thought atheists, are Christians, as amongst the Greeks, Socrates and Heraclitus and men like them.'
>
> **Justin, *Apology*, I.46**

Christian literature did not, however, end with the epistles (letters) and Gospels, though with the formation of what became known as the canon (or list) of scriptural books they had a special status and recognition by the church from around 350. Apart from the earliest apostolic circle of writers, others set about advocating, defending and propagating Christianity. Justin (c. 100–c. 165), a teacher and philosopher who was born in Samaria, wrote his first and second *Apology* (c. 155; c. 161), and also his *Dialogue with Trypho*, which aimed at convincing Jews. He was martyred in Rome around 165.

Of the other 2nd-century 'apologists' as they were called, the best known to subsequent generations was the North African, Tertullian (c. 160–c. 225), already mentioned, a brilliant polemical writer from Carthage. Third-century Alexandria produced a sustained attempt to bring together Christianity and Hellenistic (Greek-based) civilization, and two successive thinkers at the head of the Alexandrian school of theology, Clement of Alexandria and Origen, already mentioned above, sought to answer the arguments of the pagan philosophers such as Celsus. Origen's reply, *Contra Celsum*, was written around 250.

In answering the question as to how Christianity made such headway against an all-powerful state like the Roman empire, so that the tide turned in the early years of the 4th century, the great German historian of the church, Adolf von Harnack, listed a number of cumulative causes of significance: the care of the sick, of widows; the Christians' attitude to death, whether through burial clubs or the respect they showed through their belief in resurrection both in general and when faced with martyrdom in the arena; their provision of support networks for the poor, the disadvantaged, even slaves all made an impact on a society where such things were rare and unusual. He quoted Tertullian's epigram, so often turned cynically on Christians since but highly significant when first used: 'See how these Christians love one another', indicating the social nature of the faith. The churches provided a kind of informal employment bureau for the needy, as well as being sources of hospitality.

The ferocity of the persecution by emperors such as Decius and Diocletian gave evidence of the church as a strong alternative social association, which seemed to the emperors to be undermining the unity of the empire. Unlike the Jews, the Christians did not earn the right to be regarded as a *religio licita* (permitted religion); but they had a recognized social presence in the empire, to which even the graffiti in Rome of a crucified ass and its worshipper 'Alexamenos' who 'adores God' bore witness. Tertullian was still meeting this 2nd-century caricature in his *Apology*: 'You imagine the head of an ass to be our God.'

Roman approval

Constantine (c. 280–337), declared emperor in York in 306, transformed the situation of the church and its expansion. His great admirer, Eusebius of Caesarea, historian of the church and author of the *Ecclesiastical History* and the *Life of Constantine*, to whom we owe much of our knowledge of the period, saw him as the divinely appointed deliverer and Christian leader, though Constantine was not baptized until near death. Before the decisive battle of Milvian Bridge in 312, as described by the Christian writer Lactantius (c. 250–325), he dreamed of the cross, in a special form known as the 'Labarum', which became his standard. After his victory he issued an edict of toleration in 313, the Edict of Milan, from which Christians benefited. He did his best to bring unity to the church, both where it faced schism in North Africa and over protracted divisions over doctrine.

'Constantine now turned to his father's God in prayer . . . it would be hard to believe if the emperor himself had not told me . . . and . . . swore that this was true. He saw a cross of light in the sky and the words "in this sign conquer" . . . I have myself seen the copy which the goldsmiths made for the emperor the next morning.'

Eusebius, *Life of Constantine*, 27–28

One interesting aside on the extent to which Christianity had penetrated to the furthest reaches of the empire is that, when Constantine referred such issues to the Council of Arles in 314, we know that three British bishops attended, indicating a developed church life in Roman Britain.

'Many people are joining the church in the city which is called by my name. The number of churches must be increased. I ask you to order fifty copies of the Holy Scriptures . . . as quickly as may be.'

Constantine to Eusebius, *Life of Constantine*, 36

Constantine's greatest attempt at uniting the church doctrinally was the Council of Nicea of 325, which was to have lasting effects. Here the Arian heresy, which had the effect of turning Christ into a demigod, was repudiated. Jesus was judged to be not only of similar 'substance' to God but identical (Greek: *homoousios* meaning of the same substance). It was a triumph for the upholders of orthodoxy, among them Athanasius, although Athanasius's immediate reward was to be exiled by Constantine to avoid further disputes.

Encouraged by imperial protection and approval, people flocked to join the churches, whatever problems of nominal Christianity they brought with them.

Roman decline

After Constantine's death in 337, the Roman empire came under increasing pressure on its frontiers. Great movements of peoples, notably the Huns from the steppes of central Asia, pressed on other warrior groups such as the Goths, who had already been opponents of the Roman legions defending the empire's eastern boundaries. One section of the Goths pressed down into the Balkans in the 370s, into Greece and up the shore of the Adriatic in the 390s. It was these Visigoths, as they were called, who ultimately sacked the city of Rome itself, under their leader Alaric in 410, a leader influenced by Arian Christianity.

Other pagan peoples such as the Franks, the Alans, the Vandals and the Ostrogoths were also forcing their way into the empire. The Vandals, who originated in the steppes like the Huns, crossed the Rhine, moved into Spain and across the straits of Gibraltar into North Africa. Here they confronted a church made famous by Tertullian and the great bishop of Carthage, Cyprian, martyred in 258 after heroic attempts to restore the unity of the church, whose successor in terms of Christian stature was Augustine, bishop of Hippo (354–430). Augustine, like Tertullian a brilliant writer and rhetorician, was born in Thagaste in modern Algeria, to a pagan father but a devoutly Christian mother, Monica. In his great work of autobiography *The Confessions* he recorded how, after a time of prolonged inner turmoil, he surrendered his life to Christ in a garden in Milan in 386, after hearing a child's voice repeating again and again '*tolle, lege*' ('take and read'), which prompted him to open Paul's epistles at the verses that proved decisive for him.

Augustine was finally baptized by Ambrose, bishop of Milan, whose preaching had greatly impressed him, in 387. Augustine became one of

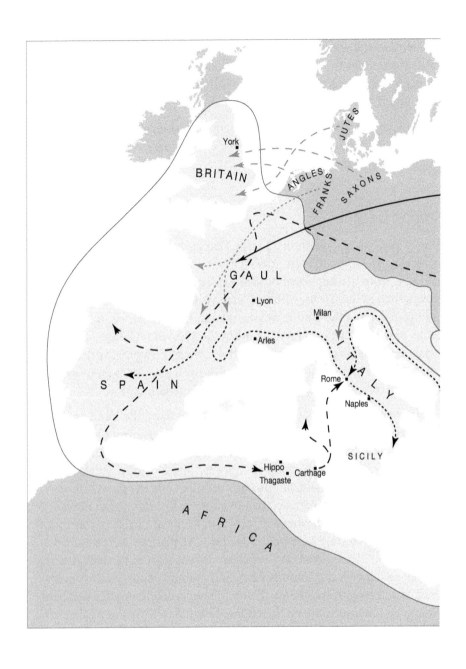

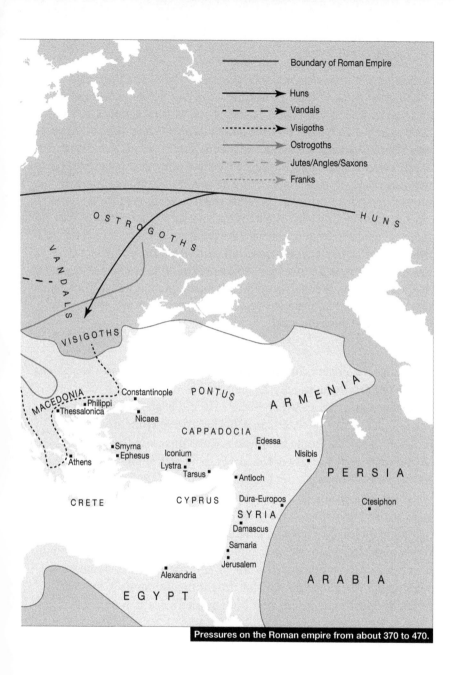

Boundary of Roman Empire

→ Huns

- - → Vandals

····· → Visigoths

→ Ostrogoths

- - → Jutes/Angles/Saxons

····· → Franks

OSTROGOTHS

HUNS

VANDALS

VISIGOTHS

MACEDONIA
- Philippi
- Thessalonica

Constantinople

PONTUS

ARMENIA

Nicaea

CAPPADOCIA

Edessa

- Smyrna
- Ephesus

Iconium

Nisibis

Lystra

Athens

Tarsus

Antioch

PERSIA

CRETE

CYPRUS

Dura-Europos

Ctesiphon

SYRIA

Damascus

Samaria

Alexandria

Jerusalem

ARABIA

EGYPT

Pressures on the Roman empire from about 370 to 470.

Monica (c. 331–87)

Augustine's mother was probably herself a native of Thagaste near Hippo. She married Patricius, a pagan, who was a potentially violent and frequently angry husband. Nevertheless, Monica appears to have been responsible for him becoming a Christian. He died when Augustine was 15, and Augustine refers to him hardly at all in *The Confessions*. Monica was a Christian of strong convictions, with a love of Augustine that was possessive but deep. She was widowed at 40, but she was prepared to deny Augustine his home when he embraced the heresy of Manichaeanism. She was ambitious for his success and followed him to Milan; here she even questioned the great Ambrose on the church's failure to fast in the way she approved. She was a strong influence towards Augustine's conversion, an admirer of Ambrose and an ally in his effect on her son. When Augustine decided to return to Africa from Italy after her prayers had been answered and he was baptized, she died at Ostia in Italy in the same year.

the greatest theologians of his or any age. In addition to *The Confessions* and *On the Trinity* he wrote a further great work *The City of God* between 413 and 426, in which he held the old pagan gods responsible for the sack of Rome by Alaric in 410. He reviewed the fortunes of secular empires like Rome but distinguished this from the image of the 'heavenly city', the city of God, only to be realized in the next life. His doctrine of the two cities became a leading influence in European thought in succeeding centuries. After Rome's fall, he could not but be aware of the 'barbarians at the gates', as the Vandals swept into North Africa and established a pagan kingdom, which included his town of Hippo, and, after his death, overcame Carthage in 439. This invasion of Latin North Africa, of which Tertullian, Cyprian and Augustine were towering figures, paved the way for the elimination of the Christian church by Muslim invasion, after Mohammed's death in 632.

CHAPTER 2
ASIA TO 1500

Thomas, the apostle of Christ, is linked by tradition to the spread of Christianity to the East. The Christian scholar and translator of the Bible, Jerome (c. 345–450), wrote in a letter: 'He [Jesus] was present in all places with Thomas in India, with Peter in Rome, with Paul in Illyria, with Titus in Crete, with Andrew in Greece, with each apostle and apostolic man in his own separate region' (*Letter to Marcellus*, 59). Eusebius of Caesarea, to whom, as we have seen, we owe much of our information on the period between Luke's writings and the time of Constantine (70–300), also connected Thomas with the spread north-east to the buffer kingdom of Osrhoene. Much of the early tradition about this kingdom and its capital, Edessa, and its reception of Christianity, is legendary, although there is no doubt that Edessa became an extremely important centre of Christian vitality later.

According to Eusebius, Thomas received a request from Abgar, king of Edessa, for healing and responded by sending Thaddaeus, one of the 72 disciples mentioned in Luke 10, to the king. Eusebius also included in his history the legend of a letter from Abgar to Jesus himself, again requesting healing, but this letter and Jesus' reply are spurious.

Nevertheless, geographically Edessa was on the old silk road north from Antioch, such an important early centre of Christian life, and there is a tradition of martyrdoms in Edessa contemporary with Pliny's persecution on the borders of the empire in 112. It is thought that Abgar VIII may have become a Christian in 177. We know of a very early Christian church, destroyed in Edessa in 201, the oldest Christian public building beyond the borders of the Roman empire yet known.

Adiabene and Armenia

Before pursuing the tradition of Thomas's travels in India, two other kingdoms deserve mention, both centres of Christian life in early days. Osrhoene (and Edessa) was a 'client kingdom', a buffer between two mighty empires, Rome to the west and Persia to the east. The Parthians,

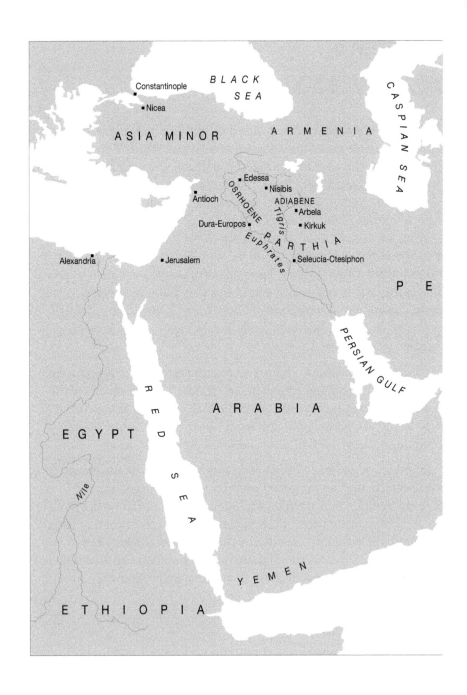

Constantinople

Nicea

BLACK SEA

CASPIAN SEA

ASIA MINOR

ARMENIA

Edessa

Nisibis

OSRHOENE

ADIABENE

Antioch

Arbela

Dura-Europos

PARTHIA

Tigris

Kirkuk

Euphrates

Seleucia-Ctesiphon

Alexandria

Jerusalem

P E

PERSIAN GULF

ARABIA

EGYPT

RED SEA

Nile

YEMEN

ETHIOPIA

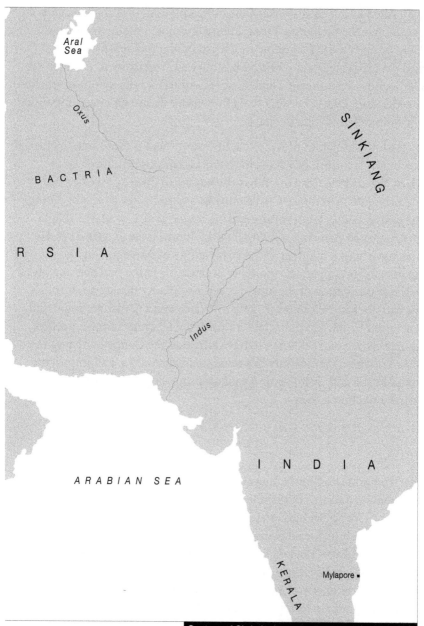

Centres of Christianity under Parthian rule, 30 to 226.

who ruled in Persia, also maintained the kingdom of Adiabene, with its capital Arbela, further east than Edessa and north of the River Tigris. Here again there is a tradition of Christian martyrdoms between AD 117 and AD 123. Uncertain tradition has linked Christianity in Adiabene to Osrhoene – a disciple of Thaddaeus (or Addai) was said to have reached the kingdom and, according to a 6th-century document, even appointed a bishop called Pkidha in 104.

With the kingdom of Armenia, however, there is more solid historical ground. It lay north of Edessa in the mountainous area between the Black Sea and the Caspian. It has the historical distinction of being the first state to embrace Christianity as a national religion, pre-dating the conversion of Constantine and his imperial victory of 312. The missionary to Armenia was Gregory the Illuminator (c. 240–332). He may have been a member of the royal family of Armenia but had grown up in exile in Cappadocia, possibly because his father had been involved in the assassination of the king. He returned to Armenia and, through his witness King Tiridates (c. 238–314), became a Christian, so possibly converted by the son of his father's assassin. Gregory's son succeeded him as bishop and is known to have attended the Council of Nicea in 325. Armenian Christianity has remained a distinctive and important brand of the faith, with some 5 million professing allegiance to the Armenian church today.

India

The traditions linking Thomas to India are more than Jerome's letter but they remain a source of dispute. There are still so-called 'Thomas Christians' in South India today, who use a Syriac form of worship (Syriac being a branch of Aramaic, probably the language spoken by Jesus himself, used in Edessa and its surroundings) and based as a very ancient Christian community in south-west India in Kerala. There is a tomb and shrine in honour of Thomas at Mylapore, built of bricks used by a Roman trading colony but not in use after AD 50. A song, written down in 1601 but passed on in Kerala for 50 generations, would also place Thomas around this date. It is known that many trading vessels crossed to India in the 1st century,

> 'He [Pantaenus] preached Christ to the Brahmans and philosophers of India.'
> Jerome, c. 400

when the secret of the monsoon winds was discovered, a discovery that led to over 100 such trading vessels a year crossing from the Red Sea to India. Seventh and 8th-century crosses have been found and the shrine of Mylapore was revered and seen by Marco Polo (c. 1254–1324).

Alongside the southern tradition, Thomas has also been connected to the north of India and to King Gundaphur. An inscription discovered in 1890 and coins suggest a 20-year reign from AD 19, giving external confirmation to the somewhat discredited document, the *Acts of Thomas*, written in Edessa, with its reference to the 'Great King Gundaphora', in whose kingdom in North India Thomas was said to have worked. It is not impossible, but historically unproven, that Thomas visited North India but died in South India, where by tradition he was martyred. One hundred years later, according to Jerome,

> 'He [Pantaenus] was a most learned man . . . he taught at the Christian college at Alexandria . . . sent as far as the land of the Indians. He found the people there who knew of Christ and already had St Matthew's Gospel.'
>
> Eusebius, *Ecclesiastical History*, 10.1–3

Pantaenus, the head of a great school of theology in Alexandria before Clement and Origen, left Alexandria to 'preach Christ to the Brahmans' of India, a development recorded by Eusebius. He wrote of Pantaenus in the *Ecclesiastical History* that he was 'a herald of the gospel of Christ to the nations of the East . . . sent as far as India'. India may have been evangelized by an apostle and visited by a famous Alexandrian theologian by the year AD 200.

Persia and the church of the East

The Persian empire, as much as the Roman empire, was the scene of expanding Christianity in the first three centuries, as it was also the source of persecutions of even greater severity than those of imperial Rome before Constantine. The Parthian dynasty, which had used Osrhoene and Adiabene as client kingdoms, gave way to the Sassanids after AD 226. By then, Christians had not only reached Persia but the steppes of Asia, and even Bactria, an area of northern Afghanistan today – this according to the Christian scholar, Bardaisan, writing around 196 in Edessa, where he wrote of Christian 'sisters among the

> 'Christ has planted the new race of Christians in every nation.'
>
> Bardaisan, Christian nobleman and scholar of Edessa, c. 190

Gilaurians and Bactrians'. An inscription, discovered by W.M. Ramsey in 1883, appears to point to a bishop from Asia Minor who met Bardaisan of Edessa and also found Christians beyond the River Euphrates with whom he shared the eucharist; the inscription could date as early as 150–200.

Nisibis was to replace Edessa as the great theological centre of the East; but the capital of the Sassanid empire, Seleucia-Ctesiphon, south of modern Baghdad, became the centre of church authority. On the disputed border of the two empires the victorious Persians overcame the fortress town of Dura-Europos in AD 250 near to the River Euphrates. This site has since revealed a very early Christian church, transformed from a private house into a full-scale church around AD 230–50, with a baptistery and wall paintings of Christ the Good Shepherd and a mural of the women at the tomb of the resurrection. A hundred years later Eusebius the historian met a bishop at the Council of Nicea in 325 whom he described as 'bishop of the whole of Persia and in the great India'. There is other evidence for a missionary bishop, David, around 300 in Basra at the head of the Persian Gulf. By the early 300s, bishops of Seleucia-Ctesiphon had national authority in Persia.

> 'There were bishops in other cities, too. Nisibis and Ctesiphon did not yet have bishops because of fear of the pagans.'
>
> **Chronicle of Arbela**

Whereas the Parthian rulers of Persia had been religiously tolerant, there was a change of front after Constantine under the Sassanids. The Persian empire had been a place of refuge for Christians from Roman persecution, although Zoroastrianism remained the religion of Persia. While Rome was the enemy of both Persian and Christian alike all would be well. Now, however, Constantine made no secret of his links with Christians in the Persian empire, which made Christians a potential fifth column as viewed by Persian rulers. One Christian theologian was unwise enough to prophesy Persian defeat by Rome. After 340 persecution of bitter ferocity was fuelled by the enmity of Zoroastrians. On Good Friday 344, 100 Christian priests were beheaded in front of their bishop, Simon, and then he and other bishops were executed. The historian of the times, Sozomen, who tried to provide a

> 'God added to their [missionary monks'] years for the sake of religion. He used them to lead nearly all the Syrian nation and many Persians to the true faith.'
>
> **Sozomen on early monastic missionaries**

sequel to Eusebius's history by covering the period 323–425, wrote of many thousands of Christians being martyred up to a possible total of 190,000. The worst persecution seems to have lasted for 40 years (339–79) until the death of Sharpur II. Although more severe than that of the Roman emperors, accounts of apostasy by Christians of the East are few by comparison. Further periods of persecution followed, less long but no less severe, in 419–20, 420–22, 445–48. In one case alone, at Kirkuk in northern Mesopotamia, 10 bishops and 153,000 others were massacred.

Theological division

In a century in which Alaric the Goth sacked Rome in 410 a highly significant date for the church of the East was that of the Council of Chalcedon in 451. We have seen earlier that debate about the deity of Christ had been central to the Council of Nicea in 325, when he was declared to be of the same substance as the Father and Arianism was denounced. At Chalcedon the debate centred on the two natures of Christ, divine and human, and it was highly significant for the church of the East because the position it held was judged to be unorthodox.

The debate was sophisticated and complex but the loser in it was the Christian leader Nestorius, patriarch of Constantinople. Broadly, those who emphasized the unity of the two natures (*monophysite*: single nature) regarded Nestorius as in error for emphasizing the two natures too heavily, to the point of separation. It is by no means certain that this is what Nestorius taught but in so far as the church of the East took a Nestorian position it was regarded by those in the West to be heretical. Many writings will still refer to the Christians of the East as 'Nestorians'.

> 'To put it pictorially, the Monophysites followed the tradition of "wine and water" – that in the incarnate Lord the divine and the human merged into one . . . the Nestorians that of "oil and water" – in Jesus the divine and human remained distinct.'
>
> **Stephen Neill, *Christian Missions***

By the year 500 there were effectively three main branches of the Christian church: the church of the West, which looked to Rome and Constantinople; the church of Africa, with its great centre in Alexandria and with the church in Ethiopia; and the church of the East, with its centre in Persia and its great missionary school of theology transferred from Edessa to Nisibis around 471 led by the famous theologian Narsai, who died in 503. At its largest this school had 1,000 students. The church of the East mounted successful missions among nomad peoples after 450 and spread Christianity across central Asia between 450 and 650. These included missions among the Huns, west of the Caspian Sea, conducted by Nestorian bishops and priests. Another missionary leader, Abraham of Kaskar (491–586) revived the monastic communities of the church and provided further spiritual vitality.

In addition to suffering schism from the West, the church of the East now had to endure the invasion of the Persian empire. Arabia had not been without Christian influence and there had been a bishop from Qatar present at the Council of Nicea in 325. There had also been a Christian ruler. Queen Mawwiyya, whose forces defeated those of Emperor Valens after her husband's death in 373, had insisted on receiving an orthodox bishop before she would make peace. There were Christian missions in the south-east of Arabia in Yemen: before the birth of Mohammed in 570 both Nestorian and monophysite missions had established themselves around 500.

The development of Islam in the next century was to have far-reaching effects in Persia and on its capital, Seleucia-Ctesiphon, which fell to the Arabs in 637, as on the church of the East as a whole. Muslim authorities could be tolerant of religious minorities but, as communities known as *dhimmi*, they often became religious ghettoes sapped of their vitality. Nevertheless, contemporary with the Muslim invasions, the church of the East had made its greatest leap forward, with its missionaries entering China at the same time as Aidan was taking the mission from Iona to Northumbria in Britain in 635.

China: the first entry

There have been few more dramatic archaeological finds or inscriptions than the stone of Hsianfu in China. This was a black limestone monument just under nine feet (three metres) tall, which was discovered by Chinese workmen in 1623 when digging. It told of Christian mission in the person of one Alopen, who was in the capital of the

T'ang dynasty in 635. Up to its discovery, the earliest-known Christian presence in China of missionaries was that of the Franciscans from 1245. The monument had been erected in 781. It commemorated the arrival of 'the Te-chin (Syrian) illustrious religion' in China and was written in Chinese characters under the symbol of a cross emerging from a lotus blossom. It advanced Western knowledge of Christianity in China by hundreds of years. Nestorian Christians may have been in China as early as 450 and there is evidence of a Persian missionary in China outside the Great Wall at Wei in 455: but the mission of Alopen received imperial favour from an emperor of the T'ang dynasty.

'Having carefully examined the scope of his [Alopen's] teaching we find it mysteriously spiritual and of silent operation . . . this teaching is helpful to all creatures and beneficial to all men. So let it have free course throughout the empire.'

Edict of Toleration of 638 in China

T'ai-tsung (emperor 627–49) owned a library comparable to the great library of Alexandria, with some 200,000 volumes; he may have had a special interest in the addition of Christian literature to this collection. He set Alopen to translate the Christian scriptures and published an edict of toleration in 638, which is recorded on the monument. His capital had Buddhist and Taoist temples built with imperial funds – support he also extended to the Christians for the building of a church. The edict also told of 21 monks in China in 638, probably all Persian. It is likely that they travelled over 4,000 miles (6,400 kilometres) from their church's main centre in Seleucia-Ctesiphon.

'The Persian scriptural religion began in Syria. By preaching and practice it came and long ago spread to China . . . it is necessary to get back to the original name. Its Persian monasteries shall therefore be changed to Syrian monasteries throughout the empire.'

Chinese Edict of AD 754

By the time the tablet was erected in 781 the Christian church had made considerable advances, especially between 712 and 781. An example of this was the Christian leader called Issu, who had caused the stone to be put in place, and was both a general in the Chinese army and also a Nestorian Christian priest. One sign of China's awareness of political realities in the west of Asia was an edict to show that Christianity went behind a Muslim-dominated Persia to origins in 'Syria'. So, in 754 all Christian monasteries previously known as Persian were to be known as Syrian.

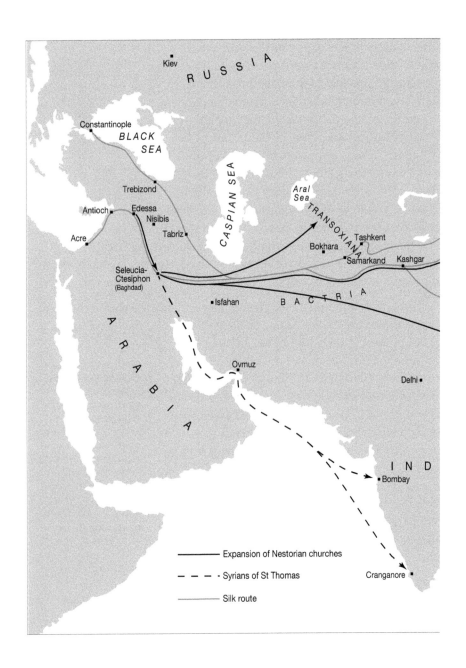

THE EXPANSION OF CHRISTIANITY – CHRISTIANITY AND THE CELTS

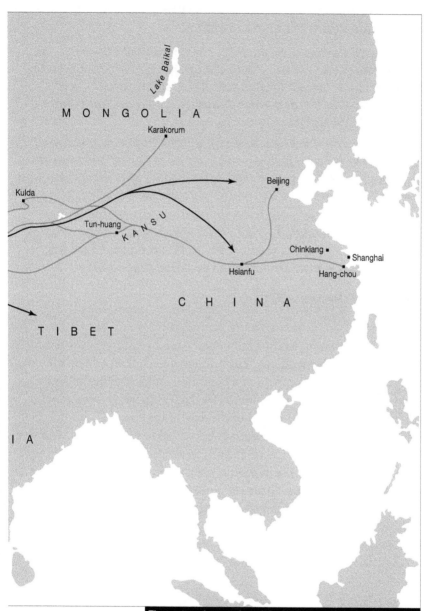

The eastward expansion of the Nestorian churches, 150 to 780.

There was in Persia a Lofty Virtue [i.e. a bishop] named A-lo-pen . . . he brought the true scriptures . . . rode through hardship and danger and in the ninth year of Cheng-Kuan [AD 635] arrived at Ch'ang-an . . . the Emperor received him as guest in the palace . . . the scriptures were translated in the library.

One Person of our Three-One became incarnate, the illustrious honoured one, Messiah, hid away his true majesty and came into the world as a man. An angel proclaimed the joy. A virgin bore a Sage in Syria. A bright star was the propitious portent, Persians saw its glory and came to offer gifts.

He hung, a brilliant sun, which scattered the regions of darkness. The devil's guile, lo, he was utterly cut off. He rowed mercy's barge, to go up to the course of light. The souls of men, lo, he has already saved. His mighty task once done, at noonday he ascended into heaven.

Text of Hsianfu Monument of 781

After 781, however, and the fall of the T'ang dynasty, the Nestorian church in China vanished, perhaps through overdependence on the T'ang rulers. There is a record of a Nestorian monk meeting an Arab called Abdul Faraj, who told him in 987 that Christianity was extinct in China. It was not to reappear until the days of the Great Khans and the Mongols and then through Franciscan missionaries. Meanwhile, between 500 and 1000, Nestorian Christianity, if weakened in China, had shown an extraordinary resilience in central Asia, so that the seven metropolitan areas based on Adiabene, Nisibis and other centres, became 15 by AD 1000 and included areas such as Turkestan and Samarkand by 781, India by 800 as well as outreach around the Caspian Sea and to the north. All this meant a strengthened church organization, despite the influence of Zoroastrianism and Islam in the Persian empire.

China during the Mongols

Among the tribal groups reached by Nestorian missionaries in central Asia were a people known as Keraits, who had settled near Lake Baikal. Some 200,000 of these people including a Kerait prince sought baptism, according to a letter to John VI, the Nestorian patriarch in Baghdad, in 1009. Nearly 200 years later, a tribal chief and Christian leader of this people became patron of a young man who was the son of a chief of a subordinate clan. This young man, known as Temujin, became in due course Genghis (Chinghis) Khan (1162–1227). He was never a Christian but, like other Mongol rulers, he was not opposed to Christianity. He moved first to the east in conquest towards Pekin (Beijing) but then to the west in overrunning Transoxiana, northern Iran and Persia. He destroyed Bokhara and Samarkand, defeated the Georgians in 1221 and the forces of southern Russia in 1223.

Although he died in 1227, his son returned to the west and invaded Russia in 1236, took Kiev and invaded northern Poland, Hungary and Austria; a raiding party even reached Albania. Genghis Khan himself was buried with traditional Mongol 'shamanistic' ceremony, which included the sacrifices of 50 young women and equivalent numbers of horses towards the next life. His successors remained tolerant of Christians and Kublai Khan (1215–94), whose territorial dominions stretched from the Pacific to Constantinople and who ruled both China and Persia, was to welcome Franciscan missionaries from the West.

Pope Innocent IV (Pope 1243–54), confronted by Mongol presence in Europe, sent the first emissary and missionary to the Mongol court in 1245. He was a Franciscan, who had known the founder of the order and was called John of Plano Carpini. After this there were more approaches by western Christians to the Mongol court, which were as much political as missionary in a religious sense, made up of Franciscan and Dominican friars. William of Rubruck, who visited between 1253 and 1255, left accounts of the Mongols and of religious debate before the Great Khan, in which Muslims, Nestorian Christians, Zoroastrians and his own brand of western Catholicism took part. William had a personal conversation with Mongke, grandson of Genghis Khan and Great Khan from 1251–59, who displayed characteristic Mongol openness to the friar but left him in no doubt that traditional Mongol shamanism was his own choice.

'In Xanadu did Kubla Khan a stately pleasure-dome decree, where Alph the sacred river ran, through caverns measureless to man, down to a sunless sea. So twice five miles of fertile ground with walls and towers were girdled round and there were gardens bright with sinuous rills, where blossom'd many an incense-bearing tree.'

S.T. Coleridge, *Kubla Khan*

William of Rubruck (c. 1215–c. 1260)

William came from Rubruck (Rubroek), a Flemish-speaking village in northern France. He joined the Franciscan order, and he became acquainted with Louis IX of France, the devout king later to become St Louis. His visit to the Mongol court was made with the king's blessing, after Louis had heard that a Mongol prince had become a Christian. William travelled from Acre in 1252 and reported to the king on what he found at the Mongol court in his *Itinerary of Friar William*. As a Franciscan western Catholic, he was severely critical of what he found of Christianity in China, whether among the Uighurs and other tribal groups, or at the court, where he did, however, recognize a better-grounded Nestorian Christianity. In his view, perhaps biased, the Nestorian priests engaged in magic themselves and failed to condemn it in others; and indulged in raucous drunkenness, while Nestorian Christians were pictured as polygamous, corrupt, untrustworthy and given to usury. He returned to Acre in 1255 and later visited Paris, where he shared his knowledge with the Englishman Roger Bacon in 1257.

In addition to the Franciscan missionaries, the famous Italian merchants and travellers the brothers Polo, father and uncles of Marco, reached the court of Kublai Khan in 1266. Kublai Khan welcomed the brothers and showed great interest in their religion. He sent a letter to the pope that requested 100 missionaries.

The pope's response was to send two Dominican friars with the Polos (Marco accompanied his uncles on this journey) in 1275 but the Dominicans turned back. This was an opportunity lost, as the Great Khan had shown sympathy, but after 1280 his power began to wane. By the time the fresh missionaries arrived from Rome in 1294 the last of the great Mongol Khans had died in that year. According to Marco Polo's accounts, after spending some 16 years in China, he estimated some 700,000 Christians were in the region that he knew and it is possible that some of these were survivors from earlier Nestorian missions, commemorated by the monument of 781. He reported on three beautiful

> 'You shall go to your High Priest [the pope] and shall pray him to send me a hundred men skilled in your religion . . . so I shall be baptized and then all my barons and great men and then their subjects.'
>
> **The Polos**

churches in Kamsu province and Christian churches in another 11 cities. Independently of Marco Polo, it is known that there was a Christian community of 2,000 in Chinkiang, a city of hundreds of thousands, where the Yangtse and the Grand Canal intersected.

Marco Polo told of a Christian prince, George, who was the issue of one of Genghis Khan's daughters and a Christian father, who first married Kublai Khan's granddaughter and then, after her death, married the daughter of Timur (Timur Lang) (1336–1405). This is the man known to history as Tamerlane, following the English playwright Christopher Marlowe, the ravager of China. Under the influence of the Franciscans, George the prince became a follower of western Christianity and built the first Roman Catholic place of worship in China when king of the Ongut tribe. He died later in battle, leading one of Timur's armies.

The Franciscan missionaries, notably John of Montecorvino (1246–1330), who had been himself a soldier, a doctor in the service of the emperor Frederick II in Europe and finally a friar, claimed to have 6,000 converts in China by 1305. Pope Clement V created him archbishop of Peking in 1307. He was reinforced by three more bishops around 1313 in a party of seven missionaries sent to help him, some of whom were martyred by Muslims en route near Bombay. Another Franciscan, Odoric of Pordenone (c. 1265–1331), who wrote a popular account of his visit to China for European consumption, may have been the source of an estimate of 30,000 Christians in China.

The 12th century is considered the period when Nestorian Christianity spread most widely in Asia during the so-called *pax Mongolica* (Mongol era of peace). It was a time when the Mongol patriarch Mark (Maryaballah III) had a wider authority than the pope himself from his centre in Baghdad. His friend and associate, the Nestorian bishop Samma, visited Rome, Paris and Edward I's court in French Gascony; and was invited to celebrate mass according to the Eastern rite in Rome by Pope Nicholas IV on a visit in 1287–88.

Before the end of the Khans, one reign of savagery remained. Timur the Great (Tamerlane) has been judged to have possessed even greater ferocity than Genghis Khan but with none of his statesmanship. He conquered Persia in 1379 after ten years as ruler of Samarkand; he sacked Delhi, killing Muslims and Christians indiscriminately; he incorporated

Mesopotamia in his empire and defeated the Ottoman Turks in 1402 and the Egyptian Mamelukes. Unlike Genghis Khan he was no friend to Christians. His campaigns, coming on top of the withering of Christian communities under Muslim rule, meant that Nestorian Christianity was destroyed. The same went for those communities known as the Jacobites, who had emphasized the single nature of Christ. Only two enclaves of any strength remained in the East: Malabar, where the 'Thomas Christians' remained and the centre of Cisre on the Upper Tigris. Timur had prepared the way for further Muslim advances, which led to the loss of the great cities of Jerusalem, Antioch and, finally, Constantinople, which fell to Muslim Turks in 1454.

The church of the East had shown great vitality, never more so than in the Mongol period. Despite the benevolent neutrality of the Great Khans, however, it had never had a Constantine in the alternative empire of Persia, let alone in imperial China. The history of the Nestorian missions was still a very notable one, not least in reaching out with success to nomadic peoples like the Keraits. It had many great achievements before the advent of the church of the West in the Franciscan and Dominican missions in China, themselves limited in their impact. Asian Christianity had a remarkable history from the early days in Antioch, Edessa and Nisibis (from, say, AD 40–500) right up to the Great Khans of 1150–1300. As this historical reflection switches to the modern period, launched by the voyages of Vasco da Gama to India of 1498 and followed by the advent of Jesuits and others in India, China and Japan, those great achievements over some 1,300 years by Nestorian Christians over the vast distances of the Asian continent should be remembered.

CHAPTER 3

EUROPE TO 1500

Turning from the East to mainland Europe, the spread of Christianity after Constantine's conversion can initially be viewed in the two corners of Europe. In the south-east corner, an influential mission was mounted among the Goths by Ulphilas (311–83). He was born in a country peopled by the Goths, Cappadocia, now part of northern Turkey. Although living in Constantinople as a young man, he absorbed the language and culture of this pagan people. He was made a bishop in Constantinople but he returned to his homeland as a missionary. Like so many missionaries, then and now, he became a translator of the scriptures. According to one Christian writer, he deliberately omitted the books of Kings, realizing that the Goths, a warlike people, needed no further encouragement to do battle. In theology he became Arian. As we have seen, the effect of Arius's teaching on Jesus was to turn him into a kind of demigod, a position ultimately repudiated by orthodoxy. The effect of Ulphilas's mission lasted for centuries but it included this Arian influence on the tribes of the Goths that he touched.

> 'They followed him . . . for he had faced danger for the faith, while many Goths were still heathen.'
>
> **Sozomen on Ulphilas and the Goths**

Irish missionaries

In the extreme north-east of Europe, there was the romantic story of Patrick (c. 450). He had been brought up in the west country of Celto-British England, the son of a town councillor and Christian deacon, who was also a landowner and farmer. Aged 16, Patrick was kidnapped by Irish pirates and spent some years as a shepherd in Ireland. He escaped to Britain with, as he felt, divine assistance and decided to study for the Christian ministry. He returned to Ireland and spent the rest of his life as an evangelist, Christian educator and promoter of communities of monks and nuns. In Trinity College, Dublin, there is a

> 'I came to the Irish peoples to preach the gospel and endure the taunts of unbelievers . . . losing my birthright of freedom for the benefit of others.'
>
> **Patrick, Confession**

1,000-year-old manuscript, copied from his own writing, it is claimed, giving the defence and account of his life, his *Confession*. The hymn known as St Patrick's Breastplate, which begins, 'I bind unto myself this day, the strong name of the Trinity', is thought to date some three centuries after his death.

Patrick was the first of a large number of saints and missionaries connected with Ireland. Perhaps the most considerable of these was Columba (c. 521–97), a prince of royal blood, who left Ireland in 563 to found the famous monastery on Iona. From this foothold off the Scottish coast, he worked among the North Picts as the British missionary, Ninian (? 390), according to Bede, worked among the South Picts, in the neighbourhood of Whithorn. Again according to Bede, Columba was responsible for the conversion of the king, and it was from Iona that Aidan (d. 651), another Irishman and monk, went to Northumbria in response to a request for help from King Oswald (c. 605–42). The monks of Iona had been instrumental in Oswald's conversion when he was in exile in Scotland. Aidan became bishop of Lindisfarne, like Iona an island retreat but, unlike Iona, connected to the mainland at low tide. Aidan, we are told by Bede, through his holy life, gentleness and 'grace of discretion', won over the Northumbrians, despite being warned against them by a previous missionary as being intractable, harsh and barbarous in disposition. It is an interesting parallel that Aidan's mission to Northumbria was contemporary with that of Alopen in China noted in the last chapter.

> 'He never sought or cared for any worldly possessions and loved to give away to the poor.'
> **Bede on Aidan**

Aidan was succeeded by another great figure, Cuthbert (c. 636–87), who became bishop of Lindisfarne in 685 and, after a period as a hermit on the Farne Islands, was buried at Lindisfarne two years later. As a sign of the ravages of the Viking raiders in the succeeding centuries, his body (a precious relic to northern Christians) was exhumed and found its ultimate resting place in Durham Cathedral. Here his tomb can be seen today, with other visible reminders of Celtic Christianity in Northumbria, a culture that produced treasures such as the Lindisfarne Gospels (c. 696). Like the Irish Book of Kells (c. 800), this illuminated manuscript of great beauty somehow escaped the depredations of these centuries. While Columba and Aidan went to Scotland and Northumbria

Bede (673–735)

Known to us as the Venerable Bede, he was the outstanding scholar of Anglo-Saxon England. He was put in the care of the monastery of Wearmouth and its abbot, Benedict Biscop, at the age of seven. When the new Benedictine monastery of Jarrow was founded in 682, Bede became a monk there for the rest of his life. He wrote on a variety of subjects but biblical commentaries and history were his main works. Among the first, he wrote expositions of the Gospels of Mark and Luke and the Acts of the Apostles. He is most widely remembered today for his remarkable *Ecclesiastical History of the English Nation* (finished in 731), still our chief source of knowledge of its period, which justly earned him the title of the 'father of English history'. It bears comparison with Luke's Acts, with its striking word pictures of leading figures and its vivid set pieces. Like Luke, his careful accounts do not baulk at the miraculous. He wrote also the life of Cuthbert, both in verse and prose, and was responsible for creating a Europe-wide cult of the saint. Appropriately, the tombs of Cuthbert and Bede lie now at the east and west end of Durham Cathedral.

as Irish missionaries, another Irish saint, Columbanus (d. 615), left Ireland around 590 to spend the rest of his life in *peregrinatio* (wandering pilgrimage) in modern France, where he founded monastic communities in the Vosges region of Gaul at Luxeuil and elsewhere, before ending his days in a monastic house at Bobbio in northern Italy.

Evangelizing Europe's tribes

Mainland Europe was peopled by largely pagan tribes, of whom the Franks later assumed great importance; but Friesians in the Netherlands, Saxons further east, Burgundians and Lombards in northern Italy all invited evangelization. As well as the Irish pilgrim missionaries, two highly significant Englishmen left their stamp on the tribes of northern Europe, both also doing much to enhance the authority of the popes in Rome on their missions. Willibrord (658–739) was a Northumbrian Christian, educated at Ripon, where he knew another famous churchman, Wilfred. Willibrord became a missionary to the Friesians. In

695 he was consecrated as their archbishop by the pope and subsequently founded a cathedral at Utrecht and a famous monastery at Echternach in Luxembourg. He also carried out missionary work in Denmark and elsewhere.

Boniface (c. 675–754) was probably born in Crediton in Devon, then in the kingdom of Wessex. He helped Willibrord in Friesia and carried out successful missions to the Hessians further south. He was made a bishop in Rome in 722 and earned undying fame by the symbolic act of cutting down the Oak of Thor at Geissen. Thor was the pagan god from whose name we still have our Thursday ('Thor's day'). This decisive and revolutionary action caused many Hessians to acknowledge the superior power of the

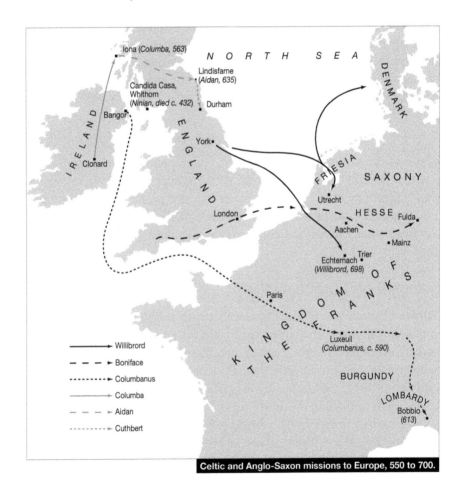

Celtic and Anglo-Saxon missions to Europe, 550 to 700.

Christian religion. In 746 Boniface became archbishop of Mainz. He worked hard to re-establish the organization of the church east of the Rhine but after some years resigned in order to return to his missionary work. In Friesia, while awaiting a large confirmation at Dokkum in 754, he was set upon by a marauding party and killed in his 80th year. The book he held up to protect his head from the sword, bloodstained and deeply cut, was a collection of the writings of Ambrose, bishop of Milan (d. 397) and mentor of Augustine of Hippo, which survives among other relics of this 'Apostle of Germany'. The English historian Christopher Dawson wrote of Boniface that he was 'a man who had deeper influence on the history of Europe than any Englishman who ever lived'.

The influence of the popes had already reached Britain. One of the greatest of all popes, Gregory I, 'the Great', loved to play on words. It is known that he made a pun of Angli (Angles, another northern people) as placed 'at the angle of the world'. It is by no means impossible that he also made the famous remark attributed to him on seeing fair-haired Anglo-Saxons in the slave market at Rome: '*Angli sunt, angeli fiant.*' ('They are Angles, they may become angels.') Legend or not, this missionary-minded pope dispatched a group of missionaries to Britain in 596 under another Augustine to the court of the kingdom of Kent, where a Christian princess had married a pagan king, Ethelbert (c. 560–616).

Hilda of Whitby (614–80)

Leadership by Christian women was known early in the church's life. Hilda was a Northumbrian princess, who was among the many baptized by Paulinus in 627. When her sister became a nun in France, Hilda intended to join her, but Aidan wanted to secure her gifts for the English church. Through his influence, she became abbess of a monastery at Hartlepool, but in 657, she herself founded a religious house for men and women at Whitby, of which she became abbess. Here the famous synod of 664 was held. Hilda supported the Celtic side of the debate but, when the Roman way was adopted, she accepted the decision loyally. Bede wrote of her that her acquaintances called her mother because of her wonderful devotion and grace and as one who brought about the amendment of many from a distance 'who heard the inspiring story of her industry and goodness'.

Gregory showed great missionary acumen, advising that heathen places of worship could be used for Christian services and pagan feasts and festivals incorporated into the Christian pattern.

In due course, as in so many tribal missions, Ethelbert as king and tribal chief was converted and baptized along with 10,000 of his subjects. Augustine became the first archbishop of Canterbury. Paulinus, a missionary monk who had joined the Roman mission, went north and baptized Edwin, king of Northumbria, and thousands of his subjects in 627, becoming bishop of York. Bede tells us that he did nothing but baptize for 36 days in a river near York, where the local centre for the worship of Woden (from which we derive our Wednesday) was set on fire and destroyed. Paulinus's baptisms prepared the way for Aidan's Celtic revival after 635 in Northumbria. The two traditions, Celtic and Roman, with their different customs, especially over the timing of Easter, met in conference at the Synod of Whitby in 664, when the Roman way on the celebration of the great festival and other things was accepted.

> 'The heathen temples of these people need not be destroyed, only the idols which are to be found in them.'
>
> **Gregory the Great**

Charlemagne and Europe

It was not only the popes who were a growing authority in Europe. The Franks were developing into a dominant influence, whose political history was to be intertwined with the spiritual authority of the papacy. Charles Martel (c. 689–741) was strictly the mayor of the Frankish palace and court, but his prowess as a soldier and leader made him effectively ruler. Islam had penetrated into Spain and Muslim armies reached into southern Gaul. In a decisive battle, Martel (literally, the Hammer) defeated the Muslim forces at Tours in 732, pinning Muslim influence south of the Pyrenees and ending the prospect of an invasion of Gaul and northern Europe. Charles Martel sent his sons to be educated in the famous monastery of St Denis. One became a monk, but the other, Pepin, with the agreement of the pope, became king of the Franks not only by possession (like his father) but by right in 753. He repaid the church's support by helping the development of the church put in hand by Willibrord and Boniface. His more famous son, Charlemagne, again allied himself with the pope and was crowned as emperor in Rome by Pope Leo III on Christmas Day 800.

Charlemagne's rule was strong but often ruthless. He was in favour of Christian learning and employed the scholarly Northumbrian theologian, Alcuin (c. 740–804), to foster learning at his court. Nevertheless, those Saxon tribes vanquished by the Frankish armies were often confronted with the choice of forcible baptism or death. Alcuin, to his credit, remonstrated against such practices, knowing that true faith cannot be imposed by force, but Charlemagne was determined to reduce the Saxons by a combination of military power and religious conformism. He subdued the Saxon tribes between 772 and 785, followed by Bavaria, before he turned his attention to Spain (785–801), a campaign that culminated in the capture of Barcelona in 801. Although he was unable to write (though he could read), his respect for learning was genuine and he encouraged Alcuin and a community of scholars in their Bible translation, teaching and writing. The creation of a palace library, his support for reform of the Frankish church and the beautiful artefacts that survive from his court at Aachen show that this period has deserved the title of the 'Carolingian renaissance' of culture and learning.

In King Alfred the Great (849–99) Britain too benefited from this Christian and Carolingian inheritance later in the same century. Alfred, a more educated man than Charlemagne, who himself translated Gregory the Great's pastoral classic *Regula Pastoralis* for the use of bishops and clergy of his kingdom, had the same cultivating effect. A circle of scholars, translators and copyists was formed at his court, who maintained Christian learning and culture against a background of Viking and Danish pressures.

> 'Let schools be established in which boys may learn to read. Correct carefully the psalms . . . the calendar . . . the Catholic books.'
>
> **Charlemagne on education,**
> ***Admonitio Generalis*, CAP. 72**

Russia

The 9th and 10th centuries were important also for the development of Russian Christianity. Russia was peopled by northern tribes from Scandinavia who moved down the great rivers Dnieper and Volga to the surroundings of the Black Sea and the Caspian. Two heroic Greek missionaries had undertaken embassies to the Khazar people at the bidding of Patriarch Photius in Constantinople and the emperor in 860. They were Constantine (826–69), later named Cyril, and Methodios (c. 815–85). Now they were asked to respond to a request from Ratislav, prince of Moravia, for teachers. Constantine believed on principle that the Slav peoples should have the Bible in their own languages rather than, for instance, in Latin. He duly translated the Gospels, daily services and the liturgy (communion rite) of John Chrysostom (c. 347–407), one of the great figures of the eastern church known as 'golden tongue' (Greek: *chrysostomos*) for his eloquent preaching, for the use of the Slavs. Constantine had composed a special script, Glagolitic, (Cyrillic script, named after him may not have been his creation, though contemporary with him). He and his partner Methodios completed the Slav Bible in 881.

From 870 Bulgaria and its king Boris became an important Slav kingdom to identify with Greek or eastern Christianity and after 900 Kiev became the cradle of Russian Christianity. A reigning queen there was baptized at Constantinople in 957; her grandson, Vladimir, seen still by many Russians as the founder of Russian Christianity, was baptized after marriage to a Christian princess, Anne, sister of the emperor, around 988. The Russian church identified with Constantinople and its tradition of eastern orthodoxy. It was to survive Mongol invasions and Muslim pressures from the Turks as an enduring Christian tradition of worship, monastic life and peasant piety, giving also national coherence and unity.

> 'The Greeks took us to their church and we did not know whether we were in heaven or earth. We only know that their God dwells among men.'
>
> **Vladimir's envoys on the Great Church of St Sophia in Constantinople**

The impact of the monasteries

One of the methods by which Christianity spread and maintained itself in Europe was through monastic communities. Their origin, as we have seen, was in the Egypt of Antony around AD 300, conveyed to Europe by such figures as John Cassian (c. 360–440), who experienced monastic communities in both Egypt and the Holy Land before founding monasteries near Marseilles around 415. Nevertheless, the true founder of European monasticism was Benedict of Nursia (c. 480–550). Like

Antony, he began as a hermit in a cave at Subiaco, but around 529, he moved with other monks to Monte Cassino, a magnificent mountain site, which, because of its strategic eminence, was to be the scene of fierce fighting in the 1940s battle for Italy.

Benedict formed his rule for his own monks, which has been praised for its balance, moderation and stability. It is based on the call to obedience (to God but expressed also through the rule of the abbot), chastity and poverty, there being an absolute ban on ownership of possessions. The basic provision of daily chapel services (seven during the day and two at night), combined with set hours for manual work, meals and study has met the demands of many communities for a balanced Christian life. In so far as the Benedictine ideal of dividing daily life by set times of prayer was also taken up by the non-monastic or 'secular' priests, Benedict may be judged to be the individual who has shaped the spirituality of western Europe.

In considering what became a dominant tradition, it is important not to forget the very different Celtic monasteries with their clusters of small beehive-shaped huts in stone or timber, often at remote spots lashed by the Atlantic as at the Irish site of Skellig Michael. According to Kenneth Clark, the art historian, such communities were vital centres of civilization as Viking looting, killing and destruction engulfed much of northern Europe.

Hundreds of Benedictine monasteries spread across Europe, with Christianizing effect, between 700 and 1000. In 910 an important monastic foundation was created at Cluny in northern France, from which a reform movement was launched to renew the Benedictine communities. For some, however, this Cluniac reform was not enough and a fresh foundation at Citeaux, near Dijon in France, provided a more austere model with a stricter observance of the Benedictine rule. Between 1100 and 1400 these Cistercian foundations grew to number 694 communities and produced in one of their abbots, Bernard, abbot of Clairvaux (1090–1153), one of the outstanding figures of the medieval church. A product of Citeaux, he was the ally and critic of popes, a preacher of the second crusade and a writer of Christian theology and devotion. The hymn 'Jesu, the very thought of thee', attributed to him, may not be his composition, but its expression of warm devotion to the person of Jesus was of the kind for which he stood.

Rule of Benedict

The Abbot and the Brethren

III. 'Whenever matters of importance have to be dealt with in the monastery, let the abbot summon the whole congregation and himself put forward the question that has arisen. Then, after hearing the advice of the brethren, let him think it over by himself and do what he shall judge most advantageous. Now we have said that all should be summoned to take counsel for this reason, that it is often to the younger that the Lord reveals what is best. But let the brethren give advice with all subjection of humility, so as not to presume obstinately to defend their own opinions; rather let the matter depend on the abbot's judgment, so that all should submit to whatever he decide to be best . . . let no one in the monastery follow his own inclinations and let no one boldly presume to dispute with his abbot . . .'

XXII. How the monks are to sleep: 'Let them sleep in separate beds and let their beds be suitable to their manner of life, as the abbot shall appoint. If possible, let them all sleep in one room . . . let a candle be kept burning in the cell until morning. Let them sleep clothed, girdled with belts or cords – but without knives at their sides lest they injure themselves in sleep. And let the monks be always ready; and when the signal is given, let them rise without delay and rival one another in their haste to the service of God . . . let not the younger brethren have beds by themselves but dispersed among the seniors. And when they rise for the service of God let them gently encourage one another, because the sleepy ones are apt to make excuses.'

Scandinavia

This account of the Christianization of Europe by AD 1000 has shown something of the struggle to evangelize pagan tribes. A further example, ending in the collapse of Christian hopes, was in Scandinavia. Here, the great pioneering missionary, Anskar (801–65), a monk from modern France, founded the first church in Stockholm; he had already been expelled by pagan tribes from the area known as Schleswig-Holstein. He was responsible later for the conversion of Erik, king of Jutland in Denmark, but despite the efforts of a lifetime of missionary work in the Scandinavian countries there was a relapse into paganism after his death.

In Sweden an English monk, Sigfrid, re-established Christian mission and baptized King Olov around 1000. It took a further two centuries for Christianization to be complete.

In Norway, two Christian monarchs, both converted from the lives of Viking raiders, made a Christian impression on their people. Olav Tryggvasan (king of Norway 995–99) had a memorable meeting with a Christian hermit in the Scilly Isles, when still a Norse raider. Olav Haraldsson (c. 995–1030), king of Norway from 1016 to 1028, adopted a strongly Christian stance, which provoked much resistance. Denmark, partly due to the efforts of Anskar and an ally in the Danish chief, Harold, who had been baptized while visiting the Frankish court, became Christian effectively by 1035, over a century after Anskar's death.

Progress was often slow, there were frequent lapses into heathenism and in the very far north the Lapps (Sami people) remained unevangelized for centuries. Norwegian missionaries reached Iceland in Olav Tryggvasan's reign (following earlier Irish hermits) and Christianity replaced paganism there, the home of the earliest parliament, the Thing, in the early 11th century. In Greenland, Vikings led by Erik the Red had been exiled from both Norway and Iceland and Christianity advanced in the 11th century there, too, through the adherence of Erik's son, Leif.

Norsemen may have reached Newfoundland and North America long before Columbus. Their own community in Greenland received a bishop as head of the community in 1123.

Later developments

The final 500 years covered by this chapter saw a number of important developments in the Christianization of Europe. Various popes strengthened the hold of the papacy on the church and over political authorities. Europe has been left an indelible example of the growth of the spiritual power of the papacy under Gregory VII (d. 1085), known also as Hildebrand: threatened with excommunication and with it the dispensing of his subjects from their oaths of allegiance, Henry IV, the emperor, stood for days with his family in the snow at Canossa in 1017, until the pope relented.

Innocent III (1160–1216) proved an even more able and far-sighted pope. He asserted successfully the papal right to approve the appointment of emperors and, as we shall see, strengthened the church through his wisdom in patronizing the new orders of Franciscan and Dominican friars, the kind of fresh departures that a less visionary church leader might have stifled.

Before 1500 the papacy was to suffer various indignities, including exile in Avignon between 1309 and 1377 and schism, with one pope vying with another claimant for authority; but Hildebrand and Innocent III had strengthened its hold on church and rulers considerably.

The church was also largely responsible for the flowering of Europe's universities. Bologna, Paris and Oxford were founded before 1200 and by 1400 there were over 40, a number of them being in France, Italy and Germany, two in England (Cambridge was founded in 1209) and two in Scotland. Christian theology held a central place, along with law, medicine and the arts.

Friars: Franciscans and Dominicans

Two men were responsible for the creation of mendicant (begging) orders. Francis (1181–1226), who has arguably left a deeper impression than any Christian since apostolic times, was the son of a wealthy Italian textile merchant from Assisi. After living the life of a polished young man of privileged background, he felt increasingly called to a life of compassion for people like the beggars he met in Rome when on pilgrimage and the leper he embraced in order to overcome his fear of leprosy. Disowned by his father, he responded to the call to total poverty when hearing Christ's words to the rich young man of the Gospels (Mark 10:17–22). He collected 12 followers, an apostolic band, and secured approval from Innocent III to form an order in 1209. The friars were sent out to preach in pairs. Francis himself tried unsuccessfully to make his way to Muslims in North Africa through

'Those who have now promised obedience shall have one gown and those who really need them may wear shoes.'
Rule of Francis

France and Spain in 1214–15, but he did succeed in visiting the sultan in 1219. In an era of crusades, he believed in dialogue and persuasion of Muslims. His order grew rapidly in his lifetime. It was to provide many adventurous and heroic missionaries of the Roman Catholic church, whether in China, Latin America, California, India or Africa. A women's order, founded by Clare (1193–1253), was another result of Francis's teaching, known popularly as the 'poor Clares'. Later a so-called 'third order' developed, whereby lay people could associate themselves with the order.

Dominic (c. 1172–1221) was a Spaniard, born near Castile. Like Francis, he had shown his care for the poor during conditions of famine that caused him to give up his possessions. His call to mission preaching was in the context of the church's attempts to persuade the Albigensians, a deviant movement in the south of France, to return to orthodoxy. Again, Innocent III was responsible for persuading Dominic and his fellow missioners to adopt a rule and become an Order of Preachers between 1216 and 1218. Where Francis had somewhat distrusted learning, as distracting from simplicity of life, the Dominicans had an intellectual interest from the first. Certain of them made notable contributions to the universities of Europe. Albert the Great (Albertus Magnus, d. 1280), who taught in Cologne and Strasbourg among other places, was a leading Dominican scholar, and the greatest of all, who left an indelible mark on western and Roman Catholic theology, was Thomas Aquinas (c. 1225–74).

He was an Italian from Aquino in the kingdom of Naples from an aristocratic family, who taught at Cologne and Paris. His great work *Summa Theologiae* was a compendium of theology written for his fellow friars and is still influential. His own and his order's missionary vision was expressed in the *Summa contra Gentiles*, written to assist Dominicans in their work among non-Christians. Like the Franciscans, the Dominicans supplied the church with ready and adventurous pioneers in far-distant China and the East as well as in Europe. Their concentration was on study and preaching. In England they were know as the Black Friars to distinguish them from the Franciscans – they wore a black mantle over a white habit.

> 'All I have written seems like so much straw compared with what I have seen and what has been revealed to me.'
>
> **Thomas Aquinas, after a spiritual experience in the last year of his life (1273–74)**

Ramon Llull (c. 1233–c. 1315)

Bishop Stephen Neill has described Ramon Llull as 'one of the greatest missionaries in the history of the church'. Llull was a layman from Majorca, who married and lived the life of a knight and courtier until the age of 30. At this time he had a vision of Christ crucified, which caused him to consecrate his life to Christian mission, in particular towards Muslims, who had ruled Majorca for centuries but whose rule had now ended. Llull studied Arabic and sought the support of popes and royal courts in Aragon and France for his plans towards Islam. He succeeded in receiving royal support to establish a centre in Majorca for Franciscans to study oriental languages. He himself made three missionary journeys to North Africa to preach in dangerous circumstances. He was successful in establishing the study of oriental languages in the universities of Paris, Oxford, Bologna and Salamanca and in obtaining support for his missionary objectives at the Council of Vienne in 1311–12. His overall aim was to bring Christian, Muslim and Jew together from a basis of shared monotheism, 'that in the whole world there may not be more than one language, one belief, one faith', to which end his life and writings were devoted. He is respected still as a contemplative and mystic and joined the third (tertiary) order of the Franciscans. His last visit to North Africa may have resulted in his death from injuries sustained in the cause of his mission.

Monasteries, popes, universities and preaching orders all contributed strongly towards the Christianization of Europe. In addition, it is impossible to neglect the psychological effect of the amazing outburst of Gothic architecture that resulted. Cluny itself possessed the largest abbey church in Europe, over 400 yards (365 metres) long and 100 yards (90 metres) wide, mostly built between 1050 and 1110, though the abbey had been founded in 909. What must have been the effect on the ordinary man or woman to see structures of the size of Westminster Abbey (where the new nave was completed around 1085), Ely Cathedral (begun in 1080), Lincoln Cathedral (begun in 1086), or Durham, built in a single lifetime between 1098 and 1140 in England? Or the wonders of Chartres (1130–1230), St Denis in Paris (consecrated in 1144) and Vézelay, not to mention the glorious but imposing structures of the monastic foundations at Citeaux (1098), Clairvaux (1115) and, in

England, at Rievaulx (1131) and Fountains Abbey (1132), all Cistercian foundations? The spread of such imposing stone constructions was matched across northern Europe by thousands of village churches before 1500, many of them miniature masterpieces of design and craftsmanship by stonemasons and carvers of genius. Wordsworth's 'sermons in stones' spoke of nature's appeal: but these buildings proclaimed the strength, creativity and often soaring aspirations of medieval Christendom. They preached as eloquently to those who saw them as St Sophia, the great Byzantine church of the 530s, had done to its Slav visitors in the 10th century.

The power and wealth of the church led, however, to both corruption and envy before 1500. For an institution founded on apostolic poverty, its landholding, the lifestyle of many of its office-holders and its social and political influence led to unease and unrest. Signs of dissatisfaction among churchmen themselves pre-date the Reformation and Martin Luther. John Wycliffe (c. 1330–84), a Yorkshireman by birth and Oxford don by profession, was Master of Balliol College, Oxford (1360–61) and an intellectual critic of medieval theology. A somewhat opaque person to understand, Wycliffe believed before his time in the translation of the scriptures into the tongue of the people and a return to primitive Christianity from contemporary abuses. His approach was popularized by Wycliffite preachers, the Lollards, many of whom were vigorously persecuted by the church authorities, though Wycliffe himself died naturally as rector of Lutterworth.

In Eastern Europe, a more influential figure was Jan Hus (1372–1415) in Bohemia. He became a great preacher and critic of abuses in modern Czechoslovakia, who, as rector of the University of Prague, knew and translated Wycliffe's writings and propagated his views. Church authority was sufficiently alarmed to put Hus on trial in 1414 and he was burned at the stake in 1415. It was an example of the power of the church leading to intolerance of ideas seen as subversive on such matters as property holding. In time, these attitudes led to the much greater intellectual and spiritual explosion of the Protestant Reformation.

Were this a conventional church history, men such as the great Dutch scholar Erasmus (c. 1466–1536), with his influence on New Testament scholarship and Christian humanism; Martin Luther

(1483–1546), German scholar, monk and reformer, remembered for his 95 theses pinned to the door of the church at Wittenberg in 1517 and his rediscovery of justification by grace through faith; and John Calvin (1509–64), humanist, French prose stylist and systematician, author of the *Institutes of the Christian Religion*, who made Geneva a centre of theology and who influenced the Netherlands, France (the Huguenots), Germany and Scotland would all feature as leading thinkers. For this book, however, as important as these towering individuals of the 16th century are men such as Prince Henry 'the Navigator' (1394–1460), who prompted the Portuguese exploration of Africa; Vasco da Gama (c. 1460–1524), who reached India; and Christopher Columbus (1451–1506). For with these Europeans of the age of exploration went also the Christian faith as Franciscans, Dominicans and later Jesuits and members of other orders sought to propagate the faith to the Indies (East and West), in North and South America and in Africa.

CHAPTER 4

AFRICA

North Africa has already been noted as one of the cradles of Christianity, with Tertullian, Cyprian and Augustine of Hippo among the great Latin Fathers of the faith. Egypt too was highly influential, not least through the lives of the 'desert fathers' such as Antony and Pachomios. In this chapter, the rooting of African Christianity in Ethiopian Orthodoxy will be outlined. This highly indigenous form of Christian faith and practice has survived until today with an estimated 36 million adherents. We will then consider the pioneering efforts of the Portuguese captains, inspired by Henry the Navigator, which resulted in early penetration of the continent and the extraordinary story of the Christian kingdom of Kongo after 1487. The churches of the Reformation then attempted to convey the faith to Africa – Anglicans and Methodists in West Africa; Moravians, Dutch and other Protestants in South Africa; J.L. Krapf in East Africa; and the epic journeys of David Livingstone in central Africa. Later came the influence of Cardinal Lavigerie and the White Fathers and of Anglicans in Uganda. And finally the whole stirring story of Madagascar, which laid hold of the imagination of the Victorian public only a little less than Livingstone himself.

Ethiopian Christianity

An Ethiopian appeared early in Christian documents through the vivid story in Acts (8:26–40) of the eunuch and treasurer baptized by Philip the evangelist. The beginning of the Ethiopian church, however, is thought to have resulted from the influence of an enslaved captive, Frumentius, around AD 300. Frumentius was captured while on a trading voyage and taken to the local king in Axum. Here he helped the government and was allowed to leave around 340. He presented himself to Athanasius, then bishop of Alexandria according to the historian Rufinus (345–410), who, hearing of Ethiopia's need, consecrated him as bishop of Axum. Thus began a long tradition, whereby Ethiopian Orthodoxy looked to Alexandria and its Egyptian Coptic church until as recently as 1959. Alexandria provided the church's leader, the 'abuna', an arrangement that made for great difficulty and a shortage of clergy when the appointment of an ordaining abuna was delayed. Frumentius's work is said to have been furthered by the 'Nine Saints' from Syria around 480, who extended Christian life and became greatly revered in the Ethiopian church. Ethiopia became a Christian kingdom, which in many periods of historical upheaval remained focused on the Christian monarch up to the times of Haile Selassie in the 20th century.

Certain characteristics of Ethiopian Christianity deserve to be noted. It was an extremely Jewish form of Christian tradition and for long periods observed the Sabbath rather than Sunday (and at one point both). It shared with the Falasha Jews great respect for the history of King Solomon and his visitor, the Queen of Sheba; and there was a tenacious legend that, after their meeting, the ark of the covenant had been procured from Jerusalem and taken to Ethiopia. This resulted in miniature 'arks', called the 'tabot', being displayed in places of worship. The classic account of the royal meeting is the document known as the *Kebra Nagast*, which may date as early as the 6th century. Ethiopian Christians saw themselves as Jews, having a Jewish inheritance, before they were Christians. They retained the practice of circumcision as well as practising baptism. Monarchs regarded their dynasty as from Solomon and in modern times one of Haile Selassie's titles was 'Lion of Judah'.

The Ethiopian church also had a strong monastic tradition. The 'Nine Saints' were said to have founded a number of communities around Axum, among them Dabra Damo, which lasted 1,000 years; and around 1270 a famous monastery, Dabra Libanos, became a centre of renewal. Axum itself had a very large, five-aisled cathedral, but this was destroyed in a Muslim jihad in the 16th century. At this point the whole kingdom could have become Muslim permanently had it not been for Portuguese military assistance in a decisive battle of 1543. Much credit for the survival of Ethiopian Orthodoxy has been given to their ancient translation of the Bible into Ge'ez; their strong musical tradition in worship maintained by the laity; and the deeply indigenous Ethiopian and African character of their worship and church life.

'From your lips sweeter than the scent of myrrh . . . came forth books from Arabic to Ge'ez.'

On the Bible translator, Abuna Salama (1348–88), in the *Synaxarion*

Helped by various Roman Catholic agencies, notably the Capuchins and Jesuits, they have nevertheless resisted attempts to align the church with Rome.

The extraordinary persistence of Ethiopian Christianity with, among other symbols, its rock-hewn underground churches from the reign of Lalibela (1190–1225) and its colourful processions is underlined by the fate of another flourishing Christian kingdom of the 8th to the 12th centuries in Nubia. This was a territory around modern Khartoum, whose bishops were also consecrated by the patriarch of Alexandria but were indigenous to Nubia. It had a cathedral at Faras and, like Ethiopia, the monarch was central to religion. In this case, inheritance by a Muslim king led to the demise of Nubian Christianity. This had dated from a mission initiated by Emperor Justinian and his wife Theodora in 543 in Constantinople; but by 580 the whole population had followed their rulers into Christian faith. We know of a bishop of Qasr Ibrim as late as 1372; but by 1500 the area was Muslim and what had been a flourishing church gradually disappeared. Excavations in the 1960s, prior to the flooding of northern Nubia for the Aswan dam, revealed the rich remains of Nubian churches.

> 'At length the sheep of Ethiopia, freed from the bad lions of the West, securely in their pastures feed.'
>
> **Popular chant against the Church of Rome, c. 1640**

The kingdom of Kongo

Portuguese progress down the west coast of Africa resulted in trading forts at Elmina on the Gold Coast (Ghana) in 1482 and expeditions up the River Zaire by Diego Cao in 1483, 1485 and 1487. After a further expedition in 1491, the local king, Mbanza Kongo, was baptized as Joao I, after the reigning Portuguese king (Joao II). Christianization proceeded apace under the king Mvemba Nzinga, renamed Afonso (1506–43), who made Christianity the religion of the nobility, taking their titles of marquises etc. from the Portuguese aristocracy of the day. In the capital of Sao Salvador there was an influential Portuguese presence of about 100 traders. Afonso's son, Henrique, was sent to Lisbon for education and made a bishop in 1521; but he died soon after his return to Africa in 1530. Afonso made frequent appeals to the king in Portugal for assistance in establishing Christian faith and life from 1514 onwards. A Portuguese priest of the time has left a vivid, if hagiographic and idealized, portrait of this African monarch, still regarded in Congolese tradition as 'apostle of the Kongo'. We are told that he preached to the people with great skill and clarity, a tradition of royal preaching confirmed elsewhere. Father d'Aguiar described him 'not as a man but as an angel sent by the Lord to this kingdom to convert it, especially when he speaks and when he preaches . . . better than we he knows the prophets and the gospel of our Lord Jesus Christ'.

After the death of this remarkable African convert in 1543, the story of Kongo is one of missed opportunities. Many Spanish Capuchins offered to go to Kongo after the foundation of the Propaganda de Fide in Rome in 1622 as a means of directing missionary orders, but the Portuguese resisted any Spanish incursion. Jesuits based in the Portuguese territory of Angola at Loanda offered help and there were some indigenous priests including canons of the cathedral in Sao Salvador. The Jesuits opened a seminary there in 1624. There was even a visit from a Kongolese ambassador to the pope, commemorated in frescoes in the Vatican library, but no sooner had this African met the pope, Paul V, than he died while still in Rome in 1608. The Portuguese hold was broken in 1640 after their defeat by the Dutch and a party of Capuchins led by Bonaventura d'Alessano began 200 years of mission in 1645; but of the original party many died within two years and others were withdrawn on grounds of ill health. Some Capuchin help continued from a base in Loanda but by 1700 the Christian presence in Kongo, even in the most favourable area of Soyo, was fading. It would take the introduction of Baptist missionaries in the Congo of the 1870s in the shape of men such as George Grenfell (1849–1906) and Holman Bentley (1855–1905) to cause the king, Pedro V, to recall the nation's Christian past.

'At Mbanza Zolu I sent word to the king to tell the fetishists to stop their dances . . . I beat the heads of two idols . . . and threw them into the fire.'

Diary of Fr Caltanisetta, Capuchin Missionary in the Kongo Kingdom of the 1690s

West Africa

By the late 18th century the trade in slaves from West Africa to the new world ran into thousands. After the successful campaign for abolition led by William Wilberforce and Thomas Clarkson, with the help also of a remarkable African in England, Olaudah Equiano, a British naval squadron patrolled off the slaving coast from 1807. The Portuguese were still exporting many thousands across the Atlantic to the slave fields of Brazil, as the English had done to the sugar plantations of the West Indies by the notorious 'middle passage', the noxious holds of the slave ships that caused so many to die in transit. One early governor of Sierra Leone, Zachary Macaulay, father of the historian T.B. Macaulay, actually experienced the horrors of the middle passage for himself. It was Sierra Leone that provided the answer as to what to do with the 're-captives' of the slave trade. The 'province of freedom' became a dumping ground for the navy's spoils from the slavers. The English Church Missionary Society, founded the same year as Zachary Macaulay became governor in 1799, continued its work there after Sierra Leone became a crown colony in 1807. By 1860, some 60,000 recaptured slaves had been landed through Freetown. Uprooted from their tribal structures, they were gradually settled in what in some cases became model Christian villages. One such was Regent, where the German-born missionary, W.A.B. Johnson (1787–1823), was pastor. An early recruit to CMS, Johnson was one of a number of his countrymen willing to serve with CMS at a time when home-grown missionaries were hard to find.

> 'We looked more to Mr Johnson than to Jesus.'
>
> **A Sierra Leonean Christian of Regent after W.A.B. Johnson's Death, 1823**

One unexpected injection to Christian life in Sierra Leone was the arrival of 1200 freed American slaves. These organized themselves into 15 ships at Halifax, Nova Scotia, and arrived singing hymns as they came ashore with their Baptist, Methodist and other pastors, some from the so-called Countess of Huntingdon's Connexion, leading them. In time, Methodist life was greatly strengthened by the arrival from England of Thomas Birch Freeman (1806–90), the son of an African father and English mother, previously head-gardener at a Norfolk country house before becoming a missionary with the Wesleyan Methodist Missionary Society in 1837. He was able to survive the West African climate, which was fatal for many European missionaries, and gave long service in West Africa.

Some of the re-captives in Sierra Leone caught the vision of returning to their own tribal people with the Christian gospel. Among them was the Yoruba-born Samuel Adjai Crowther (c. 1806–91). Crowther had been recaptured from the Portuguese slaver *Esperanza Felix* in 1821.

Mary Slessor (1848–1915)

Mary Slessor is said to have learnt some of her toughness as a missionary pioneer by leading a group of youngsters in a Christian youth club in Dundee. Her father was often drunk and Mary, like David Livingstone, worked in a mill while still a child. She was accepted for missionary service by the United Presbyterian Church in 1876 and sent as a teacher to Calabar, teaching in Duke Town and Creek Town. She moved to work alone among the Okoyong people, saving twins from their traditional fate of death and making a home for them and tribal women. She lived very simply, settled quarrels and, as a consular agent of the Niger Protectorate, administered justice. She was an example of identification and cultural adaptability as a missionary, responsible for a whole people's adherence to Christianity.

He became one of the first students at the new CMS college at Fourah Bay, later associated with the University of Durham for the granting of degrees in 1876. Crowther became a missionary to his own branch of the Yoruba, the Egba, in the 1830s, while also translating books of the New Testament into Yoruba. Crowther's friend and mentor in London, Henry Venn (1796–1873), secretary and chief executive of CMS, like the American Rufus Anderson (1796–1880) of the American Board of Commissioners for Foreign Missions, sought to create indigenous churches that were 'self-supporting, self-governing and self-extending', leading in Venn's thinking to the *euthanasia* of the mission.

In 1864, Venn persuaded a reluctant Crowther to become bishop on the Niger to mark the crown of Venn's endeavours to build the 'native' or indigenous church in West Africa. Although the decision was to lead to great heartache for Crowther, Bishop Bengt Sundkler, himself both bishop in Africa and a leading historian of its church life, wrote of it: 'This appointment was one of the most far-sighted ecclesiastical decisions in African church history.' In the Roman Catholic world, the Jewish convert and mission inspirer, Francis Libermann (1802–52), leader of the Holy Ghost Fathers, sought an indigenous African church in a similar way.

The Anglican CMS was perhaps the leading Christian influence in West Africa (although the Scotland Presbyterian mission of Hope Waddell and Mary Slessor in Calabar deserves mention), but it was the

Netherlands Missionary Society and the London Missionary Society (LMS) that provided some great pioneers in South Africa, by then Dutch-controlled. Moravian Christians formed a model Christian community at Genadendal under Georg Schmidt (1709–85), which is still a place of peace, tranquillity and sense of order today.

South Africa

Johannes van der Kemp (1747–1811) was a founder of the Netherlands Missionary Society. He had been a soldier and became a qualified doctor before arriving in Cape Town in 1799. He was a brilliant man, who upset conventional Boers with his marriage to a Malagasy slave girl, his opposition to slavery and to the oppression of African peoples. The LMS also provided some great figures. Robert Moffatt (1795–1833), who arrived in Cape Town in 1817, John Philip (1775–1851), who came two years later and David Livingstone (1813–73). Moffatt, like T.B. Freeman, had been a gardener, coming from Overtoun in Scotland. He gave 50 years to mission north of the Orange River, mostly based at his station of Kuruman from 1821. His daughter Mary married Livingstone; and Moffatt guided Livingstone in his early years in the field. John Philip, also a Scotsman, in his case from Aberdeen, was sent by LMS as a mission administrator. He was an ordained Congregationalist minister, who combined work for the mission with a pastorate of a Congregational church in Cape Town. He, too, like van der Kemp, was a doughty opponent of what he saw as white oppression of the black population and like the Dutchman aroused deep hostility among Boers and other colonialists, including the British, for his political stance for indigenous Africans.

David Livingstone was the child of a poor home in Blantyre, Scotland. He worked in a cotton mill for 13 years before offering for missionary service and qualifying as a doctor in London. He joined Moffatt at Kuruman and spent 11 years with him (1841–52). Here he conceived his plan of exploration, which took him west to the Loanda coast of Angola and east to the mouth of the Zambezi at Quelimane, journeys achieved between 1852 and 1856. The extraordinary physical and geographical feat made him a hero in Victorian Britain. He had a

'I go back to Africa to try to make an open path for commerce and Christianity. Do you carry on the work which I have begun!'

David Livingstone at the University of Cambridge, 1857

David Livingstone (1813–73)

Livingstone was born in the mill town of Blantyre, near Glasgow, Scotland. Having left the Kirk (the Church of Scotland), his father, Neil, brought up his family in an independent congregation in Hamilton, which resulted from the evangelical revival. As a boy, after a 12-hour day in the mill, Livingstone was offered two hours' schooling, during which he studied such texts as Virgil and Horace. In his twenties, he was fired by stories of Karl Gutzlaff's work in China, and in 1837, he offered himself to the LMS and trained as a missionary and a doctor. After a meeting with Robert Moffatt, during the Opium War in China, he decided for Africa. He qualified as a physician in Glasgow in 1840 and arrived in Cape Town in 1841, before joining Moffatt, whose daughter, Mary, he married. Their first child died in 1846 and they lost another child in 1850. During the period after 1852, Mary took the family to Scotland, but this proved a very unhappy episode, when her relationships with Livingstone's parents became strained, and she herself resorted to drink in her loneliness. After Livingstone's epic journeys of 1853–56 and his triumphant reception in the home counties, they were reunited. Mary accompanied him on his Zambezi expedition of 1858, but she died during it. Livingstone's eldest son, Robert, died in 1864 as a soldier in the Union cause (the abolition of slavery) during the American Civil War, a cause close to his father's heart. Livingstone was found by H.M. Stanley in 1871 and died in April 1873. His funeral, paid for by the government, was held in Westminster Abbey on 18 April 1874, with two royal carriages for the principal mourners, who included Moffatt, two of Livingstone's sons, Tom and Oswell, and his daughter, Agnes, to whom he had been particularly close in his last years.

triumphant tour, which included an enthusiastic reception at the Senate House in Cambridge, where his inspiring address effectively launched the Universities' Mission to Central Africa.

Two other missions of note also took their inspiration from Livingstone. The Free Church of Scotland's Livingstonia Mission was launched in 1875 and, soon after, the Church of Scotland began its Blantyre Mission south of Lake Nyasa, both missions being in modern Malawi. It was during yet another daunting journey of exploration that

Henry Morton Stanley (1841–1904)

Stanley is known to missionary history for his famous greeting of 1871, 'Dr Livingstone, I presume?' He had been born in Denbigh, North Wales and brought up in a workhouse before emigrating to the United States in 1858. He became a journalist and the *New York Herald* sent him in search of Livingstone. The story made him famous. In 1875 he visited the Kabaka of Buganda, Mutesa, and published an appeal for missionaries to be sent to Uganda, which prompted the CMS mission of 1877. Later, Stanley played a part in opening up the Belgian Congo to Christian missionaries when employed by Leopold II, the king of the Belgians.

H.M. Stanley, representing the *New York Herald*, found Livingstone at Ujiji in 1871. Two years later, in modern Zambia, Livingstone finally died in May 1873. There followed one of the great African epics, when his two helpers, Susi and Chuma, carried his body at great risk to themselves over hundreds of miles to the coast. Livingstone was buried finally in Westminster Abbey on 18 April 1874.

Debate about Livingstone will continue. Was he a missionary or an explorer? How far was his hope of opening up the interior of Africa to commerce and civilization as an antidote to the slave trade a legitimate and reasonable aim? What of his treatment of Mary and his family in his single-minded pursuit of his goals? Such issues cannot be handled here, though they will continue to fascinate and perplex. C.P. Groves, a widely versed historian of Christianity in Africa, wrote of him:

The great trans-continental journey . . . was an achievement that marks a watershed in the history of the continent and . . . meant more for the expansion of Christian missions in Africa than any other single exploit. It was a breaking of the lock that opened a door inviting advance . . .

Or, in Livingstone's own words, 'The end of the geographical feat is the beginning of the missionary enterprise.' What is clear is that Livingstone, unlike many Europeans, had an instinctive affinity with Africans based on mutual respect, eliciting extraordinary loyalty and enduring friendship in response.

East and Central Africa

The Portuguese had taken Mombasa in 1591 and there had been some Christian penetration by the Augustinian order, some of whom became martyrs, leading to African converts in the early 1630s. Protestant work had to wait until J.L. Krapf (1810–81) arrived there in 1844. Krapf was another German recruit to the CMS, who had been sent first to Ethiopia. He lost both his wife and infant daughter in Mombasa and was joined in his lonely service by another German, Johannes Rebmann (1820–76), with whom he became the first European to see Mount Kenya. To this Rebmann added Kilimanjaro in 1848. Both missionaries studied Swahili and Rebmann translated the Gospels of Luke and John. North of Lake Victoria lay the kingdom of Buganda in modern Uganda. Here too the CMS gained entry in 1877, not least in the person of the Scottish engineer and lay missionary, Alexander Mackay (1849–90).

> 'Tell our friends that in a lonely grave on the African coast there rests a member of the mission.'
>
> J.L. Krapf to CMS from Mombasa, 1844

Islam was also present, introduced by Arab traders. Uganda occupied the mind of one of the greatest Roman Catholic missionary strategists and animators in Cardinal Charles Lavigerie (1825–92), then archbishop in Algiers. He was founder of the Missionaries of Our Lady of Africa, known as the White Fathers. In 1878, a party of them came to the kingdom led by Father Lourdel. The Baganda and the reigning Kabaka, Mutesa (d. 1884), proved open to the missionaries and many of the young men, who, as king's pages, lived in close proximity to the court, became Roman Catholic and Anglican Christians. Mutesa's successor, Mwanga, had learnt homosexual practices from the Arabs and he became enraged that Christian youths would not participate in his tastes. A number of 'boy martyrs' were speared to death in 1885. Anxiety about Christians acting as a potential fifth column in a threatening situation may have contributed to a fresh atrocity in 1886, when 32 men were burned to death. There was much jostling for position by Muslims, Roman Catholics and Anglicans in the years that followed but through the intervention of Captain (later Sir) Frederick Lugard, acting for the Imperial British East Africa Company, a decisive victory at Mengo in 1892 led to a British protectorate in

1893. The colonial period that followed was a time of mass response to Christianity in the country.

Before turning to Madagascar, certain general comments about Christian advance can be made. First, as the cases of Mutesa and Mwanga indicate, the response of rulers to the missionaries and their message could be all-important. Moffatt had a strong relationship with the Ndebele chief, Mzilikazi, while his successor, Lobengula, another astute and powerful chief, prevented the great French missionary, François Coillard (1834–1904), from advance. Nevertheless, Coillard, Eugene Casalis and Adolphe Mabille of the Paris Evangelical Mission were very influential, not least through Casalis's relationship with the great Sotho chief, Moshoeshoe, and Coillard's with Lewanika, chief of the Lozi people in modern Zambia.

> 'If I adopt your law I must entirely overturn all my own and that I shall not do.'
>
> **Chief Ngqika of the Xhosa people to van der Kemp, 1799**

The Zulu leaders, Dingane and Cetshwayo (the latter imprisoned by the British in 1879), were not responsive to the missionaries, although among them they had one of the most radical and imaginative representatives of Christianity in Bishop Colenso (1814–83). His ideas on the Bible caused great anxiety at home but to the Zulus he was 'Sobantu', the father of the

François Coillard (1834–1904)

Coillard was born in Asnières-les-Bourges to a French Huguenot family. He arrived in Cape Town in 1857. He spent 20 years in Leribe in Sotho territory, where his missionary work was interrupted by Boers. In 1877 he tried to reach further north but was arrested by Lobengula. While in the chief's custody he learned of the Lozi people in modern Zambia. He was refused entry at first in 1878 by chief Lewanika but reached the territory in 1886. Lewanika used his good offices to approach Queen Victoria for a treaty, which was achieved in 1890. Coillard was invited to become a British resident but refused. His wife, the daughter of a Scottish minister in Edinburgh, whom he married in 1861, died in 1891 but Coillard continued and greatly reinforced the mission with another 15 missionaries in 1898. One of Lewanika's sons became a Christian. Coillard was one of the most outstanding of all missionaries to Africa in a remarkable group from the Paris Evangelical Mission.

people. After his death, his daughters, Harriette and Frances, continued his campaign for Zulu rights. Livingstone was able to baptize a chief in Sechele of the Kwena people, though he later withdrew his support over marriage discipline. Polygamy in Africa was a continual problem to the missionaries.

In a different case, not involving a chief, van der Kemp's lasting influence was seen through the conversion of the African Ntsikana (1760–1820), whose hymn-writing and profound reinterpretation of Christianity in African terms meant much to the Xhosa and Khoi peoples. Robert Lawes (1851–1934) of the Livingstonia Mission established a strong relationship with Mbelwe, chief of the Ngoni.

Africans showed themselves responsive to the education offered by the missions at institutions like Lovedale, where James Stewart presided, and none more so than the ordained African Tiyo Soga (d. 1871), as influential in the south as that product of Fourah Bay, Samuel Crowther, had been in the west. These and others were a standing contradiction to Europeans who maintained that it would take generations of 'civilization' to produce an educated African leadership.

Madagascar

As in South Africa, it was the LMS who provided the missionary pioneers to the Malagasy people in the early 19th century. Portuguese religious,

Jesuits and Lazarists, had made attempts between 1587 (a Portuguese missionary was killed after brief service in that year) and 1674; but the first churches were founded by David Jones (1797–1841) and Thomas Bevan of the LMS, between 1818 and 1835. They did their work well. For a period of intense persecution followed under Queen Ranavalona (reigning 1828–61), with Malagasy Christians hurled to their deaths over precipices or burned or stoned.

> 'Christians had been speared, smothered, starved or burned to death, poisoned, hurled from cliffs or boiled alive in rice pits.'
>
> **B.A. Gow, who estimated 150,000 deaths, 1979**

Incoming Holy Ghost Fathers and Jesuits were forced to keep to the coastal areas. The constancy of Malagasy Christians caught the imagination of the missionary public and provided an example (which modern China reproduced after 1949) of the removal of expatriate missionaries leading to considerable indigenous growth – often to the surprise of the missionary agencies. After 1860 other Protestant missions entered, among them Norwegian Lutherans in 1866. Madagascar became a French colony in 1896 and the LMS, whose churches at their peak had a membership of some 300,000 looked to the French Paris Evangelical Mission to assist them, with its fluent French-speakers. Although at first the colonial administration was anti-clerical, Roman Catholic advance was considerable, with much work done by the Jesuits. Today some 44 per cent of Malagasays are Christian, while most others follow traditional religions.

Before leaving 19th-century Africa, it is important to emphasize that the spread of Christianity was again and again an indigenous African enterprise, independent of the missionary. Sometimes it could result from the dynamism of a particular people like the Mfengu, who initiated Christian response in different areas. Sometimes it resulted from African clergy and missionaries like the Sierra Leoneans. Sometimes it was the direct effect of gifted individuals like the prophetic figure of Ntsikana among the Xhosa and, as will be seen in the final chapter, Prophet Harris on the Ivory and Gold Coasts. Africans began to look to indigenous forms of Christianity, independent of European influence. One such pioneer of what became known as 'Ethiopianism' was Mangena Mokone, originally an ordained minister in the Wesleyan Methodist church, who became dissatisfied with the paternalism of the missionaries. This led him to found an 'Ethiopian' breakaway church, which was given formal recognition by the Boer leader, Paul Kruger, in the Transvaal as 'the Ethiopian Church of South Africa' in the 1890s. Ethiopianism and 'Zionism' (African charismatic groups with emphasis on healing) have led in the 20th century to large numbers of African Independent Churches (AICs), a phenomenon that will recur in the final chapter.

CHAPTER 5

AMERICA

The expansion of Christianity after Columbus's epoch-making voyages of the 1490s to the Caribbean and what is now known as Latin America was heavily dependent on the two great colonial powers of Spain and Portugal. From the beginning there was a religious intention to the efforts of the conquistadors, however subordinate it may have become to conquest and treasure-seeking for themselves and their royal masters. By means of the papal bull *Ceteris Partibus* of 1493 (such documents being known by the initial words of the Latin text) the pope, Alexander VI, divided the world between the two spheres of influence. Although the map was altered later to enable Portugal to colonize Brazil, the original division was along a line drawn from the North to the South Pole west of the Azores, with Spain given the West Indies and the Americas; and Portugal, which had already explored the west coast of Africa in the time of Henry the Navigator (1394–1460) and moved towards India through Vasco da Gama (c. 1460–1524), Africa, India and the East. Priests accompanied da Gama's voyages and they were equally part of Spanish colonization, combining the roles of missionaries, explorers, secretaries and chroniclers. Often they belonged to religious orders, Franciscans and Dominicans at first and later, with special missionary emphasis and success, the Jesuits.

> 'It is the Holy Trinity in his infinite goodness who has led your Highnesses to this enterprise of the Indies. The Trinity has made me his messenger.'
>
> **Columbus on his third voyage of 1498**

Latin America

It was then with a sense of religious mission, as well as the motivation of acquiring wealth from the indigenous peoples, that men like Cortes (1485–1547) and Pizarro (c. 1475–1541) began their conquest of the Aztec and Inca empires. As in the case of Charlemagne, the goal of Christianization, if achieved by enforced baptisms at the point of the sword, appeared not to trouble the consciences of these military leaders. Cortes was born in Medellin in Spain. He attended the University of

Salamanca and left Spain for Cuba in 1511. At the age of 33 he mounted an expedition against the Aztec capital in Mexico with 700 fellow Spaniards, equipped with canons and muskets, reinforced by thousands of Indian allies.

Although he experienced a reverse after a massacre of Aztec nobles and temporarily had to withdraw from the capital, Tenochtitlan, he returned to the city in August 1520 and systematically destroyed it. He founded and built Mexico City on the same site. He became governor of New Spain and captain general of the forces in 1522, titles that were confirmed by the emperor, Charles V, when Cortes returned to Europe in 1529. He was later replaced by a viceroy and died in 1547. His contemporary, Pizarro, directed his attention to the Inca empire in Peru. He obtained authority from Spain for its conquest in 1528–29 and attacked the Incas in 1530. Again a massacre of Incas assembled at Cajamarca was followed by the capture of the Inca capital of Cuzco in November 1530.

> 'Or like stout Cortez, when with eagle eyes/ He stared at the Pacific – and all his men/ Look'd at each other with a wild surmise –/ Silent upon a peak in Darien.'
>
> **John Keats, 'On First Looking into Chapman's Homer'**

The period of the conquests, which included success in Columbia (1536–38) but failed in Chile, was followed by ecclesiastical and colonial consolidation. Under the so-called *padroado* (Spanish: *patronato royale*) the papacy devolved on the monarchs of Portugal and Spain all the ecclesiastical patronage and appointments in Latin America. The appointments to the new bishoprics of Tlaxcala (1525) and Mexico City (1526), as of Lima (1541) and Caracas, were royal choices. Another of Alexander VI's bulls allowed the monarchs to collect tithes in their colonies and so to finance further Christianization in 1501 (*Eximiae devotionis*); in 1508 a bull (*Universalis ecclesiae*) enabled them to determine the territorial areas of the bishoprics and the naming of all candidates from bishops to curates.

On the colonialist front, a system was developed with the title of *encomienda*. By this method, a number of Indians were assigned to a colonist or landlord. He was ascribed rights to both tribute and labour but it was understood that he was responsible for the Christianizing of those committed to his charge. In fact,

> 'Tell me, by what right or justice do you keep these Indians in such cruel and horrible servitude . . . are they not men?'
>
> **Antonio de Montesinos in a sermon, 1511**

The colonization of South and Central America in the 16th century.

Map labels:

San Francisco

San Diego

CALIFORNIA

NEW SPAIN

Tenochtitlan (Mexico City)
Tlaxcala
Vera Cruz

GUATEMALA

HONDURAS

CUBA

HISPANIOLA

ATLANTIC OCEAN

PACIFIC OCEAN

NEW GRANADA

Caracas

VENEZUELA

Santa Fe de Bogotá

GUIANA

Quito

Amazon

Tordesillas Line

PERU

Lima

Cuzco

BRAZIL

La Paz

SPANISH

PORTUGUESE

Recife (Pernambuco)

CHILE

PARAGUAY

Paraná

Asunción

Sao Paulo

Rio de Janeiro

Santiago

Buenos Aires

Aztec empire (destroyed by 1521)

Inca empire (destroyed by 1535)

however well-intentioned, the *encomienda* system became a by-word for oppression and cruelty by the colonists or *encomenderos* and soon resulted in the virtual slavery of the Indians after its introduction in 1503. Brave Dominican priests denounced the system, one of the earliest protestors being Antonio de Montesinos (c. 1486–c. 1530) on the island of Hispaniola in 1511.

Another Dominican, whose father had accompanied Columbus on one of his voyages, Bartholemew de las Casas (1484–1566), witnessed the burial alive of an Indian leader in Cuba. He became a champion of Indian rights for 50 years from 1514. Confronted by a philosophical position, rooted in the study of Aristotle, that viewed the Indians as slaves by nature, an inferior race intended for their menial role, he worked tirelessly in America and Spain to change attitudes and convince those in authority that the use of force was contrary to apostolic understandings and that the Indian should be respected as God's creation. His efforts to lobby support at home in influential circles, which received recognition from the emperor, Charles V, against the activities of the colonists, included a debate in 1550 at Valladolid with the Aristotelian philosopher and scholar, Sepulveda. Before he died, de las Casas's campaign for just laws for the Indians had been largely responsible for the New Laws of 1542–43, which prohibited Indian slavery and caused the Council for the Indies to be reorganized. After serving as bishop of Chiapas (1544–47), de las Casas used his pen on behalf of the Indians, most famously in his *Brief Account of the Destruction of the Indies*, a hard-hitting critique of Spanish practice, in which he was held to have exaggerated abuses in a work widely disseminated in Europe.

> 'God created these simple people without evil and without guile . . . nor are they quarrelsome, rancorous, querulous or vengeful.'
>
> **Bartholemew de las Casas on Indians**

Jesuit missions

The Franciscans and Dominicans had been first in the field among the orders from 1510 onwards; but in the second phase of the mission the Jesuits were active, in Brazil from 1549, in Peru from 1567 and in Mexico from 1572. José de Anchieta (1534–97) was one great Jesuit missionary who gave 44 years of his life and became known as the 'apostle of

Brazil'. He was one of the founders of both the Sao Paulo and Rio de Janeiro Jesuit missions. Another heroic figure and defender of Indian rights in Brazil was the Jesuit, Antonio Vieira (1608–97), who opposed the Inquisition and the colonists equally, was admired by John IV of Portugal but almost lynched by the colonists in 1661 after the king's death.

In the 17th century, Jesuits were active in Bolivia, Uruguay and Paraguay. In the early 1600s they created a missionary system known as the 'reductions', which was pioneered among the Guarani people in Paraguay but later extended to other missions. By 1623 they had created 23 settlements among the Guarani, which aimed both to protect them from colonists and to Christianize them. In total these communities comprised some 100,000 people. Each settlement had a church, school and workshops and led an ordered life, with work being obligatory for Indians, who, however, had free time and their own gardens allotted to them as well as set periods of service to the general community. The colonists resented the removal of the pool of labour from their control but the Jesuits resisted their influence.

General agitation against the Jesuit order in Europe and in the colonies led to their expulsion from Portuguese territory in 1759 and from Spanish possessions in 1767. The order was suppressed in 1773. All this proved a disastrous blow to the reductions as a means of evangelization. It also exposed the weakness of a form of mission that was essentially paternalist, with little or no authority passed over to the indigenous people or attempt to develop Indian ministry. With

José de Anchieta (1534–97)

José de Anchieta was born in the Canary Islands and studied at Coimbra at the Jesuit College, entering the order in 1551. He reached Brazil in 1554 and co-founded a mission in the Indian village of Piratininga with his Jesuit superior. Ultimately this village became Sao Paulo. He learned the Tupi-Guarani language and taught both Guarani and Portuguese children. He wrote the first grammar and dictionary of the Tupi language, and he is regarded as the father of Brazilian literature. He became Jesuit superior of the Sao Paulo–Rio de Janeiro mission and from 1577–87 provincial of Jesuits in Brazil.

The Mercedarians

The Mercedarians were a Spanish order, dating from around 1235. Their original aim was the collection of money to ransom captives and redeem properties that had fallen into Muslim (Moorish) hands in Spain during its occupation by the Moors from around 750 to 1250. In origin it was a lay order but clergy were admitted and controlled the order in the 14th century. Members travelled to Muslim lands to seek freedom for Christian captives. Gradually academic theology and educational work was included in its work and an order of nuns was founded. Peter Nolasco (c. 1180–c. 1249) its founder was canonized in 1628.

the removal of the Jesuit leaders the reductions collapsed as a system and whole villages were engulfed by jungle after 150 years as oases of Christian community.

Modern Venezuela became an area for further Jesuit exploits. They penetrated the jungles of the Amazon to reach large numbers of Indians. The area of the upper Amazon valley was known as the Maynas. One early Jesuit pioneer, Rafael Ferrer, began a mission in 1599 that cost him his life in martyrdom in 1611. Further Jesuit efforts achieved more and by 1661 many thousands were baptized in this area. The Jesuits found that these people were less easily led than the Guarani people and there was opposition from the Portuguese; but with assistance from Franciscans, some half a million people were reached in the Maynas region.

Central America

Central America was again pioneered by the orders – Franciscans, Dominicans and Mercedarians. The first church on the isthmus of Panama was built in 1510. Missionaries entered Guatemala in 1526, and de las Casas, who had joined the Dominican Order in 1522, introduced other Dominicans to Nicaragua. Guatemala had 22 Franciscan and 14 Dominican houses by 1600.

Mexico, after the era of Cortes, again attracted the orders, so that Franciscans landed at Vera Cruz in 1524, Dominicans in 1526, Augustines in 1533 and later Capuchins (1565) and Jesuits (1572). A

Franciscan, Juan de Zumarraga (c. 1468–1548), became bishop of Mexico City in 1528 and proved to be a firm defender of Indian rights and a believer in an indigenous clergy, towards which he used his college at Tlatelolco. He became archbishop of Mexico in 1546. The University of Mexico, founded in 1553, reflected the church's emphasis on education. In the north of the country a famous Jesuit missionary, Eusebio Kino (1644–1711), Italian by blood but born in the Swiss Tyrol, arrived in Mexico in 1681 and did missionary work in lower California, in the modern state of Arizona and in Colorado. Described as a modest, gentle, humble man who was an upholder of the welfare of Indians, he travelled perpetually in the interest of the mission. He had hoped to reach the war-like Apache people but death intervened in 1711. Before their dissolution the Jesuits achieved another 37 stations in Lower California by 1767.

In the modern state of California a string of Franciscan missions are still to be found between San Diego and San Francisco. Father Juniper Serra (1713–84), born in Majorca, became the leader of the mission and founded such communities as Monterrey and Carmel (1770), San Luis Obispo (1772), Santa Barbara (1786), still an impressive and active Christian community, and others. By 1800 some 100,000 Californian Indians, many from the Chumash people, had been reached by the mission and some 18 Franciscan mission compounds established. At least some of the thrust to the north was driven by Spanish fear of Russian incursion, moving south from Alaska. Father Serra also spent some years establishing work in Texas.

Canada and Alaska

Russians were not the only European power to be feared by Spain. The French had American possessions in Louisiana and French Jesuits were active in the Mississipi valley. Some dreamed of a link between French Canada and the south down this waterway. Father Marquette (1637–75), a gifted linguist, moved down the Mississipi from the north and attempted a mission among the Illinois Indians. While based in Quebec he had made himself master of seven Algonquin languages and he gained a considerable reputation as an Indian-style orator. He was in turn preacher, pastor, explorer and geographer, whose writings contributed to local knowledge of Indian peoples and horticulture. In the political

Jean de Brébeuf (1593–1649)

Jean de Brébeuf was born to a family of the French rural nobility and entered the Jesuit order in 1617. He reached Canada in 1625. He learned one of the Algonquin languages and lived among the Huron people of the north-west, adding their language and staying for three years (1626–29). After capture by the British, he returned to France but renewed his mission in Canada from 1633. He founded the mission 'St Marie among the Hurons' in 1639, destroyed by Iroquois warriors in 1649. He was tall and strongly built and became known as the gentle giant. Like the Jesuits in Paraguay, he favoured withdrawing the Hurons into a missionary settlement. He is an example of the heroic pioneer Jesuit, whose missionary life ended in martyrdom in the field.

struggles of the day, the French were to lose New Orleans and West Mississipi to Spain and Eastern Mississipi to the British; but French Carmelites, Recollects (a 16th-century branch of the Franciscans) and Jesuits achieved much in the French possessions before the Jesuits' expulsion in 1763. French Jesuits had attempted but failed in a mission to the Sioux but in Canada French Roman Catholic influence remained strong. The explorer, Jacques Cartier, had placed a cross when on an expedition to Canada in 1534–36 and then arranged for three native Canadians to be baptized on his return to France.

> 'We folded our hands and venerated the Cross in the presence of a large number of savages in order to show them . . . that our salvation depended only on the Cross.'
>
> **Jacques Cartier in Canada, 1534**

In 1611 two Jesuit missionaries settled in Canada but their mission ended with an English attack. In Quebec, the Recollects began work in 1615. An outstanding priest, Joseph le Caron, began among the Huron people, who were mainly situated north of Lake Ontario, between Georgian Bay and Lake Simcoe, down the St Lawrence River from Quebec and Montreal. They numbered around 20,000 at the time. François de Laval, a missionary-minded vicar apostolic in Canada (vicars apostolic being Roman Catholicism's representative figures before dioceses are formed), became bishop of Quebec in 1674. He was a founder of the Société des Missions Étrangères of Paris, and he gave a fresh impetus to mission by linking his seminary in Quebec to the society in Paris.

Jesuits, who had favoured his appointment, had begun work among the Hurons, chief among them being Jean de Brébeuf (1593–1649). He had learned the Huron language between 1626 and 1629 but was taken prisoner by the English before returning to the Huron mission in 1633–34. This mission was tragically overwhelmed by the war-like Iroquois in 1649 and he and another Jesuit leader of 'St Marie among the Hurons', Gabriel Lalemant, were captured and tortured to death by the victors. Both martyrs were canonized by Pius XI in 1930. Quebec was the scene of a further initiative in 1639, when a wealthy noblewoman, Madame de la Peltrie, was instrumental in French nuns, Ursulines, opening a school for native Canadian girls, a successful piece of missionary work by women.

The British General Wolfe secured Canada, after his victory over the French General Montcalm on the 'Heights of Abraham' of Quebec in 1759; and in 1763, at the Treaty of Paris, Canada became British. At about this time the Jesuits, on the verge of their dissolution, expanded their work among native Canadians and Americans to include various sub-groups of the Iroquois in the Mohawks, the Oneidas, the Cayugas and the Senecas, as well as working among the Algonquins at Sillery near Quebec and a related clan, the Abenaki. But the missions struggled with Iroquois resistance, problems of disease (introduced by the missionaries themselves), and the influence of brandy and other strong drink (also brought in by Europeans) to which the Indians became addicted. Although thousands of Iroquois were baptized, the large majority remained pagan. Bishop Laval was responsible for another famous Jesuit missionary, Claude Allouez (1622–89), initiating missionary work west of Montreal and north to Lake Nipigon in 1667. Jesuits reached the Hudson Bay area and baptized there. Even after the British had won Canada and their order had been suppressed in Europe, some Jesuits remained in Canada as late as 1789.

In the far north, Russians had entered Alaska in 1741. Russian Orthodox Christianity had begun work on Kodiak Island, off Alaska, in 1794. By 1796 some thousands of the islanders and the population of the Aleutian Islands had been baptized. They met hostility from the Russian American Company but the mission received fresh invigoration by the arrival of Innocent Veniaminoff (1797–1879), an Orthodox priest from Siberia, who reached the Aleutian Islands in the 1820s.

Ursulines

This order of nuns was founded in 1535. It developed into an educational order, working in girls' schools, not least in 16th-century France. Marie Guyard ('Marie of the Incarnation', 1549–1672), who founded the house in Quebec in 1639, was one of the most famous members of the order. She and two other sisters of the house in Tours, with Madame de la Peltrie, accepted the Jesuit invitation to assist the mission in Canada through a convent based in Quebec. Marie was the first superior of the Ursulines. She was also a religious visionary and mystic, whose letters and writings were published after her death.

He mastered the Aleutian dialect well enough to translate the Gospel of Matthew and to write a devotional tract that became a classic, *An Indication of the Pathway into the Kingdom of Heaven*. After working among the Aleutians for some years, he served among the Tlingit people. After his wife died, the Orthodox Church appointed him as bishop of an area that included California. Between 1840 and 1868 he continued notable work. Although 40 years of missionary service, often in conditions of great physical hardship, had left him exhausted and ready to retire, he was appointed metropolitan of Moscow, a position he used to found the Russian Missionary Society as a means of support for Orthodox missions. His outstanding service was recognized in 1977 by the Orthodox Church of America conferring on him the title of 'Evangelizer of the Aleuts and Apostle to America', while the Russian Orthodox Church made the 200th year of his birth (1997) 'the year of St Innocent'. Alaska was sold to the United States in the 1870s but the Holy Synod created an independent bishopric to include Alaska in 1872. By 1900 there were some 10,000 Orthodox Christians in the diocese. Of the 65,000 Alaskan and Aleutian people today, some 70 per cent claim to be Christian and many of these belong to the Orthodox community.

America and Protestant missions

Roman Catholic orders were often heroic pioneers in the continent of America and from 1622 Roman Catholicism had the great advantage of a central organizing body for missions in the Sacred Propaganda for the Faith (today's Congregation for the Evangelization of the Nations). By contrast, the churches of the Reformation had comparatively little missionary vision in the 16th century and no directing agency in the 17th. French Protestantism, led by the Huguenot Admiral Coligny, attempted a short-lived experiment off Rio de Janeiro where Admiral Villegagnon established a settlement with Calvinist worship and church life at its heart between 1555 and 1560, until the French were expelled by the Portuguese. A longer-lasting Calvinist settlement was initiated by the Dutch after their capture of Pernambuco, which remained Calvinist for 40 years. Jan Maurizius created a number of Calvinist centres in the north-west of Brazil, in what had been Portuguese settlements. Some 20 Reformed congregations developed in Brazil, with 50 pastors employed, one of the larger congregations being in Recife.

North America presented a different scene. The symbolic event of the voyage of the *Mayflower* with its 'Pilgrim Fathers' in 1621 was a historical pointer to the strong influence of Calvinist Protestantism in New England. The states of Massachusetts, Connecticut and New Hampshire were strongly Congregationalist and Presbyterian in church life and heavily influenced by English Puritanism. Some, at least, of these pioneering people felt a responsibility for spreading the Christian faith to the native American indigenous peoples. John Eliot (1604–90) is regarded as the chief initiator, when acting as Presbyterian pastor of Roxby, near Boston in Massachusetts from 1632. He taught himself the Iroquois language, and, like the Jesuits in Paraguay but probably with no knowledge of them, founded 'praying towns', communities that, over 40 years, included over 3,000 Christian Indians in Natick and other settlements. Eliot translated both the New Testament (1661) and the Old Testament (1663) and showed far-sightedness in preparing an indigenous Christian ministry of native American preachers, of whom there were 24 by his death.

A remarkable family called Mayhew were also pioneers in missionary work, their field being Martha's Vineyard, Nantucket and the Elizabeth Islands off Cape Cod. Thomas Mayhew bought the islands in 1641 with an Indian population of around 5,000 people. His son, Thomas (1621–57), began a mission among them and by 1651 around 200 had responded to his work. After the death of both generations, John, youngest son of the younger Thomas and his son Experience Mayhew (1673–1758) continued the mission, Experience having the advantage of fluency in the language and ability to write in it. Zechariah, his son, carried on a tradition that lasted from 1641–1806 and produced Indian clergy and one Harvard graduate. Of this family, Kenneth Latourette has written: 'Not even the line of Gregory the Illuminator in Armenia was so prolonged in its leadership.' Gregory's mission began in 280, and was continued well into the next century by his son, but was eclipsed by the Mayhews.

We have already mentioned the Moravian community in Georg Schmidt's mission at Genadendal in South Africa, but here we should note an early Moravian mission among Eskimo (Inuit) people in Labrador, as well as Moravian missionaries founding communities of Christian native Americans. (Their origins as a Christian community will be examined in the next chapter.) Their own leader in Europe, Count Zinzendorf, had been in North America in Philadelphia from 1741 to 1743 and prompted work among indigenous people and colonists alike. The leader in America became August Spangenberg (1704–92), who organized missionary preparation for Moravians at their centre at Bethlehem, Pennsylvania. A mission was founded in the same state named Gnadenhütten (dwellings of grace). David Zeisberger (1721–1808) gave a lifetime of missionary service from 1745, but disaster struck at Gnadenhütten when, in his absence in Detroit to convince the British of the neutrality of the mission, 96 of his Indian converts were massacred by American troops in 1782, innocent casualties of the war of American Independence. Zeisberger started again, giving a total of 62 years to missionary work, during which he mastered several indigenous languages and produced dictionaries and other essential linguistic aids.

David Brainerd

A New England figure who was to become a missionary icon to many, including William Carey and David Livingstone, was David Brainerd (1718–47). He was born in the farming country of Haddam, Connecticut and studied for the ministry at the then Yale College, from which he was somewhat unjustly expelled in 1741. He impressed the local leadership of the

'There is one thing in Mr Brainerd easily discernible, that is, that he was one who by his . . . natural temper was . . . prone to . . . dejection of spirit.'

Jonathan Edwards's preface to the _Account_ by David Brainerd

Scottish Society for the Propagation of the Gospel enough for them to employ him for missionary service from 1742, when he worked among the Indians of Stockbridge and then, after Presbyterian ordination, in western Massachusetts, Pennsylvania and New Jersey. In the last setting he experienced scenes of religious revival among the Delaware Indians, which he recounted in his journals, as well as his own spiritual history, with all its fluctuations of mood in spiritual exaltation and despair.

Brainerd died young but his journals and the account of his life by the great preacher and philosopher, Jonathan Edwards (1703–58), became immensely influential in the Protestant world. Edwards, also a student at Yale and citizen of Connecticut, was himself a missionary at Stockbridge among the Indians from 1750–58. His eminence as a leading philosopher, theologian and president-elect of Princeton lie outside the limits of this book, but he was one who combined the life of scholarship with extensive efforts for the Indians. His life of Brainerd was published in 1749.

'Rode several hours in the rain through the howling wilderness.'

David Brainerd on his way to the Delaware Indians, *Journal*, 1 May 1744

The New England Presbyterians and Congregationalists were not matched by other non-Roman Catholic churches in their efforts among native Americans, although Episcopalians and the missionary society of the Church of England, the Society for the Propagation of the Gospel, did achieve some work among native Americans. Work among the Iroquois of New York was initiated by the then governor, Lord Bellomont, and one converted Mohawk chief, Joseph Brant, helped to establish a Mohawk church. Queen Anne of England even presented some communion silver to four Mohawk Christians in London in 1704 for use in her 'Indian chappell of the Mohawks'.

In Virginia the royal charter declared one of the aims of the settlement to be the conversion of the Indians. The first minister of Henrico, Alexander Whitaker, did act as a missionary and introduced the Indian princess, Pocahontas, to the faith. A college was founded at Henrico for the education of Indians and there were appeals for funding for Indian missions at home by King

'To settle the State of Religion as well as may be for our own people . . . and then to proceed in the best methods . . . towards the conversion of the Natives.'

Annual sermon of 1701 expressing the aims of the SPG

James I and his archbishops, so that one of six professorships at the College of William and Mary was set apart for the teaching of Indians.

Methodists had behind them the experience of John and Charles Wesley when acting as Anglican priests and missionaries of the SPG in Georgia from 1735. John Wesley had sought to reach out to the Choctaw and Chickasaw peoples, despite being principally a chaplain to English settlers, but he had little response. After his breach with the Church of England over irregular ordinations, his chief lieutenant in the New World, Thomas Coke (1741–1814), became a driving force for Methodist missionary work, attempting a mission in Nova Scotia in 1786 before being deflected to the West Indies by his wind-driven ship. Methodist missions really came into their own in the 19th century after Coke's death and took the form of frontier preachers and 'circuit riders' under the direction of his great collaborator, Francis Asbury (1745–1816), who himself travelled some 300,000 miles (480,000 kilometres) on horseback in the cause of the gospel and whose vision included both native Americans and African Americans for Methodist outreach. By the time of Asbury's death in 1816 Methodist membership had moved from 13,000 in 1784 to 200,000, a sign of growing influence.

Expansion north

The 19th century in North America saw the further extent of the north reached by Roman Catholics, Anglicans and Methodists. Two priests reached Red River (Winnipeg) in 1818 and by 1843 a large number of people in the settlement became Roman Catholic Christians. The Order of the Oblation of Mary Immaculate (OMI) was assigned western Canada, and Albert Lacombe (1827–1916) became a leading missionary in the north-west, who won the confidence of native Canadians and was known as the 'apostle of the Blackfeet' and by them as 'the man with the good heart'. In 1820, the Anglican CMS took responsibility for the evangelization of the west and the north. William Bompas (1834–1906) worked heroically among the people of the extreme north-west up to the Arctic ocean from 1862 and was consecrated bishop of Athabasca in 1874, publishing works in seven different Indian dialects. Most Eskimo (Inuit) people became Anglican in allegiance. They received their first bishop in Archibald Fleming (1883–1953) in 1933, who signed himself

James Evans (1801–46)

James Evans was born in Hull, England. In 1822 his family emigrated to Canada. After some years as a teacher he was converted at a Methodist camp meeting and began to teach Indian children at the Rice Lake school in 1828. His facility in language led him to construct an Ojibwa alphabet and syllabary and he translated scripture and wrote hymns in their language. In 1833 he was ordained into the Methodist ministry and was appointed to the St Clair River. After 1839 he travelled north of Lake Superior and applied his skill to the Cree language. He was involved in the tragic and accidental death of a teacher, Thomas Hassall, and returned to England leaving much creative work as his memorial. His *Cree Syllabic Hymnbook* of 1841, printed by his own hands, is thought to be the first book printed in the Canadian north-west.

'Archibald the Arctic', by which time 80 per cent were Anglican and 20 per cent Roman Catholic. In Labrador, where once again Moravians had been the pioneers, one losing his life in 1752, CMS took up the work in the person of Edmund Peck (1850–1924), previously a Royal Navy sailor for ten years, who baptized some 100 Eskimos between 1876 and 1882. Methodists made contact with the people of the far north through their representatives at the posts of the Hudson's Bay Company after 1840, the most widely known missionary being James Evans (1801–46) among the Ojibwa people of St Clair River.

The 19th century was a period of extraordinary development in North America, despite the ravages of the Civil War of 1861–65, especially in the United States. Great numbers of immigrants flooded into the country from Europe, estimated at 33 million between 1820 and 1950. Of British emigrants between 1815 and 1900, 65 per cent found their way to the USA. Of African Americans, whereas only some 12 per cent had belonged to any sort of church life in 1860, by 1910 the number was 44 per cent. Many joined the Baptist and Methodist congregations of the southern states after the abolition of slavery. In the nation at large, the extraordinary achievement to any non-American was the blending into one nation of so many disparate peoples, so that their American citizenship was more prominent than whether their roots were Italian, Irish, Jewish, German, Scandinavian or English. The influx posed great challenges to the churches but Americans became a church-going people. The treatment of native Americans, however, as of many slaves of African origin, had often been shameful.

There were many parallels in the treatment by the British of aborigines in Tasmania and Australia and the activities in Spanish, Portuguese and Dutch territories, where European ascendancy resulted again and again in oppression of indigenous peoples. As we have seen, from time to time brave missionary figures rose up in protest, like Bartholemew de las Casas or, in the previous chapter, John Philip in South Africa, to champion the rights of those suffering at the hands of the colonists. Yet in many cases these brave men were themselves subject to obloquy and social ostracism by people of their own race.

'The Great Spirit has made the Red Man and the White man brothers and they ought to take each other by the hand . . . the White Man has robbed us.'

Chief Sitting Bull of the Sioux to Queen Victoria, 1877

CHAPTER 6
EUROPE FROM 1500 TO 1900

The period after 1500 in Europe left it in the throes of the Reformation. The churches that resulted from this religious upheaval, Lutheran, Calvinist, Anglican, Anabaptist, had to devote their energies to their own church life. There was little to match the Roman Catholic outreach to the world through the orders, who accompanied the empire building of Spain and Portugal as Franciscans, Dominicans, Augustinians, Jesuits, Capuchins and others. In the last chapter we noted the exception to this Protestant vacuum in the French Huguenot settlement off Portuguese Brazil in the time of Admiral Coligny's leadership; and the Dutch efforts that resulted in Calvinist congregations in Penambuco and in the north-east of Brazil. The 17th century saw little change. John Eliot was an exception as a Calvinist pioneer in his work among the unevangelized native Americans. It was not, however, until the emergence of the Moravians that the churches of the Reformation developed missionaries with the kind of vision of Jesuits such as Francis Xavier (1506–52) and Robert de Nobili (1577–1656) or the kind of considered missionary strategy represented by the Propaganda (1622) under its Italian head, Francesco Ingoli, which will be examined in the next chapter.

Moravian missionaries

The Moravians had an interesting history. They originated as a reforming movement, which owed its impetus to Jan Hus, the Czech reformer, who was executed for pursuing a Wycliffite programme in 1415. A group called the *Unitas Fratrum*, who stood in the Hus tradition, were greatly reduced in numbers in the 17th century in their native Bohemia at a time of Roman Catholic resurgence, known as the Counter Reformation. A German aristocrat, Count Nikolaus von Zinzendorf (1700–60), born in Dresden and in the service of the government of Saxony from 1722, welcomed the remnant of them on his estates. He had been influenced by the warm devotion to Christ in the movement known as Pietism in Lutheran Germany, centred on the remarkable work of A.H. Francke (1663–1727), who founded the school Zinzendorf had attended and taught at the University of Halle. He also founded other institutions, including a large orphanage, and has led a recent historian of Pietism, W.R. Ward, to describe him as 'one of the great visionaries and . . . most remarkable organizers in the whole history of Christianity'.

Zinzendorf created a religious community on his estates known as Herrnhut. His interest in mission appears to have been inspired by seeing two baptized Greenlanders when attending the coronation of the king of Denmark in Copenhagen. He became a man of consuming missionary vision, often critical of what he saw as the dry orthodoxy of the Lutheran church. His ardour that Christians should win 'trophies for the Lamb' by the conversion of individuals was shared by the Moravian community.

> 'The enthronement of the Lamb of God as the sole creator, sustainer, redeemer and sanctifier of the entire world.'
>
> **Zinzendorf on the missionary aim**

Their very understanding of the church was that it be missionary. Christian life for believers was understood as a missionary calling for all. Although Zinzendorf laid emphasis on winning individuals, Moravian missions developed a strong and deep emphasis on Christian fellowship in community, with warmth of devotion and worship. As noted in previous chapters, Moravians reached South Africa in the person of Georg Schmidt (1709–85) in 1739, who created a Christian community at Genadendal; and among native Americans in North America through the work of the Moravian leader August Spangenberg (1704–92), and great missionaries like David Zeisberger (1721–1808) and the Christian Indian communities of the Gnadenhütten in Pennsylvania. Moravians strongly influenced John Wesley through their missionary Peter Böhler, during and after his service in Georgia.

> 'On shipboard . . . it pleased God . . . to give me twenty-six of the Moravian brethren who endeavoured to show me "a more excellent way".'
>
> **John Wesley, *Journal*, May 1738**

Farflung Moravian missions were to be found in the West Indies (1732), Greenland (1733), Labrador (1752) and among Tibetan people. K.S. Latourette has written of the Moravians in his *A History of the Expansion of Christianity*:

Here was a new phenomenon in the expansion of Christianity, an entire community, of families as well as of the unmarried, devoted to the propagation of

A.H. Francke (1663–1727)

Francke was born in Lübeck and became a lecturer in Leipzig. He was deeply impressed by P.J. Spener (1635–1705) and his spirituality as an early leader of Pietism, who sought the renewal of the Lutheran Church while acting as court chaplain at Dresden. The University of Halle was founded through Spener's influence. Francke became professor of Greek and Oriental languages there in 1691, while also acting as pastor and preacher locally. As well as his orphanage he opened a poor school, a publishing house and a dispensary. He became professor of theology in 1698. He pursued Spener's aims of deepening Bible study, lay priesthood, the regulation of theology in the universities, the renewal of preaching and practical Christianity.

the faith. In its singleness of aim it resembled some of the monastic orders of earlier centuries but these were made up of celibates. Here was a fellowship of Christians, of laity and clergy, of men and women, marrying and rearing families, with much of the quietism of the monastery and of Pietism but with the spread of the Christian message as a major objective, not of a minority of the membership but of the group as a whole.

Before turning to the development of the Protestant missionary societies, which were to become so influential after 1800, certain other Protestant pioneers deserve mention. Hans Egede (1686–1758) was born in Norway. He became a Lutheran missionary in Greenland and a pioneer among Eskimo people there; it was two of the converts of this mission that Zinzendorf saw in Copenhagen. In Greenland the local shamans, known as *angakut*, were the dominant religious force but Egede secured a response to his work, not least through the care he and his wife exercised through a smallpox epidemic in 1733. Egede experienced some tensions with Moravian missionaries who arrived in that year but his son, who had been brought up in Greenland, mastered the language and produced a New Testament for Greenland in 1766. By then Egede had founded an institution for the training of missionaries in Copenhagen in 1736 and the work prospered.

Denmark, whose Lutheran church had been influenced by Pietism, was the country that sent out two other early pioneers to India – Bartholemäus Ziegenbalg (1682–1719) and Heinrich Plütschau

(1677–1752) – both Germans and both educated at Halle. From Copenhagen they settled in the Danish settlement of Tranquebar as the first Protestant missionaries to India in July 1706. They were 'royal Danish' missionaries, with their salaries paid by King Frederick IV of Denmark. Both owed much to A.H. Francke but on arrival were wise enough to seek help with the Tamil language from Jesuit missionaries. Ziegenbalg produced the first Tamil New Testament in 1715. He died four years later, aged 36.

The Danish example of royal influence is a reminder of the kind of monopoly on all kinds of overseas enterprise that operated in Europe. In England, for example, such trading bodies as the East India Company or the Hudson's Bay Company, in an era of what became known as mercantilism, were granted monopoly trading agreements directly from the crown by royal charter. The same principle held true for the Society for the Propagation of the Gospel (SPG), incorporated by royal charter in 1701.

As an economic system it was to be dissolved by the new economics of Adam Smith and his *Wealth of Nations* as part of the movement known as the Enlightenment in Europe, during which royal monopolies gave way to the kind of free economic competition of the new capitalism. The joint stock companies of the 19th century, with their boards of directors and basic voluntary principle, became a model for missionary societies, which stood in a voluntary relationship to their churches, as did the Church Missionary Society to the Church of England.

> 'Pietism caused Germany to be Protestantism's leading missionary country . . . [and] demonstrated in a remarkable way what total dedication meant.'
>
> **David Bosch, Transforming Mission**

Despite its foundation date of 1701, SPG was not the earliest missionary society in England; that distinction belongs to the Society for Promoting Christian Knowledge of 1698. Like SPG it owed its existence to the vision of an English rector, Thomas Bray (1656–1730), who had himself acted for the bishop of London in seeking to meet the needs of the colonists of Maryland in 1699. SPCK and SPG were both active in North America and SPCK was prepared

> SPG was to 'supply the want of learned and orthodox ministers' in the colonies and in 'factories beyond the seas'.
>
> **Royal Charter of William III, 1701**

to employ German Lutherans, some ordained, maintaining strong ties with A.H. Francke and German Pietism, while also giving support to the Danish-Halle mission in Tranquebar where Ziegenbalg and Plütschau served. A series of German missionaries, often selected by Francke, went from Halle to this mission, of whom possibly the greatest of all was Christian Friedrich Schwartz (1726–98), who served in India for nearly 50 years (1750–98). Schwartz was influential in South India generally and was admired equally by the Hindu prince, Saraboji, and the East India Company, both of whom commemorated him with monuments in marble.

The era of voluntary societies

The end of the 18th century in England was a time of a fresh set of missionary initiatives through the foundation of the voluntary societies. Here were concentrated missionary-minded individuals, who formed organizations that, like the missionary orders of the Roman Catholic church, often acted independently, while still maintaining links with denominational churches. One of the first of these was the Baptist Missionary Society, which was organized to

> 'Expect great things. Attempt great things.'
>
> **William Carey in a sermon on the text 'Enlarge Thy Tent' (Isaiah 54:2) at Nottingham to the Northamptonshire Association, 30 May 1792**

support the great Protestant pioneer William Carey in 1792. Carey and his Baptist co-workers, Joshua Marshman (1768–1837) and William Ward (1769–1823), with their base at Serampore, will feature in the next chapter, but it is interesting to note here that they sailed to India in a Danish ship because of prejudice against their aims in England and among the East India Company. Here was a clash between the royal charter monopoly and the voluntary missionary agent.

In 1795 the London Missionary Society (LMS) was founded. Although it had a Congregationalist core, it was non-denominational and open to evangelical membership from all churches, being committed to a policy that no particular form of church government would be pursued for its missions. It was the society that supported Robert Moffatt and David Livingstone in Africa and the lonely pioneer Robert Morrison (1782–1834), who retained a foothold in China from 1809, engaged in Bible translation. It was also to be influential in Madagascar and Oceania.

In 1799, evangelical Anglicans, many of whom had supported LMS, decided to form their own society, the Church Missionary Society (CMS). Like the SPCK, CMS found itself employing German Lutheran missionaries in its early days, when missionary recruits were hard to find. In its important early work among the freed slaves of Sierra Leone, it was a German missionary, W.A.B. Johnson, who was a typical if exceptional figure, as were the Germans J.L. Krapf and W. Rebmann in East Africa. Both SPG and CMS were active increasingly in areas of the British empire after 1800.

Missionary societies also developed in mainland Europe. Johannes van der Kemp (1747–1811), who has appeared in these pages as a pioneer in South Africa, was co-founder of the Netherlands Missionary Society in 1797, before arriving in Cape Town as a NMS missionary in 1799. In Basel, the German Christian Fellowship founded the Basel Mission in 1815 with C.G. Blumhardt (1779–1839) as its first director. It was in the mission seminary of this society that many of the early CMS missionaries received their training, Krapf and Rebmann among them. In all, the seminary supplied 88 of the early CMS missionaries. It was another indication of the close links between German Pietism and the English societies.

Germany also produced the Leipzig Society, whose first director was Karl Graul (1814–64), a notable missionary thinker; the Rhenish Society (1828), which worked in South Africa and elsewhere; the North German Society (1836), which worked in West Africa; the Gossner Society (1842), with work in Bengal; the Herrmansburg Mission (1849), working in South Africa and British India; and the Neuendettelsau Society (1849), which worked in New Guinea and among Australian Aborigines. Among many great pioneers from these missions, particular mention is made later of Ludwig Nommensen (1834–1918), sent by the Rhenish Society to the Bataks of Sumatra; Christian Keysser (1877–1961) of the Neuendettelsau Society among the Kate people of New Guinea; and Bruno Gutmann (1876–1966), sent by the Leipzig Society to work among the Chagga people of Mount Kilimanjaro.

One famous German-speaking missionary from Alsace, who chose to associate himself with a French society, was the renowned theologian and musician Albert Schweitzer. As a missionary doctor in West Africa at Lambarene his links were with the Paris Evangelical Missionary Society.

Albert Schweitzer (1875–1965)

Schweitzer was the son of a Lutheran pastor in Alsace. He became famous both for his New Testament writings and his brilliant musicianship, not least his interpretation of J.S. Bach's organ works. In 1906 he published the German edition of *The Quest of the Historical Jesus* with its view of the subject as dominated by the end-time. It had a great impact on the theological schools of Europe and is still influential. In 1913 he decided to forsake the academy to work in Africa as a medical doctor and established a hospital at Lambarene in French Equatorial Africa (Gabon). This work was based on his principle of reverence for all life. Although linked to the Paris Society he provided his own support and sat loose to doctrinal orthodoxy. He was awarded the Nobel prize for his humanitarian efforts in 1953. The first of his books on his African experiences was *On the Edge of the Primeval Forest*.

This was founded in 1819 as an international and inter-denominational body. It was the society that gave much notable service in Africa through those outstanding Frenchmen mentioned earlier, François Coillard, Adolphe Mabille and Eugene Casalis. It took over much of the LMS work in Madagascar after 1896. The Scandinavian nations also developed missionary societies: the Swedish Missionary Society (1835); the Norwegian Missionary Society (1842); the Finnish Missionary Society (1859); and a further Swedish body, the Svenska Missionsförbundet of 1878, which broke away from the Church of Sweden and formed a free Lutheran church in that year. Swedish missions have worked in Ethiopia, Zaire and Tanzania; and Norwegians in Madagascar and Zululand.

For Protestantism, the influence of Pietism and its propagation through Moravian missions provided one source of missionary stimulus. The evangelical revival, connected with the activity of John Wesley and George Whitefield, provided another. John Wesley's decisive spiritual experience of 1738 arose from his friendship with the Moravians and their roots in Pietism.

The Methodist Missionary Society can date its beginnings to 1786, although it began more

> 'When I met Peter Bohler again he consented to put the dispute upon the issue I desired, namely scripture and experience . . . I felt my heart strangely warmed. I felt I did trust in Christ, Christ alone, for salvation.'
>
> **John Wesley, *Journal*, May 1738**

D.L. Moody (1837–99)

Moody was born in Northfield, Massachusetts. He began work aged 17 in his uncle's shoe store in Boston. He did Sunday School and evangelistic work in Chicago from 1858 and acted as a YMCA relief worker during the US Civil War. He toured England, with Ira D. Sankey as organist and soloist, on an evangelistic journey in 1873–75, attracting very large crowds (the Sankey and Moody hymnbook dated from 1873) and returned in 1881–84 after a number of urban missions in the USA. In 1880 he founded the Northfield Conferences, at which many student participants discovered a missionary vocation. In 1886 the Student Volunteer Movement for Foreign Missions (SVM) was formed with its watchword 'the evangelization of the world in this generation'. He founded the Moody Bible Institute in 1889, which has been judged to have made a larger contribution to foreign missions than any other Protestant institution in the USA.

formally in 1819. In the 19th century, fresh impetus was provided by the American preacher and revivalist D.L. Moody, who favoured inter-denominational evangelistic work, which in turn gave rise to missionary societies of this kind. Societies like the China Inland Mission, founded in 1865 by James Hudson Taylor, were an inter-denominational meeting ground of Baptists, Anglicans, Methodists and others. CIM may have been the largest of these societies but others like the Africa Inland Mission (1895) and the Sudan Interior Mission (1893) were similarly constituted, often known as 'faith missions' because of their policy and practice of making no public appeal for funds.

Although Roman Catholic missionary work had languished somewhat in the 18th century (one sign of which being the suppression of the Jesuit order in 1773), as with European Protestantism there was fresh infusion of missionary enthusiasm in the 19th century. The importance of Cardinal Lavigerie and his White Fathers has already been mentioned, but in addition the foundation of the Marists ('the Society of Mary') in Lyons in 1816, the Picpus Fathers confirmed by the pope in 1817 (both congregations active in the Pacific), the Holy Ghost Fathers ('Spiritans') in their merger with the Immaculate Heart of Mary in 1841, the Mill Hill Missionaries ('St Joseph's Society for Foreign Missions') founded by Cardinal Vaughan (1832–1903) in London in 1866 and the Society of the Divine Word (Societas Verbi Divini – SVD) in Steyl, Holland in 1875 were all signs of renewed missionary vigour. French, English and Dutch orders were reviving the missionary vision of the Church of Rome during Latourette's 'Great Century' of Christian expansion.

Cultural impact and missionary thinking

Two final subjects deserve attention in this chapter. First, in this European missionary awakening, it can often seem that European culture and values (for example, Victorian English forms of clothing) were as important to the missions as the Christian gospel. Such a judgment has to be balanced, however, by the recognition that some of the profoundest understandings of alternative societies and peoples were provided by missionaries. So, a Jesuit like Jean de Brébeuf, through his extraordinary facility in the Huron language, provided the indispensable tools for the understanding of the Huron people; William Ward, companion of William Carey, produced a study of Indian language and religion *The History, Literature and Religion of the Hindoos* (1817–20) far ahead of its time as a study of an alternative religion; James Legge (1815–97), LMS missionary in China, was the leading Sinologist of his day, ultimately recognized for his expertise by an Oxford professorship in 1876; the missionary tradition produced anthropologists of world stature in Henri Junod (1863–1934) with his *Life of a South African Tribe* and R.H. Codrington (1830–1922), who produced ground-breaking studies like *The Melanesians* when working for the Anglican Melanesian Mission. Again and again it was missionary translations, dictionaries and tribal descriptions that laid the groundwork for wider cultural studies. Much sensitivity to language and culture accompanied much insensitivity in the inculturation of the Christian gospel.

Secondly, the 19th century in Europe was also a time of development in reflection of the theory and practice of mission and its subjection to a fresh analysis. Propaganda in Rome had reflected fruitfully on mission for the Church of Rome since its inception in 1622, some of the results of which will appear in the next

> 'Every period of mission leads to Christianization of the ethnic group . . . [it] begins with the conversion of individuals . . . the church in every nation conveys the native traits and characteristics of the whole ethnic life.'
>
> G. Warneck, *Missionslehre*

chapter. In Protestant circles Gustav Warneck (1834–1910) established mission studies, becoming the first professor of mission at Halle, which had provided so much of the vitality of Protestant missions after 1700. Reflection on the indigenous church as the goal of mission, to be 'self-supporting, self-governing and self-extending' came from mission directors like Henry Venn of CMS (1796–1873), views shared outside Europe by the director of the American Board of Foreign Commissioners, Rufus Anderson (1796–1880) and Karl Graul of the Leipzig Mission. For Gustav Warneck, the Pietist and Moravian stress on winning individuals to salvation had to be combined with planting churches and churches that were 'of the soil', sharing the culture, national character and life of indigenous people.

This kind of emphasis, as also the increasing cultural sensitivity of the missionary anthropologists to the cross-cultural element of missionary work and evangelization, was the most promising legacy of European missionary expansion towards the 20th century.

CHAPTER 7
ASIA FROM 1500 TO 1900

Christian expansion into Asia after 1500, in sharp contrast to that achieved by the church of the East up to the time of Alopen, was heavily European, related to the expansion of the Portuguese and Spanish empires in the 16th and 17th centuries and to the Dutch, English, French and Danish trading interests in the 18th and 19th centuries. The Jesuits, and their 'Visitor to the East', Alessandro Valignano, and later the 'Propaganda Fidei' under Francesco Ingoli (1578–1649), tried hard to detach Christian mission from the stranglehold put on it, for example, by the authorities in Lisbon, who tried to ensure that all missionaries and all correspondence on missions passed through their hands. In the later period, the relationship between the East India Company and its Dutch equivalent with missionary work was often to regard it as a threat to maintaining undisturbed relationships with the indigenous peoples on which trade could flourish. European trading and political weight, as in the time of the British 'Raj' in India (1857–1947), was by no means always advantageous to Christian mission.

Francis Xavier and Jesuit mission

Even before the Jesuit order had been finally recognized by Rome, its founder, Ignatius Loyola (1491–1556), became aware of the need for an able overseer of Asian missions. Reluctantly, and under pressure of circumstances, he sent his ablest lieutenant and close friend, Francis Xavier (1506–52), to Portuguese Goa in 1540. Xavier remains one of the greatest of all Christian missionaries, possessed it seems of an immensely attractive personality and a Pauline determination to preach the gospel where it had not been named.

Xavier moved from Goa to the Parava (Bharathra) fishermen of the Coromandel coast of India, where he baptized thousands and was

'Many out here fail to become Christians simply because there is nobody to make them Christian. I have [wanted] often to go round the universities of Europe to bludgeon those people who have more learning than love . . .'

Francis Xavier to Ignatius Loyola in a letter

Alessandro Valignano (1539–1606)

Born into the Italian nobility, Valignano obtained a doctorate of law at the University of Padua. After a profound religious experience, he entered the Society of Jesus in 1566. He was appointed Visitor to the Eastern Missions in 1573. He sailed to Goa from Lisbon in 1574. A period of study in Macau led him to the influential decision that the Jesuit mission in China should concentrate on Chinese language, script and the understanding of Chinese custom and literature, a policy followed through by Michele Ruggieri and Matteo Ricci, the Jesuit pioneers of it. Valignano set his face against any conquistador approach to the high civilizations of China and Japan and set out his views in the work *Il Ceremeoniale per i Missionari del Giappone* of 1581, prepared with help from Japanese Christians. He paid two further visits to Japan in 1590–92 and 1598–1603. In China, Ricci, who studied Confucianism deeply enough to be accepted by the Chinese Confucian *literati*, both exemplified Valignano's policy and in his *Journal* regarded him as founder of the Catholic church in Japan of the time.

active in catechizing, though on his own account with a poor grasp of the language. He visited Sri Lanka (1541–45) and Indonesia (the Molucca Islands) for two years before entering Japan in 1549. He established Jesuit missions in Japan and had two catechetical books translated into the language. Exposure to Japan, with its deep respect for all things Chinese, made him determined to enter China. He was poised to do so on the off-shore island of Shang-Chiuan when he died in 1552.

Although Xavier failed to enter China, Valignano, who reached Japan in 1578, became equally convinced of its importance as a mission field and that neither Japan nor China were to be approached (as the Spaniards had approached the Philippines since Magellan made contact in 1521) as if by conquistadors. Instead, careful accommodation to their highly developed civilizations would be needed. This led Valignano, an Italian, to resist the introduction of missionary orders influenced by such a conquistador mentality from the Spanish and Portuguese possessions. Two remarkable Jesuits followed through this policy in imperial China.

Inroads into China

Matteo Ricci (1552–1610) and Michele Ruggieri (1543–1607) entered China in 1583. In due course, they and their successors were to earn the deep respect of the Chinese, not least for their mathematical and astronomical abilities. Ruggieri, a lawyer from Puglia in Italy, worked with Ricci in Portuguese Macau before moving to the mainland. Together, they produced a Portuguese–Chinese dictionary, and Ruggieri later composed the first Chinese Catholic catechism; he was sufficiently proficient in the language to write Chinese poetry. Ricci, an outstanding intellectual, mastered the Confucian classics and came to believe that the kind of grounding he had received in the works of Thomas Aquinas and his use of Aristotle was compatible with the moral ideals set out by Confucius. Ricci's work of 1603 *Tiangzhu Shiyi* (The Meaning of the Lord of Heaven) adopted this approach in reaching out to the Chinese intelligentsia. Ricci believed that participation by Christians in Chinese ancestor rites did not compromise their Christian belief.

From 1600 Ricci had been permitted to reside in Beijing. His successors, like Father Ferdinand Verbiest (1623–88) and Father Schall von Ball (1592–1666), also greatly admired, were given official positions by the first Q'ing emperor, Kangxi (1654–1722; emperor 1662–1722) and they were able to cast the mantle of their positions of honour to protect other missionaries. Schall von Ball, however, narrowly escaped execution in 1664 in an often volatile situation. It was a tragedy that, after the combined influence of Valignano's policy of accommodation had been followed through with such success by Ricci and his Jesuit companions, even Propaganda Fidei's defence of the policy was eventually overturned in Rome. The so-called Rites Controversy, which hinged on how far the honouring of ancestors was a civil or religious act, involving Christians in superstitious practice (at its height between 1693 and 1704), in which dispute Rome ruled against the kind of accommodationist position advanced by Ricci, alienated the good-will gained by the Jesuits and dissipated its effect, so that Christianity became viewed as foreign and a religion of foreigners. The issues raised by the rites dispute were not finally laid to rest until

'In no way . . . can Christians be allowed to preside . . . at the solemn sacrifices . . . at the time of each equinox to Confucius and other departed ancestors.'

Pope Clement XI in a decree, 1704

1939, when Catholics were finally allowed to take part in ancestral veneration and the rites were accepted as civil demonstrations of honour, which had lost any earlier pagan associations.

India

In India another apostle of accommodation and a Jesuit, Robert de Nobili (1577–1656) had immersed himself in Hinduism, both its philosophy and its way of life. He, like Valignano an Italian by birth, intended to detach himself from strongly Portuguese and European models of Christianity. He succeeded in commending his form of Christian faith to Indians and became responsible for a number of high-caste Brahmins becoming Christians. His methods, however, raised controversy among his superiors and for a time he was forbidden to baptize.

'Father Nobili said, "I too shall become an Indian to save the Indians" . . . he introduced himself to Brahmins . . . as a sannyasi i.e. a penitent who has renounced the world.'

The Jesuit Provincial's description of de Nobili, 1609

Like Ricci in China, de Nobili in Madurai stood for great sensitivity towards the culture and life of the host country and suffered misunderstanding from co-religionists through their fears of compromise. Alexandre de Rhodes (1591–1660), a Jesuit pioneer in modern Vietnam, made himself persona non grata with the Portuguese for his firm advocacy of indigenous clergy, which they understood as a breach of the *padroado*. Missionary initiatives and deep identification with alternative language and culture were often met by disapproval from the authorities, political or religious. Despite problems with both Portuguese and Vietnamese authority, including de Rhodes's expulsion, by 1640 there were some 100,000 Christians as fruit of the Jesuit mission in Vietnam.

Japan

Japan, too, after Xavier, enjoyed a period of great progress. Valignano, visiting in 1580, declared himself deeply impressed with the quality of Christian life to be found in Japan. By 1583 there were 200 churches and some 150,000 Christians. In one town south of Kyoto around 8,000 had been baptized in 1579. The Jesuit mission was well led by Francisco

Cabral (1528–1609), a leader of Portuguese noble extraction, between 1570 and 1583. Ultimately, however, he and Valignano differed over the advance of the Japanese indigenous ministry (espoused as ever by Valignano) and Cabral left. There was a sharp change in the attitude of the political authorities later in the century and in 1614 there was an expulsion order on all Jesuits. Fierce persecution then followed on the 300,000 Japanese Christians (in a population of some 20 million). Christians were crucified in Nagasaki in 1597 and there were further mass executions in 1622. The policy was pursued with great savagery between 1627 and 1634 and resulted in many 'hidden Christians', whom 19th-century missionaries found had retained their knowledge of many of the symbols of the Christian faith, when Japan opened two centuries later after 1859. Despite the tragic outcome of their work, one recent authority from outside Roman Catholicism, Andrew Ross, has judged the Jesuit mission in Japan to have been the most successful approach to a sophisticated society of any since the conversion of the Roman empire.

> 'Do not attempt in any way to persuade these people to change their customs . . . what could be more absurd indeed than to transport France, Italy or some other European country to the Chinese?'
>
> **Propaganda Fidei instruction of 1659**

Protestants in Asia

From 1600 both Dutch and English trading interests became increasingly important in Asia, not least because of their nations' maritime superiority. The Dutch established themselves in Indonesia and created a centre at Batavia (Jakarta). Their trading company, Verenigde Oost-Indische Compagnie (VOC), founded in 1602, meant that Reformed religion reached the East Indies, though it did not conduct significant missionary work among indigenous peoples. Its English equivalent, the East India Company, founded in 1600, although highly suspicious of missionaries, appointed chaplains to their trading communities. This provided an opening for those with missionary vision in England and India such as William Wilberforce and Charles Grant, an employee of the company.

Two outstanding EIC chaplains were Henry Martyn (1781–1812) and Claudius Buchanan (1766–1815). Martyn had been one of the leading young Cambridge intellects of his day and was a winner of university prizes. He and other Cambridge men of his time had been influenced by the long ministry of Charles Simeon (1759–1836), with his preaching of the gospel for all peoples. Martyn proved a brilliant linguist and translator. He was appointed a chaplain in 1805, translated the New Testament into Urdu and Persian and prepared an Arabic version before his early death from tuberculosis aged 31. His Indian assistant, Abdul Masih (1765–1827), converted from Islam to become a Christian missionary colleague and notable advocate of the faith, and was eventually ordained in 1825 as the first Indian Anglican clergyman. Others were inspired by Martyn's life of scholarship and devotion.

Claudius Buchanan was a Scotsman. Leading evangelicals arranged for him to attend the university of Cambridge; he joined other 'Sims', as Simeon's followers were called, in India, in particular David Brown, on his appointment as EIC chaplain. Buchanan served as vice-provost of Fort William College, Calcutta, founded by the Duke of Wellington's elder brother, Lord Wellesley, then governor general of India, and showed his missionary vision by endowing essay prizes on missionary subjects at the universities of Oxford and Cambridge, the Scottish universities and Trinity College, Dublin. In 1806 Buchanan was invited by the archbishop of Canterbury to become the first bishop in India but declined. A missionary-minded chaplain who did become a bishop and was also a 'Sim' was Daniel Corrie (1777–1837), the first Anglican bishop of Madras.

The East India Company

The East India Company was the source of British influence in India until the Crown took direct responsibility after 1857. It was run by a court of directors in London. The company's main rivals in India were the French but it raised its own army under its employee Robert Clive (1725–74) and defeated them at Plassey in 1757, one of the decisive battles of world history, which led to the control of Bengal and British supremacy in India. For 100 years the company effectively ruled Bengal, though from 1784 British politicians created a system of dual control. Great fortunes were made by returning Englishmen, known as the 'nabobs', and there were accusations of peculation, most famously in the case of Warren Hastings (1732–1813). The 'Indian Mutiny' of 1857 led to government by the crown after 1858 until Indian independence in 1947.

William Carey (1761–1834), who had been both a shoemaker and a Baptist preacher in Northamptonshire and is often regarded as the father of Protestant missions (though John Eliot, Ziegenbalg and others could be said to have a prior claim), arrived in India in 1793. He was soon joined by two other Baptist giants in Joshua Marshman (1768–1837) and William Ward (1769–1823), making up what became known as the 'Serampore trio', when they settled in the Danish possession. It is clear that they greatly admired the Moravians and tried to shape their own community life on Moravian models. Carey had been denied a passage by the EIC and his calling was derided by critics like Sydney Smith, the satirical writer and clergyman who wrote for the *Edinburgh Review* at home.

> 'A nest of consecrated cobblers.'
>
> **Sydney Smith, Edinburgh Review, April 1809**

Carey, however, by steady perseverance, not least in monumental labours at biblical translation, as well as in family tragedies and losses of precious manuscripts by fire, faced down all his critics, becoming in time Professor of Sanskrit at Fort William College and earning the accolade from Bishop Stephen Neill, himself a missionary in India: 'In the whole history of the church no nobler man has ever given himself to the service of the Redeemer.'

> 'What a treasure must await such characters as Paul and Elliot and Brainerd and others.'
>
> **William Carey, An Enquiry into the Obligations of Christians to Use Means for the Conversion of the Heathen, 1792**

Scotland supplied a rich vein of missionaries in India after Buchanan. Alexander Duff (1806–78) won respect for his educational approach, with its equal measure of belief in the Bible and western science and literature as a means of reaching high-caste Indians. The Indian reformer, never a Christian, Ram Mohan Roy, respected and co-operated with Duff's efforts. Duff was to become the first professor of missions at New College, Edinburgh in 1866 after serving for 30 years in the field and declining the vice-chancellorship of the university of Calcutta.

Duff's service straddled the period when the EIC gave way to the Raj. Between 1857 and 1947 a number of outstanding Scottish missionaries and educators served in India, including John Wilson (1804–75), who became vice-chancellor of Bombay University; Alfred Hogg (1875–1954), principal of Madras Christian College and powerful analyst of Christian–Hindu issues; and another brilliant scholar and writer in John Nicol Farquhar (1881–1929), LMS missionary and finally professor

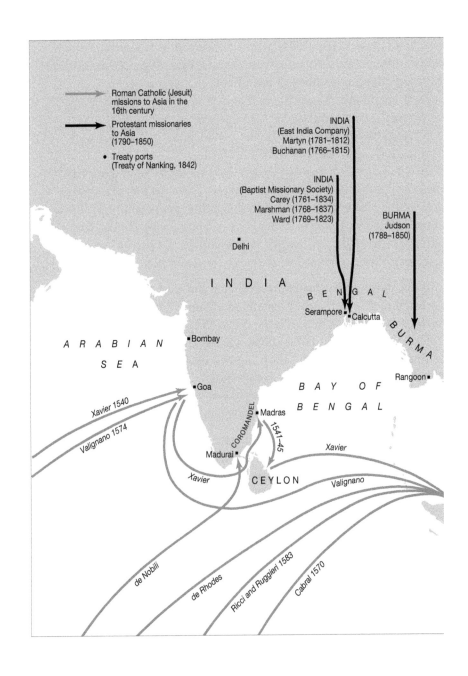

Roman Catholic (Jesuit)
missions to Asia in the
16th century

Protestant missionaries
to Asia
(1790–1850)

• Treaty ports
(Treaty of Nanking, 1842)

INDIA
(East India Company)
Martyn (1781–1812)
Buchanan (1766–1815)

INDIA
(Baptist Missionary Society)
Carey (1761–1834)
Marshman (1768–1837)
Ward (1769–1823)

BURMA
Judson
(1788–1850)

■ Delhi

I N D I A

B E N G A L

Serampore ■ ■ Calcutta

B U R M A

A R A B I A N
S E A

■ Bombay

■ Goa

B A Y   O F
B E N G A L

Rangoon ■

Xavier 1540

Valignano 1574

C O R O M A N D E L

■ Madras

1541–45

Xavier

Madurai ■

Xavier

C E Y L O N

Valignano

de Nobili

de Rhodes

Ricci and Ruggieri 1583

Cabral 1570

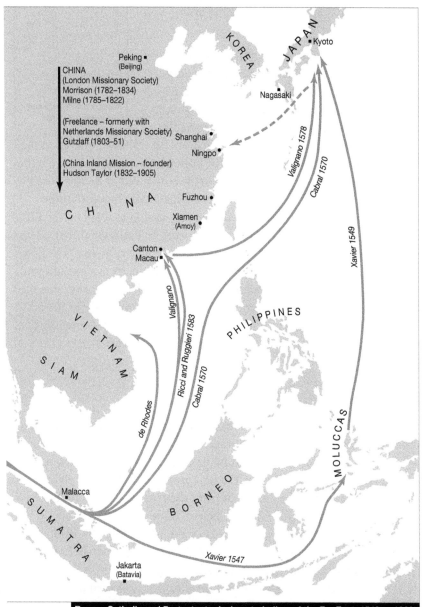

CHINA
(London Missionary Society)
Morrison (1782–1834)
Milne (1785–1822)

(Freelance – formerly with
Netherlands Missionary Society)
Gutzlaff (1803–51)

(China Inland Mission – founder)
Hudson Taylor (1832–1905)

Roman Catholic and Protestant missions to India and the Far East, 1540 to 1860.

of comparative religion at Manchester after 30 years' service in India.

For North Americans, an equivalent figure to Carey as a pioneer was the great missionary to Burma (Myanmar) Adoniram Judson (1788–1850). Judson had received missionary inspiration from reading sermons of Claudius Buchanan in 1809 and, after ordination as a Congregationalist minister, offered to the American Board of Commissioners for Foreign Missions in 1810. On the voyage out to India, he and his wife became convinced of Baptist views. On arrival in India he was baptized, having made his change of mind known to William Carey. He was refused permission to work by the EIC as a Baptist missionary in India but began work in Rangoon in 1813. His work among the Karen people met with considerable response. The first Karen baptized, Ko Tha Byu (1778–1840), who came from a background of violent crime, became a notable lay evangelist. The Karens became the largest Christian group and in modern Myanmar number some 200,000 Christians in over 1,000 churches. Judson himself became something of a missionary icon and hero in mid-century North America.

> 'In the very act of acquiring English, the mind, in grasping new terms . . . ideas . . . must be tenfold less the child of pantheism, idolatry and superstition.'
>
> **Alexander Duff, *India and Indian Missions*, 1839**

China and Japan: fresh departures

China had effectively closed its doors to foreigners of all kinds after imperial edicts against Christian preaching in 1720. Robert Morrison (1782–1834) was a lone Protestant witness as LMS missionary from 1807, often at risk of his life. Although the EIC proved hostile to his plans, from 1809 he accepted employment from them as an interpreter in order to remain on Chinese soil. With the help of another LMS missionary, William Milne (1785–1822), he translated the whole Bible by 1819 and created a Chinese dictionary between 1815 and 1823, which became a standard work. He and Milne founded an Anglo-Chinese school in Malacca, of which Milne was the first headteacher, followed by the scholar, fellow Scot and LMS missionary, James Legge in 1840, who later became the first professor of Chinese at Oxford in 1876.

All missionary incursion into wider China was impossible, however, until the treaties of the mid-century opened up the country by degrees.

First, the so-called 'treaty ports' became accessible in 1842 (by the Treaty of Nanking, a treaty forced on China by British commercial interests, not least towards the import of opium from India after the 'Opium Wars' of 1839–42); and the later treaty of 1858 (the Treaty of Tientsin), which opened the interior to missionaries, preparing the way among other institutions for the China Inland Mission's penetration after 1865.

James Hudson Taylor (1832–1905) was born in Barnsley in Yorkshire to a devoutly Methodist family. He trained as a doctor, but, before he qualified, his offer of missionary service to the China Evangelization Society was accepted. Owing to the political conditions prevailing in China during the Taiping rebellion (read by some as a movement of Christian promise), he was sent to Shanghai (Guangzhou) in 1853. The Taiping rebellion was subsequently crushed by General 'Chinese' Gordon (later of Khartoum) in 1864. Taylor joined a missionary community in Shanghai, mostly LMS and CMS, profiting from the treaty of 1842. He claimed inspiration from Karl Gutzlaff (1803–51), who had travelled to the interior of China between 1833 and 1839 as a freelance missionary.

Taylor experimented with identification in Chinese dress and 'queue' (pigtail) on the advice of a veteran missionary in China, W.H. Medhurst

Karl Gutzlaff (1803–51)

Gutzlaff was the son of a German tailor, who was educated at a Moravian school. He met Robert Morrison as a young man, which may have influenced him towards China. He offered to the Netherlands Missionary Society in 1824 and served initially in Siam (Thailand). He translated the Bible into Thai in three years. In 1828 he broke with NMS because they would not send him to China. He became a freelance missionary, distributing Christian literature along the coast. After Morrison's death he succeeded him as interpreter for the EIC in Guangzhou. He helped the EIC to negotiate the Treaty of Nanjing in 1842. He recruited various Chinese nationals as 'evangelists' to the interior and raised funds for their support through his writings in Europe, only to find that many of his recruits had deceived him and taken the money for other purposes. Although discredited in the eyes of some, Gutzlaff's probity was not in doubt nor his missionary zeal. Hudson Taylor looked on him as 'grandfather' of the CIM and its work in the interior provinces.

(1796–1857), to the dismay of many other members of the missionary community. In 1857 he resigned from the CES. Deeply stirred by the needs of the unevangelized Chinese of the interior, he founded the China Inland Mission (CIM) in 1865, aiming to put two missionaries in each province, areas now open to foreigners after the Treaty of Tientsin of 1858. By now a fully qualified doctor and married to Maria Dyer, daughter of a missionary and a leader in her own right, he set out with a party of 16 from London to Shanghai on the *Lammermuir* in 1866, narrowly avoiding total loss by shipwreck.

'Prayed for twenty-four willing, skilful labourers at Brighton, June 25, 1865.'

Note on the flyleaf of Hudson Taylor's Bible on the birth of CIM

From the beginning the CIM was to be a so-called 'faith mission', with no public appeals for funds; and its missionaries accepted the absolute, if gently exercised, authority of Taylor himself, described by the American missionary W.A.P. Martin as the 'Loyola of Protestant missions'. In time, CIM numbered over 800 missionaries, including Methodists, Baptists, Anglicans and Presbyterians and others, and it planted churches that had a membership of some 80,000 by 1897. The profile of the society had been greatly enhanced in the 1880s by the advent of the so-called 'Cambridge Seven', two of whom were well-known sporting heroes at home and held to be making very great sacrifices. C.T. Studd (1860–1931) was one of these, later to be founder of World Evangelization Crusade (WEC) and the Heart of Africa Mission, which worked in the Belgian Congo. Hudson Taylor's publication, *China's Millions*, achieved a circulation of 50,000 at this time and also helped to put the mission in front of the public. Although the society suffered heavily in the Boxer Rebellion (1898–1900), when 200 missionaries, many of them Roman Catholic, and around 30,000 Chinese Christians lost their lives (CIM lost 58 missionaries and some children out of a total Protestant loss of 130), the society refused indemnities by policy. It continued to be an influential Christian body under the second director, Dixon Hoste (1861–1946), himself one of the Cambridge Seven, but in 1949 all missionary personnel were expelled by the Communist regime. Taylor himself was described by Latourette as 'one of the four or five most influential foreigners who came to China in the 19th century for any purpose, religious or secular'.

Another influential figure, Timothy Richard (1845–1919), originally applied to the CIM for service but was finally sent by the

Baptist Missionary Society in 1869 to work in Shandung province. His reputation as a leading Christian humanitarian grew after his outstanding relief work during the famine in the province and North China in 1876–79. He had been drawn at first by the evangelical biblicism of the CIM but he moved into a liberal theology, which caused him to dissociate from the BMS and to concentrate on literary and journalistic work, aiming to reach the Chinese intelligentsia, social leaders and the source of supply for the Chinese civil service. In 1891 he became director of the Christian Literature Society, which pursued these aims, based in Shanghai. He associated with leading Chinese reformers at the turn of the century and through them his ideas became widely influential. He adopted a more collective approach to reaching the Chinese nation with the gospel and was regarded with some suspicion by those like Hudson Taylor, who placed heavy emphasis on the salvation of individuals and the planting of congregations. He was also strongly affirmative of Chinese religion, especially Mahayana Buddhism, which to him had many affinities with Christian teaching. A controversial figure, with individual perceptions and conviction, he was one of the best known Christian leaders in China by 1900.

'Hidden Christians' in Japan

Japan had been closed to foreigners since the severe persecutions of Christians and the expulsion of the Jesuits in 1614. This policy had been pursued by the Tokugawa regime between then and the 19th century. A new government, known as Meiji Restoration, responded differently to political, commercial and missionary initiatives. The government of the USA used a naval squadron under Commodore Perry to re-open trading relations with foreigners in the 1850s. By a treaty of 1859 missionaries were able to take advantage of the new situation; the edict of 1612 against Christianity was finally officially repudiated in 1873. Meanwhile, American Protestant missionaries, as well as Roman Catholic and Orthodox, discovered many 'hidden Christians', who had preserved certain forms of the faith since the 17th century.

They knew the Lord's Prayer, the Ten Commandments, the Hail Mary and the framework of the liturgical year; images of Buddha have come to light that, when reversed, reveal a crucifix. In addition to those at Nagasaki, one modern estimate has suggested 50–80,000 such Christians in island retreats on the Gotto Islands, where a lay organization consisted of various forms of responsibility such as 'father-leader' and 'teacher-baptizer'. Such groups were reluctant to re-join the Roman Catholic church, which had given them birth, for fear of losing their own developed life.

> 'There were two main leaders in most of the villages . . . the prayer leader . . . the baptizer [who] had to have with him a pupil baptizer to succeed him.'
>
> **Petitjean's description of the hidden Christians of Nagasaki, 1865**

Meanwhile, between 1860 and 1900, the Orthodox church was given remarkable leadership in mission in Japan by Nicholas Kassatkin (1836–1912), who baptized his first Japanese converts in April 1868, built an Orthodox cathedral on land overlooking Tokyo in the 1870s, and by his death had commissioned 34 Japanese evangelists and organized the church into 260 congregations served by a largely indigenous ministry, which included 35 Japanese priests and a total membership of 33,000. American Episcopalians and other Anglicans, including Canadians, and Presbyterians and others, also developed missionary work.

Korea

Until 1865 Korea had been similarly closed to foreign influences, though there had been baptisms of Korean visitors to China in the 18th century, leading to an infant Roman Catholic church with a Chinese priest (owing entirely to Korean initiative); and some missionary involvement by members of the Société des Missions Étrangères de Paris in 1835. There was persecution over the issue of ancestor worship, which Christians were held to have abolished, and a number of executions. Even in the 1860s Christians were feared as a fifth column when Russian political pressure threatened and there were estimates of thousands of martyrs. The first Protestant missionary, R.J. Thomas of LMS, paid with his life when attempting to import Chinese Bibles. Despite many difficulties and helped by toleration of religion in the 1880s, there was a remarkable expansion of the church in Korea, due in some measure to the work of the Presbyterian missionary J.L. Nevius (1829–93). His 'Nevius Plan' capitalized on the same 'three self' formula – churches becoming self-supporting, self-governing and self-extending – that was so important to the mission administrators Henry Venn and Rufus Anderson. After

1900 Korean churches experienced revivals and these, combined with Japanese attempts to stamp out Korean national culture (resulting in wider and deeper adherence to the church), made for the immense Christian population of today, when 15 million Christians in over 200 denominations are to be found, mostly in South Korea, and over 10,000 are serving as missionaries.

Although this conclusion trespasses into the subject of the final chapter on the 20th century, it may be as well to summarize the shape of Asian Christianity today, much of which has resulted from European expansion since 1500. Indonesia is largely Muslim but has some 20 million Christians who make up 16 per cent of the population. Roman Catholic life is especially present in the Philippines, a Spanish colonial possession until 1898, when the USA assumed government for a time. Twenty-seven million people regard themselves as Roman Catholic and Christians make up 90 per cent of the population. At the other end of the scale, Japan remains largely impervious to Christian influence, although there have been Christians who have been prominent in public life and others, like Toyohiko Kagawa (1888–1960) who have been internationally renowned Christian individuals. Christians, however, remain only one per cent of the population of 120 million. China presents a more puzzling picture, with details elusive from the Communist regime. There seems little doubt that Chinese Christians run into millions. By 1900 there were half a million Roman Catholics and around 40,000 Protestants. An informed and authoritative source has suggested that Roman Catholics now number between 10 and 12 million and Protestants 15 million; in addition, there are large-scale syncretistic, or religiously mixed, movements which display some Christian practices and may number as many as 50 to 100 million more than those in traditional churches. India remains 80 per cent Hindu in religion, although formally a secular state; Christians are a mere two to three per cent of the remainder, though this figure may mean as many as 27 million Christians. So, Christianity in Asia has many millions of adherents, minorities in Japan and India, probable growth in China far exceeding 19th-century levels and strong populations of Christians in South Korea and the Philippines.

CHAPTER 8

OCEANIA

Captain Cook's voyages in the South Seas were one important way that Europe became aware of the islands of Polynesia, through his visit to Tahiti in 1769 and to New Zealand and Australia, some of the coastline of which he charted meticulously. Publications based on his journals fired the imagination of missionary-minded pioneers like John Williams (1796–1839), a Congregationalist minister and LMS missionary, who was commissioned to serve in Tahiti at the same time as Robert Moffatt was commissioned for South Africa by the LMS in 1816.

'Here the natives flocked around us in great numbers in as friendly a manner as we could wish, only that they showed a great inclination to pick our pockets.'

Cook on his arrival in Matavai Bay, Tahiti, *Journal*, 14 April 1769

Tahiti

It was the LMS who provided the first pioneers earlier than this, when a party of 30 men, including four ordained ministers, sailed in the *Duff* in 1796. The rest of the party were so-called 'artisan missionaries' and the majority landed in Tahiti, though one went to Tongatabu in the Tongan group of islands and one to the Marquesas. This original party found their work sufficiently discouraging for most of the group on Tahiti to leave in 1798 to take refuge by ship to Sydney.

On Tahiti, the activities of a tribal chief became conclusive for the mission. Pomare II (1779–1821) had been forced to flee from the island, where he had befriended the missionaries and become literate through their teaching. While in exile on the island of Moorea, in company with the LMS missionary and bricklayer Henry Nott (1774–1844), Pomare was drawn increasingly to Christianity. When he returned to Tahiti and reasserted his authority in 1812 he declared for the Christian cause; and, after an attack on his life in 1815, he insisted on the destruction of idols throughout the island, so paving the way for his own continued dominance and that of the Christian faith.

It was to this prepared situation on Tahiti that John Williams came aged 20. King Pomare became a baptized Christian in 1819, though his self-indulgent life left the missionaries dissatisfied. Williams, however, was not content to be restricted to Tahiti. He was eager to evangelize the other island groups and went first to Raiatea in the Windward Islands in 1818, where he formed a church in cooperation with the chief, Tamatoa; and, after buying a ship, the *Endeavour*, reached out to more of Polynesia and then Melanesia. He worked on the island of Rarotonga between 1823 and 1833, pioneered Samoa using Polynesian Christians to assist him in visits of 1830 and 1832 and by 1834 was able to claim that no group or island of importance within 2,000 miles (3,200 kilometres) of Tahiti had been unreached. He returned to England to oversee the translation and printing of the Rarotongan New Testament (1834–38) but was back at work again in the Pacific in 1839, when he was attacked and killed on the island of Erromanga in the New Hebrides (Vanuatu) on 20 November 1839.

Australia and New Zealand

In 1788 the British government decided to use New South Wales as a convict colony and Botany Bay became their destination. William Wilberforce's Christian compassion extended to convicts as well as to slaves and he took a leading part in ensuring that the first convicts had the services of a chaplain. Richard Johnson, the chaplain, built the first church at his own expense and served until 1801. Samuel Marsden (1764–1838) his successor was physically stronger, a Yorkshireman, product of the evangelical revival and of Magdalene College, Cambridge, where he had been strongly influenced, like the chaplains in India, by Charles Simeon. Marsden established himself as not only chaplain but also a successful sheep breeder and farmer at Parramatta and became a magistrate. It was Marsden who befriended the LMS missionaries when they arrived in Sydney in 1798 and in 1804 was made LMS agent for the South Seas. He encouraged the missionaries to persist in the period before Pomare's re-emergence as a Christian chief and befriended another party forced to flee in 1810. Marsden had also met and employed some Maori at Parramatta. In 1807 he urged the CMS to mount a mission to New Zealand. This project had to be put on hold after Maori plundered the ship *Boyd* and killed its crew, probably in revenge for European aggression, in 1809; but in 1814 Marsden was able to lead a CMS party with the help of a young Maori chief, Ruatara. The party was made up of two artisan missionaries in John King, a shoemaker, and William Hall, a carpenter, and a schoolmaster, Thomas Kendall, who was ordained in 1820. Marsden preached the first Christian sermon on New Zealand soil on Christmas Day 1814, interpreted to his Maori hearers by Ruatara.

Between 1814 and his death Samuel Marsden, who was a bad sailor and suffered severely from sea sickness, made seven voyages to New Zealand and was regarded by the missionaries there (whatever his reputation as a 'flogging magistrate' in New South Wales) with the deep respect of a founding father and wise adviser to the mission. Both Methodist missions (with the friend of Marsden, Samuel Leigh, as pioneer) from 1822 and Marist (Roman Catholic) missions led by Bishop Pompallier, who arrived in 1838, were to share in the evangelization of the Maori.

> 'It being Christmas Day I preached from the second chapter of St Luke's Gospel and the 10th verse, "Behold, I bring you glad tidings of great joy."'
>
> **Samuel Marsden in his journal of his visit to New Zealand of 1814**

After isolated baptisms in the 1820s, the Maori response was increasingly remarkable. According to William Williams, one of two notable brothers who were missionaries for CMS and a reliable witness, there were 30,000 Maori worshippers in CMS churches alone in the 1840s in the North Island. The first Anglican bishop of New Zealand, G.A. Selwyn, who arrived in 1841, by a strange mistake by clerks in London preparing his Letters Patent, was given authority over large areas of Melanesia. He capitalized on the error by engaging in missionary work in the Pacific himself and by recruiting a brilliant linguist in J.C. Patteson (1827–71) to extend the work in Melanesia, of which he was created Anglican bishop in 1861. Patteson was said to speak 20 Melanesian dialects. He established a school for boys from the islands on Norfolk Island in 1865, which aimed to produce an indigenous Melanesian ministry with a minimum of European impositions by way of cultural change in matters such as clothing.

> 'All this is very surprising when it is considered that five years ago nothing but the fern flourished here . . . the lesson of the missionary is the enchanted wand.'
>
> **Charles Darwin on the CMS Mission in New Zealand in 1835**

Patteson, like John Williams, ultimately paid the price of martyrdom on the island of Nukapu in 1871, almost certainly a revenge killing for the kidnapping of five boys by 'blackbirders' shortly before his visit, taken to provide cheap labour for the plantations of Fiji or Queensland. Five wounds in his body and five fronds tied to it (held as a relic of martyrdom by the SPG) were evidence of this. Two notable Anglican priests continued Patteson's work on Norfolk Island: the first was his successor, R.H. Codrington (1830–1922), missionary and anthropologist, whose study *The Melanesians* (1891) remains important, along with his analysis of 'mana' (spiritual power) in such societies; and second C.E. Fox (1878–1977), who arrived on Norfolk Island in 1902 and earned great respect as priest among Melanesians and as a scholarly anthropologist.

Whereas the Maori were a people organized in settled communities, if warlike in character, the Australian aborigines represented quite a different challenge to missionary work. They were estimated to number some 300,000 prior to European contact and had lived in Australia for 20,000 years or more. The semi-mystical importance of the land to this nomadic people and due appreciation for their intricate culture has steadily escaped Europeans. As with the cases of native Americans and Canadians, their treatment has been marked again and again by shameful and exploitative episodes in colonial history. Tasmania presented an extreme example of the general oppression and lack of understanding. After racial clashes in the 1830s, the aboriginal population of Tasmania was hunted down, sometimes shot as prey, and finally transported to Flinders Island, numbering then about 5,000 in 1835. Here, separated from their land and ancient customs of their ancestors, they became ultimately extinct in 1876.

> 'Appalling and inhuman behaviour, which can only be called genocide, characterized settlement in Tasmania.'
>
> **Ian Breward, Australian Professor, in his *History of the Churches*, 2001**

There had been an early CMS mission to aborigines in New South Wales in 1832, which gave up in 1843; and a Methodist mission to Sydney's aborigines begun in 1821, which also failed, though Methodism had some success in Western Australia after 1840, as did Roman Catholic Benedictines north of Perth after 1847. This mission produced two candidates for the priesthood, who sadly both died in Europe. Both Moravians and Lutherans in Queensland tried to reach out to aborigines. By 1850, the original population had been reduced to 10,000. European diseases, including smallpox, typhoid, tuberculosis, measles and influenza, to which they had no immunity, contributed to a decline, in which cultural dislocation and land disputes were also factors.

Polynesia and Melanesia

Of the three ethnic groups in the Pacific, Polynesian, Melanesian and Micronesian, the Polynesians were both the first to receive the Christian gospel and frequently responsible for its extension to their own islands and those of Melanesia also. If the islands of Hawaii and the special case of Pitcairn are discounted, LMS had begun work in islands like the Marquesas as far to the east of Australia and New Zealand as any in the Pacific. For our purposes, a treatment that works its way towards Australasia and the great land mass of New Guinea from further east can make for clarity. Tahiti, the original base for LMS missionaries, was reinforced by men like William Ellis (1794–1872), whose *Polynesian Researches* (1829) was probably second only to Cook's journals in bringing life in the Pacific to a wider public. Tahiti supplied John Williams with numbers of Polynesian evangelists and teachers. It became a French possession and in 1863 the LMS decided to hand their work over to the Protestant Paris Mission (Société des Missions Évangéliques de Paris).

Tahitian teachers had been established on Samoa by Williams in the 1830s and LMS work there began in earnest in 1836. The two sets of Samoan islands had a total population of around 200,000 people and so constituted a larger field than Tonga (50,000). In Tonga, however, the Methodist WMMS (Wesleyan Methodist Missionary Society) had remarkable success. Although Walter Lawry of their mission had landed as early as 1822, it was Tahitian converts like Hape, Tafu and Borabora who were effective between 1822 and 1827. Two important Europeans did arrive, John Thomas (1796–1881) on Tongatabu, a blacksmith become missionary who served from 1826–59, and Nathaniel Turner (1793–1864) who already had experience of the Methodist mission in New Zealand and arrived with three Maori assistants in 1827. In Tonga, the breakthrough, as in so many African cases, came with the conversion of the chief Tupou (Taufa'ahau) in 1830, who took the name of King George. In what became essentially a Methodist kingdom, with 90 per cent Methodist adherence, one missionary, Shirley Baker, was to resign his ministry to become prime minister of the island kingdom and adviser to the king on constitutional matters from 1860–90. Eventually, however, he was judged a liability and deported by the British High Commissioner. King George died in 1893 and Tonga became a British protectorate after 1900.

Two Roman Catholic missionary orders were active in the Pacific. One, the Marists (Society of Mary), already mentioned here as in New Zealand, had its origin in the missionary vision of Père Colin in France in 1815. It was active in the Marquesas and in Futuna and Wallis Islands, whose populations became entirely Roman Catholic. It had its martyr in Father Pierre Chanel (1803–41), recruited for mission by Bishop Pompallier and a man described as serene and gentle in character, who was killed on Futuna after enduring much isolation and illness. He was canonized in 1954. The second order were the Picpus Fathers (the Congregation of the Sacred Heart of Jesus and Mary), confirmed as a missionary congregation by the pope in 1817 and given responsibilities in Oceania by the Propaganda in 1825.

Where the Marists were assigned western Oceania, the Picpus missions worked in islands like Easter Island and Hawaii. Here their most famous missionary was Father Damien (1840–89), Flemish in origin, who devoted himself to the lepers on the island colony of Molokai from 1873. He himself contracted the disease in the 1880s. By 1884 there were estimated to be 17,000 Roman Catholics on Hawaii. The pioneers there, however, had been the Protestant missionaries of the American Board of Commissioners for Foreign Missions. They had arrived in 1820, seen baptisms of the royal house in 1823 and by 1870 felt able to withdraw in the light of Christianization achieved, much of it through the assistance of Tahitian Christian chiefs and evangelists. Christian missions here, however, did not prevent a catastrophic decline in indigenous population: Polynesian numbers dropped from some 400,000 prior to European contact to 30,000 by 1900.

Space forbids attention to all the island churches and missions but Fiji (population 775,000), the Solomon Islands (368,000) and the New Hebrides, especially New Caledonia (200,000), deserve treatment before moving on to the larger land mass of New Guinea. The Solomon Islands have become a field of indigenous mission, not least through Anglican

Gauguin and Tahiti

Paul Gauguin (1848–1903), the French artist who has left enduring images of Tahitian and Polynesian life on the European imagination, had worked in banking and finance in France. He abandoned this life for that of a painter. He reached Tahiti in 1891, where he produced a series of masterpieces that spoke of a vision of the 'noble savage' beloved of European philosophy but also of the sense of a Polynesian paradise lost. His work was not acclaimed in his own lifetime and he died heavily in debt. His work will now fetch millions in any currency.

Melanesian missionaries, who have provided as many as 1,000 workers, a reminder that again and again in the Pacific it has been the initiative of native peoples that has been as influential as European missionaries. In recent times, the Melanesian Brotherhood, an Anglican order with simple vows, which include a given number of celibate years for mission, have followed up the earlier initiatives of Bishop George Selwyn and Bishop Patteson, and of Bishop John Selwyn, son of the bishop of New Zealand. They built on the work done on Norfolk Island by Patteson, R.H. Codrington and C.E. Fox, himself the only European to be a member of the order. Methodists were active in the western Solomon Islands, and the Roman Catholic Father Epalle, first vicar apostolic for Micronesia and Melanesia, worked on the island of Ysabel, while the South Sea Evangelical Mission, with its remarkable founder, Florence Young, expanded its work among expatriate Melanesians and others in Queensland into the Solomons in 1904.

Fiji had an exceptional Tongan missionary in Joeli Bulu, who showed great awareness of the need to inculturate Christianity in Fijian forms, composing Fijian hymns and settings for the Lord's Prayer, the Creed and the Te Deum in Fijian chants, while also adapting their traditional funeral dirges to Christian use. John Hunt (1811–48), a Methodist missionary who arrived with Bulu in 1838, was equally and exceptionally sensitive to cultural issues in his decade of service. Again the breakthrough came with the conversion of the chief, Cakobau, who after early hostility, was greatly influenced by the conversion of his friend Varani through Hunt's ministry in 1845. Cakobau himself was finally baptized in 1854. Two years later there were some 30,000

Florence Young (1856–1940)

Born into a wealthy Plymouth Brethren family in Nelson, New Zealand, Florence Young began her work as a Sunday School teacher on their Queensland estate. This included working among Melanesian labourers. Some of these returned to their islands and formed Christian fellowships, who then appealed to Miss Young for teachers. She visited the Solomon Islands in 1904–1905 and founded the South Seas Evangelical Mission. She also served with CIM for some years in China. Today the SSEM, with some 63,000 members, is second only to the Anglicans in the number of Solomon Islanders who are members of its 600 congregations.

church attenders and, even more significant, a social and cultural transformation in process, where the strangling of widows, polygamy and traditional cannibalism were steadily eradicated. Fiji became British in 1874. By 1914 there were around 80,000 Methodists and 7,000 Roman Catholics, the results of Marist work from 1842 onwards. Methodists still predominate today, with around half of the population affiliated to them.

The New Hebrides and New Caledonia have special associations and famous names in their Christianization. The first, a largely Polynesian population with some Melanesians, contained the island of Erromanga, scene of John Williams's martyrdom in 1839. A total of six European missionaries lost their lives in this group of islands between 1839 and 1872. Samoan and Rarontongan missionaries were influential, beginning with the three Samoan Christians landed by Williams on Tanna. A very famous missionary, based on Tanna, was John G. Paton (1824–1907), a Church of Scotland minister who began work there in 1858. Paton's fame rested on his success in fundraising for the Pacific in tours of Australia, Canada and Britain and through his widely read autobiography. His fundraising paid for ships for missionary work, called successively *Dayspring*, and the fund continued to be the resource for five stations in the New Hebrides into the 20th century. Anglicans were also active after initial visits by G.A. Selwyn in 1848 and 1849; and Marists had some 1,000 baptisms and 3,000 catechumens by 1900. Politically the islands became a shared condominium between France and Britain from 1906.

New Caledonia became a French possession. Melanesian evangelists with connections to LMS had been pioneers here. The same combination of French government and LMS mission had been true of Vanuatu, where John Williams had planted some Samoan teachers in 1839. The French annexed the islands in 1853 and by 1900 there were some 11,000 Roman Catholics. The Paris Society (Protestant) had an outstanding missionary and anthropologist in Maurice Leenhardt (1878–1954), who joined the mission in 1897 and did notable missionary and anthropological work among the Kanaks. In company with R.H. Codrington, Leenhardt was among the foremost interpreters of the Melanesian world to the western universities and became a professor of the Sorbonne and friend of Lévy Bruhl. He has been described as 'the greatest ethnologist among Pacific missionaries'.

> 'God is not an import. He reveals himself.'
> **Maurice Leenhardt**

New Guinea missions

Papua New Guinea, the eastern part of what in the west is part of Indonesia (Irian Jaya), with a population of 4 million people, was a major mission field. Once more, LMS were the early arrivals. In 1871, Samuel Macfarlane (1837–1911) established himself on Darney Island in the Torres Straits, which he hoped to turn into a kind of Iona for the mainland. He was joined by A.W. Murray (1811–92), another Scotsman from Jedburgh, who had served with the Samoan mission of LMS. W.G. Lawes (1839–1907), an even more influential figure, who had worked for LMS on the island of Niue, now became the first white man to live permanently on the mainland at Port Moresby in 1874, from which base he trained native Papuans to serve as missionaries. Lawes persuaded the British to create a protectorate, to defend Papuan rights against land-hungry Australians, in 1884 and he continued to press the administration towards guaranteeing Papuan rights thereafter. James Chalmers (1841–1901), another Scot and in his case a Congregationalist minister who had worked on Rarotonga for ten years training Polynesians to be evangelists in New Guinea, joined the New Guinea mission himself in 1877. Like Lawes, he supported the British protectorate as a means of defence of Papuan rights. He became a friend of Robert Louis Stevenson and is said to have changed the writer's

> 'Here he lies where he longed to be; home is the sailor home from the sea and the hunter home from the hill.'
> **Robert Louis Stevenson's chosen epitaph for his grave on Samoa**

views of missionaries and their work. Chalmers was martyred by Papuan cannibals in 1901, while working to train Papuans and Polynesians for mission at Saguane on the Fly River. With him another 10 teachers and a young European missionary, Oliver Tomkins (uncle to an Anglican bishop of Bristol of the same name), were also murdered.

The courage involved in living among head-hunting tribes was not confined to these Scotsmen or the Englishman, W.G. Lawes. In 1886 Johannes Flierl (1858–1947), of the German Lutheran Neuendettelsau mission, left work among the Australian aborigines for Finschafen, a station on one of the eastern tips of New Guinea. His work as a pioneer was followed by Christian Keysser (1877–1961), who earned a formidable reputation both as a missionary to the head-hunting Kate and Hube tribes and later as a writer and trainer of other missionaries in Germany; he had been refused renewed entry to New Guinea by the Australian authorities in 1920. Keysser, with his contemporary, Bruno Gutmann (1876–1966), who worked among the Chagga people of Kilimanjaro in Africa, pursued a corporate, tribal approach to mission work, which was widely studied. Keysser's attractively written books *A People Reborn* (German: *Eine Papuagemeinde*) and *Anutu im Papuagemeinde* (*Anutu* being the word the missionaries used for God) written in the 1920s popularized this so-called 'folk-mission' approach in Germany. As well as Finschafen, this German mission had a base in Sattelberg, while another German mission established itself in Astrolabe Bay in 1887. By 1910 the mission launched by Johannes Flierl had some 2000 baptized members and 13 different stations.

> 'The folk church or tribal church is the goal of mission endeavour as pursued by the Lutherans.'
>
> **Christian Keysser, *A People Reborn***

Of the other denominations in this large field, Methodists worked from the islands off the north-east coast from 1875; Anglicans established a mission on that coast in 1890, led by a Scottish Anglican priest, A.A. Maclaren, who died soon after his arrival. Roman Catholics entered New Guinea in 1889, led by Bishop Henri Verjus (1860–92) of the Sacred Heart Mission. His early death aged 32 did not prevent the mission receiving thousands of converts in its 25 churches. Roman Catholic work was strengthened by the arrival of SVD (the Society of the Divine Word) missions in New Guinea in 1895. This work was led by a German, Eberhard Limbrock (1859–1931), who had experience of China

Ludwig Nommensen (1834–1918)

North of New Guinea (Irian Jaya), in what in colonial days was Dutch Indonesia, lay the island of Sumatra. This was the home of the Batak tribe. In 1862, a remarkable missionary figure, native of Schleswig-Holstein and member of the Rhenish Society, began work among the tribe. Over the years, Nommensen increasingly adopted a tribal approach to this people, and he was willing to emphasize the importance of *adat*, or tribal law and custom, in their life, and the traditional structure of elders in the church's development. Nommensen lost a child six years after his arrival and another four years later, before his wife died in 1887. Although he married again in 1901, another child was murdered in Sumatra in the same year, and his second wife died in 1909. Despite these personal tragedies, Nommensen gave 54 years of service to the Bataks. Initial baptisms had been made in 1865, a translation of the New Testament in the language was published in 1878, and a constitution was drawn up in 1881, which laid stress on the formation of a 'people's church', with Batak leadership and structure. The development of the work was helped by Dutch government generosity in grants towards education; many of the teachers supported were also Christian catechists. By Nommensen's death, the Batak church had 34 Batak pastors, serving in 500 local churches and supported by over 700 Batak teachers. Total membership had reached 180,000. Nommensen must be reckoned as one of the most outstanding missionaries in Protestant mission history.

and whose exceptional leadership resulted in an integrated approach that included schools, cattle raising, bridge and road construction, saw mills, and docks and cargo ships as a way of improving the life of the people while advancing the mission's aims. The SVD had a reputation for respecting local culture and custom, a reputation shared by the Protestants of the Neuendettelsau mission; both missions produced works of value on ethnology and culture. By the time of Limbrock's death the SVD mission had some 20,000 Christians and another 5,000 under instruction.

Pitcairn Island, lying as far east of New Guinea as any Pacific island, is a special historical case. In 1789, the crew of the *Bounty*, a British ship commanded by Captain Bligh under instructions to visit Tahiti, mutinied against their captain. Bligh and the crew loyal to him were put in an open boat in which, by astonishing seamanship, Bligh crossed the Pacific to landfall. The leading mutineer, Fletcher Christian, realized that to stay on Tahiti invited recapture (Bligh did indeed return in 1792) but he had knowledge from charts of the existence of Pitcairn, to which he, with some crew and Tahitian men and women, resorted. It became a community riven by disagreements and violence before the surviving mutineers, with the aid of a Prayer Book and Bible, created a form of Christian life. In the 1890s, after a visit from a missionary ship, the community embraced Seventh Day Adventism, a denomination that has gained considerable strength in the Pacific since. Pitcairn, with its tiny population, has been administered from New Zealand as a British possession.

Cargo cults

One result of Christian mission in Oceania has been the emergence of so-called 'cargo cults' or, as they are now better known, adjustment movements. Typically these combined some Christian teaching with promises to cult members of European goods and bounty in the future. An early example was the new religion created by a Polynesian religious leader called Siovili in Samoa in the 1830s, with probable influence also on Tahiti. There was another such movement in Fiji in the 1870s. In the 20th century, cargo cults were important religious phenomena among the Melanesians of Papua New Guinea. In certain respects, the kind of missionary emphasis on material improvements noted above strengthened this connection between religion and expected material rewards. The Solomon Islands also developed such cults, examples of invigorating traditional religious ideas with a culturally adapted Christianity, sometimes in the face of misunderstandings by British, French or Australian representatives of government in their various territories.

In New Zealand, a succession of such Maori-inspired reinterpretations of religion occurred, 'Papahurihia' in the 1830s being the earliest, and 'Pai Marire' in the 1850–70 period being another. This latter movement was led by an ex-slave, Te Va Hamene, and mixed traditional practices with the biblical, so that an angelic expulsion of Europeans would lead to a Maori Canaan. Known sometimes as 'Hau Hau', the movement was held responsible for the death of the missionary Carl Volkner at Opotiki in 1865, but it now seems more likely that he had passed information to the British during the Maori wars and paid the penalty when this was discovered. 'Ringatu', which took on some aspects of the Hau Hau movement but also emphasized the Old Testament and Christian inheritance more heavily, developed in the 1860s and survives as a form of Maori church today.

Missionary impact

There has been a strand of European literature that has laid emphasis on the tragic consequences of Western contact in Oceania and Australasia and in some cases held the missionary movement responsible. The occurrence of the adjective 'fatal' in the title of a number of such studies has signified the corrupting influence discerned. There is no escaping the fact that Europeans introduced diseases to which the peoples of the Pacific had little or no resistance; populations were often decimated. It has to be remembered that crews of whalers, of sealing vessels and other European and North American incursions would have taken place with or without the missionaries' presence. The evils of prostitution, exploitative trading and kidnapping to staff the plantations were introduced independently of missionaries. Often, as has been shown, it was missionary intervention that prevented further exploitation by land-hungry colonialists in Australia, New Zealand and Papua New Guinea. Some evils can be traced back to missionary involvement. For example, the blankets with which the missionaries traded for food with the Maori were less healthy than traditional clothing – when damp and worn continually they were a probable cause of Maori susceptibility to deadly tuberculosis and influenza in the 1830s. By and large, however, missionaries were more often the protectors of the exploited than the sources of their decline.

Finally, it is important, as in the case of Africa, to underline how much of the expansion of Christianity in the Pacific was achieved by Polynesians, Melanesians and Micronesians themselves. We have noted Tahitian evangelists on Hawaii and on Tongatabu; a gifted and influential Tongan on Fiji; and Polynesians of different origins in many other island settings. Melanesians formed one highly effective indigenous agency in the Melanesian Brotherhood, with its 1,000 indigenous workers. There were well-authenticated examples in New Zealand of European missionaries finding worshipping communities of Christian Maori with no direct European contact, evangelism and teaching having been effected by Maori converts from other areas. Spontaneous expansion was an important part of the Pacific Christian experience.

'[In] the Pacific Islands . . . the people gave to the churches a larger place in their life than did the people of any other region.'

Charles Forman, *Island Churches of the Pacific*

CHAPTER 9

THE 20TH CENTURY: AN AFRICAN CENTURY

In a history of Christian expansion, the 20th century must be dominated by the extraordinary development in sub-Saharan Africa, to which much of this chapter will be devoted. The contrast in Christian life and vitality can be made between the World Missionary Conference of 1910 in Edinburgh, where the historian of this immensely influential Protestant gathering noticed just one African from Liberia among a number of representatives from the younger churches of Asia; and the African Synod of Rome in 1994, with some 200 Africans including cardinals, archbishops and bishops as well as priests. The same point can be made about African Protestant leadership in the period after 1950, when men like Archbishop Erica Sabiti and Janani Luwum, who will appear later in this chapter, led the Anglican Church of Uganda in the 1960s and 1970s in parallel with a Roman Catholic leader like Cardinal Laurean Rugambwa, who attended the Second Vatican Council of 1963–65.

In terms of wider statistics, 10 million African Christians (mostly from Egypt and Ethiopia) in 1900 became, by David Barrett's latest calculations, 335 million in 2000. Of these, some 83 million are estimated to belong to African Independent (sometimes African Initiated) Churches. These comprised 2,000 different denominations in 1968 and are well over 10,000 today. Some attempt, however inadequate, must be made to describe this extraordinary African Christian phenomenon in all its variety.

In an earlier chapter, the beginnings of 'Ethiopianism' and 'Zionism' were described, in particular the breakaway Ethiopian church founded by Mangena Mokone and recognized by Paul Kruger in the Transvaal as 'the Ethiopian Church of South Africa', which asserted an African expression of Christianity over against colonial and missionary-directed expressions. Zionism can be traced back to Zululand and a missionary, P.L. le Roux, who resigned from the Dutch Reformed Church in 1903 and called his Zulu congregation the Zionist Apostolic Church. After 1906 this became African-led and by 1930 there were Zionist congregations in Swaziland, the Transvaal and Rhodesia as well as in Zululand, laying emphasis on healing, speaking in tongues and extended times of worship. In the early years of the century, this African Christian consciousness was also experienced through a series of Christian 'prophets', religious revivalists to whom thousands of Africans responded by casting away and burning their fetishes and welcoming baptism, often also reinforcing the mainline denominations but sometimes resulting in breakaway churches.

African prophets and revival

Perhaps the most influential of all the prophets was William Wade Harris (c. 1865–1929). Harris was born in Liberia and a Methodist in background, though he was later confirmed into the Protestant Episcopal Church in Liberia. He was imprisoned in 1910 after a rebellion against the Liberian authorities by his people, the Grebo. While in prison he experienced a personal call to itinerant preaching. He wore a white robe and a turban and carried a baptismal bowl and a calabash rattle, travelling barefoot with a cross-shaped staff and a Bible. The response to his preaching over the border of Liberia in the Ivory Coast was astonishing – it is estimated that it resulted in 100,000 converts in 1913. He also had a considerable impact in the Gold Coast (now Ghana).

> 'God is all powerful, so you must burn your fetishes and love one another. Bring your idols so that I can burn them . . . thereupon I am going to baptize you.'
>
> **Preaching of Prophet Harris**

Mainline denominations profited. Roman Catholic baptisms, previously running at about 80 a year became 6,000 in 1915. The Methodist missionary, W.J. Platt, was faced with 25,000 catechumens as a result of Harris's campaigns when working in the 1920s. In addition, Harrist churches developed throughout West Africa in countries such as Ghana, Togo, Benin, Liberia and the Ivory Coast. These were led by Harris's designated successor, E.J. (John) Ahui (c. 1888–1992), who was styled 'Supreme Prophet of the Harrist Church of West Africa'. Over 300 congregations with 200,000 adherents made up this new denomination. Harris's extraordinary effectiveness as a Christian revivalist was recognized by the more traditional churches, even if, as with others of the African prophets, there were aspects of his teaching to which they could not subscribe, notably his tolerance (and practice) of polygamy.

Garrick Braide (1880–1918) was a similar figure, who originated in the Niger Delta area. He has been called the first major Nigerian independent Christian prophet. Like Harris he led a revivalist movement in 1915, which featured opposition to traditional religion and mass baptisms. He experienced imprisonment and religious resistance from Anglicans; like Harris he was tolerant of polygamy. Nigeria was also the scene of the development among the Yoruba people of the Aladura groups (literally, 'praying people'), which began as a response to the influenza epidemic of 1918 and the search for healing. Three main Aladura churches developed, the first of which, the Christ Apostolic Church, owed much to Isaac Akinyele, brother to an Anglican bishop, who became its president in 1941. A second, which broke away to form the Church of the Lord (Aladura), was led by Josiah Oshitelu, a baptized Anglican and revivalist, who, in contrast to the first church, upheld polygamy. The third was the Church of the Cherubim and Seraphim, today a church of 4,000 congregations. One informed observer, who is both a bishop and a university lecturer, has judged that the future of the church in Nigeria lies with these Aladura churches and that far from being marginal they are now a central Christian reality in Nigeria.

In Ghana, a similar figure to Harris was John Swatson (c. 1885–1925). Diplomatic handling of the revival movement that he instigated resulted in many accessions to the Anglican church during 1915–16. In Malawi, by contrast, a tragedy unfolded in connection with the work of John Chilembwe (c. 1871–1915). Between 1900 and 1914 this Baptist leader, trained in Virginia, pursued quiet missionary work in Malawi; but his following became radicalized by colonial injustice, a sense of grievance exacerbated by African conscription for the 1914–18 war. Violent insurrection followed, in which Chilembwe lost his life and, by a strange irony, a grandson of the great David Livingstone, who was a farm manager of a large European estate where working practices were felt to be oppressive, was decapitated.

The Congo and Kimbanguism

The Congo, with its very special history of European administration as a prime example of the so-called 'scramble for Africa' by the European powers in the 19th century, also provided a special case of African

Church Independency. King Leopold II of the Belgians had effectively owned vast tracts of central Africa as a private fiefdom or estate, administered through his own agents, one of whom was H.M. Stanley. The determined policy here was to make profits from rubber and ivory. On rubber collection, quotas were set to villages and savage punishments meted out where these were not met. This inhumanity provided Joseph Conrad, who visited the Congo, with the background to his novel *The Heart of Darkness*, set in the country. After a campaign mounted largely by a gifted journalist, E.D. Morel, who was able to use firsthand accounts of atrocities given to him by Baptist missionaries, the British consul Roger Casement was asked to report on the situation. He produced a document that caused a sensation in Europe and in 1908 led to the Belgian government taking responsibility for the territory.

> 'Nowhere else was there so systematic or long-standing a regime of oppression as in Leopold's Congo.'
>
> **Adrian Hastings, *The Church in Africa***

Ten years later, an African of no formal education, Simon Kimbangu (c. 1889–1951), received what he believed to be a calling from Christ towards the conversion of fellow Africans, a calling that, like Jonah, he refused, and to escape which he fled to Kinshasha. In 1921, however, he began a ministry of healing in N'Kamba (his birthplace), which turned into a mass movement of revival. Like Harris, he preached against fetishes with a simple message of repentance and faith in Christ. Unlike Harris, he stood for monogamy. Within a few months of the mission of healing in April 1921 the authorities took fright, arrested him and sentenced him to death, a sentence commuted to life imprisonment by King Leopold. For 30 years (1921–51) he remained in prison but the movement grew rapidly. In time, L'Église de Jésus Christ sur la terre par le prophète Simon Kimbangu (The Church of Jesus Christ on Earth through the Prophet Simon Kimbangu) became one of the main denominations recognized by the authorities and in 1959, the year of recognition, had 1 million members. Joseph Dagienda, Kimbangu's youngest son, was its leader and it became a member church of the World Council of Churches in 1969. Today it has 14,000 congregations, though its treatment of Simon Kimbangu as a virtual messiah has raised questions about the version of faith in Christ that it represents. Nevertheless, it is an extreme case of an African Independent Church growing from one imprisoned leader to its present position of a major denomination, accorded international recognition, with a membership of 7 million.

Growth and African leadership

There is a danger in a description of African Christian life such as the Kimbangu church for observers to neglect equivalent growth (and equivalent African leadership) in the more traditional churches. Uganda, with its strong response to Christianity since 1890, was an example where the two main traditional denominations, Roman Catholic and Anglican, benefited to the extent of millions of new adherents, so that today, of 19 million Ugandan Christians, 17 million may be regarded as either Roman Catholic or of the Church of Uganda (Anglican). The 20th century saw at least one outstanding African leader in each church. For Roman Catholics, Yohana Kitagana, in an almost Franciscan renunciation, forsook his assured position as a chief in 1901, gave away his property and became a missionary with staff and rosary in unevangelized areas of the country like the mountains of Kigezi. Among Anglicans, Apolo Kivebulaya (d. 1933) was ordained priest in 1903 and became a missionary to the pygmy people of the Congo around Mboga, where he died after 30 years of service. He laid the foundations of an entire Anglican province. Here were two African 'apostles', very different from Harris and Braide, also deeply committed to their calling, whose ministries resulted in growth and development in their traditional churches.

> 'Jesus Christ appeared to me in a dream on the night when I was doubting if I could endure being bound and prodded with spears and my house being burnt.'
>
> **Apolo Kivebulaya on his work among the Pygmies of Mboga**

Uganda was also a country touched by a movement of revival, which had profound effects in Ruanda and East Africa in the 1930s. It originated in a deeply shared European–African experience of personal renewal between an English doctor, who was a CMS missionary, J.E. (Joe) Church, and a Ugandan (Ganda) Christian, Simeon Nsimbambi, which spread among the orderlies at the hospital in Ruanda where Church was working. Great emphasis was placed by the *balokole* ('saved ones') on forgiveness through the saving blood of Christ, on personal confession of sin and testimony to personal salvation. The movement

Janani Luwum (d. 1977)

Luwum was one of the Ugandan Christians influenced by the East African revival. He was ordained into the Anglican Church of Uganda and became provincial secretary in the 1960s and bishop of Northern Uganda in 1969. In 1977 he succeeded Erica Sabiti, the first African archbishop, who had followed the Englishman, Leslie Brown. In 1971 General Amin, a British-trained soldier, supplanted President Obote while the head of state was at a Commonwealth conference in Singapore. His years of power (1971–79) were years of terror. Luwum and his fellow Anglican bishops, as critics of the regime, incurred Amin's enmity and vengeance. After arrest, Luwum was put to death in 1977 by Amin's henchmen. Sabiti preached at his funeral service outside Namirembe Cathedral in Kampala. Amin was finally defeated by the Tanzanian army and exiled. Luwum is commemorated in a chapel dedicated to 20th-century martyrs in Canterbury Cathedral and in stone carvings to them on the west front of Westminster Abbey unveiled in 1998.

had its own hymn 'Tukutendereza Yezu' ('We Praise You, Jesus, Jesus the Lamb'), and it mounted powerful Christian conventions. Many of the African leaders in East Africa, such as Archbishop Erica Sabiti and his successor, Janani Luwum, a martyr in General Amin's Uganda in 1977, Luwum's episcopal colleague, Festo Kivengere, and the Kenyan bishop of Fort Hall (Murang'a), Obadiah Kariuki, were deeply influenced by the revival. Kenya was the area where the depth of Christian life among the revival brethren was most severely tested and most impressively displayed. In the Mau Mau insurrection among the Kikuyu people of Kenya, taking the Mau Mau oath meant drinking blood and committing acts of violence. Those Kikuyu, Embu and Meru Christians who, when faced by intimidation and death, refused were in many cases *balokole* Christians. In at least one known instance, the reply was given 'I have drunk the blood of Jesus Christ and I can drink no other', to which the response was a blow intended to kill. While the East African revival had been potentially schismatic in the Church of Uganda, the stories of the Kikuyu martyrs showed the Christian depth and constancy of many of those it had reached.

Post-colonialism

After 1950, Africa entered a period of post-colonialism, as the European powers granted independence to one colony after another.

In 1952, President Nkrumah took power in the Gold Coast (Ghana), the first post-colonial African head of state. Independence and African leadership followed in Nigeria (1960), the Belgian colonies of the Congo, Ruanda and Burundi in the 1960s and the British colonies of Tanzania (1961), Kenya (1963), Malawi and Zambia (1964). The Portuguese territories of Angola and Mozambique followed in the 1970s. The leaders of these new nations had often been educated in mission schools; and in one case, Kenneth Kaunda of Zambia, the president was the son of a Presbyterian minister. Kaunda was faced with a Christian movement resulting from a 'death and resurrection' experience of a prophet, Alice Lenshina (c. 1925–78), in 1953. Once more, a movement began that aimed at the destruction of the fetishes of traditional religion, acting also against witchcraft, polygamy, beer-drinking and paganism. Alice Lenshina composed hymns and many previously Roman Catholic or Presbyterian church members joined the fold. Sadly, this 'Lumpa' church movement confronted the new government of independence with violence in 1964, over such issues as the spread of schools, and as many as 1,000 people died, Lenshina herself being imprisoned.

> 'The wind of change is blowing throughout the continent.'
>
> Harold Macmillan, British Prime Minister, to the South African Parliament in Cape Town, January 1960

> 'You who loved the land of darkness, let us break through, be saved. He will help us in everything, he will take us out of evil, when, when?'
>
> Translation of Bemba hymn composed by Alice Lenshina of the Lumpa Church

Apartheid and South Africa

This is not the place to pursue the history of the struggle against the policy of apartheid in South Africa in detail, but determined opposition of the policy by such figures as Dr Beyers Naudé of the Dutch Reformed Church, Trevor Huddleston of the Anglican Community of the Resurrection at Rosettenville and Desmond Tutu, a product of the seminary at Rosettenville and protégé of Huddleston, achieved much towards deeper Christianization in southern Africa. The Nationalist

Trevor Huddleston (1913–98)

Huddleston was an Anglican priest and member of the Community of the Resurrection, Mirfield. In 1963 he was appointed to lead the Anglican mission in Sophiatown, Johannesburg, known as the Church of Christ the King. He became one of the leading Christian campaigners against the policy of separate development adopted by the government. In 1956 he published the book *Naught for Your Comfort,* a widely read work on the South African struggle, which was critical of the government in South Africa and after which he was not permitted to return to the country. He became Anglican bishop of Masasi (Tanzania) in 1960. The young Desmond Tutu had known and admired Huddleston, who was a friend also of Nelson Mandela and Oliver Tambo. In 1968 Huddleston made way for an African successor in Masasi. He became in turn bishop of Stepney (1968–78) and archbishop of the Indian Ocean and bishop of Mauritius (1978–83) before retiring to Mirfield. From 1981 he was president of the Anti-Apartheid Movement.

party of Malan and Verwoerd had come to power in 1948 with 'separate development' as their aim, leading to the closure of mixed race institutions founded by the churches at centres like Lovedale. The policy was ruthlessly enforced by the police, for example in the shooting of African civilians at Sharpeville in 1960. Nelson Mandela's release after 27 years in jail in 1990 marked the end of a searing political struggle.

Desmond Tutu, appointed as Anglican archbishop of Cape Town in 1986, was given the task of presiding over a Truth and Reconciliation Commission (National Initiative for Reconciliation) in 1990, which attempted to heal the wounds inflicted during the struggle and which included a confession from the Dutch Reformed Church that apartheid was a sin.

Threats to Africa's future

For the missionaries of the 19th century, the Christian expansion in Africa of the 20th century would have been difficult to believe, deeply committed as they were to their task. Nevertheless, not all of the scene would be so cheering, albeit in a widely Christianized Africa. Since the early 1980s, Africa has developed a HIV/AIDS pandemic, whereby an estimated 33 per cent of the population aged 15–49 years are infected, a situation that could have catastrophic effects on both the demographic and economic future of the countries. There are gleams of hope, for instance, in the falling infection rates in Uganda, but Africa faces a tragic crisis through the disease.

Secondly, it has been profoundly disturbing to many that areas such as Ruanda and Burundi, with a 90 per cent nominally Christian population, can be the context of ethnic violence of frightening savagery. The rivalry between the ruling Tutsi clan and the Hutu in Ruanda boiled over into the slaughter of 800,000 Tutsi by Hutu extremists in 1994 during three months. Twenty years earlier, in 1973, 100,000 Hutu had been treated similarly by the Tutsi. It is this kind of phenomenon that has caused sympathetic commentators like Adrian Hastings and Bishop Sundkler to view the massive accession to the historic churches and the independents as 'terrifying'; for the issue is whether such great numbers can be rooted, taught and nurtured, so that their Christianity is not superficial adherence but a deeply implanted moral and spiritual formation. The next 100 years in Africa will be as significant, or more so, than the 20th century has so evidently been for African Christianity.

Pentecostalism and the charismatic movement

A 20th-century movement that has grown in almost African proportions has been worldwide Pentecostalism. As a denomination, Pentecostals look back to the Azusa Street Revival in Los Angeles, California of 1906 as a point of departure. A black revivalist, William J. Seymour, who had been shaped by Wesleyan teaching on holiness, began to teach a 'baptism of the Spirit', associated with speaking in tongues as evidence of it. One immediate result, surprising in its day, was that blacks, Hispanics and white Americans were found worshipping together in Azusa Street between 1906 and 1909. From these small beginnings, the movement spread to Canada, South America, Scandinavia, England and Germany. Today, analysts divide the movement into Pentecostals (a denomination), charismatics (those in mainline denominations) and neo-charismatics (groups formed since 1980 outside mainline denominations).

Since 1960, there has been much growth of the movement in the traditional denominations, termed the charismatic movement. Charismatics are found in Roman Catholicism, Anglicanism, Lutheranism and other mainline churches. Of all the areas of the world, Latin America has been the scene of the greatest development. Of the 60 million members of the churches who see themselves as sharing in the charismatic renewal, 33 million are in the Latin American countries. In Chile, some 36 per cent of all Christians are reckoned to be Pentecostal, charismatic or neo-charismatic. The proportions are similar in Colombia (30 per cent) and Argentina (22 per cent). The country with the strongest presence, however, is Brazil, where one recent estimate, possibly inflated, gives a figure of 47 per cent of all Christians in the three categories; the strength of the Assemblies of God (Pentecostal Churches) alone is said to contain 100,000 pastors and 500,000 recognized lay leaders. Even if the figure of 79 million in all three categories is exaggerated, it indicates a movement of very large numbers. The third category of neo-charismatics is a sign, as among the African Independent Churches mentioned earlier, that indigenous forms of Christianity, which bear comparison to the first two groupings with their emphasis on healing, prophecy and exuberant worship with speaking in tongues, have sprung up as independent, non-denominational expressions of local Christianity.

A new centre of gravity

These figures are a reminder of the shift in Christian population from the predominance of the north (Europe and North America) to the south in the 20th century. In 1900 the overwhelming number of Christians were in the so-called 'sending' countries of the missionary era. Now, the balance has shifted to Africa, south of the Sahara, Latin America and the Pacific in a proportion of 60–40; put another way, if Christians are estimated at two billion of a world population of six billion, well over half of these are to be found in the south, in what were traditionally regarded as the 'mission fields'. Further large numbers of missionaries, intent on expanding the influence of the Christian gospel in often post-Christian lands, are to be found in nations such as South Korea (which has around 10,000 missionaries, of whom some hundreds are to be found in Japan, Russia and the Philippines) and Nigeria, which has over 3,000

Vatican II (1963–65)

Regarded by many as the most significant religious event of the 20th century, the Second Vatican Council was summoned by Pope John XXIII (1883–1963; pope from 1958) who was over 80 years of age when it met. He gave the council the task of renewal (*aggiornamento*) of the life of the church. It was attended by 2,300 bishops from all over the world, of whom 800 came from the younger churches of Asia, Africa and Oceania. Observers from the Orthodox, Anglican and other churches were also invited. It ushered in an immense process of adjustment for the Roman Catholic church. A predominant view of the church as 'the people of God' in movement, rather than as a static and hierarchical institution, issued in vernacular (rather than Latin) liturgies, an emphasis on collegiality and shared ministry among bishops, a permanent and married diaconate (though celibacy remained the rule for priests) and a greater openness to the 'separated brethren' of the non-Roman churches.

missionaries. Although there is still pioneering work to do by such bodies as Wycliffe Bible Translators (founded in 1934), among peoples whose languages have yet to be expressed in written forms and into which the Bible has yet to be translated, the main ethnic groups have been evangelized over two millennia in terms of territorial outreach. The Christian churches are confronted with a different, if no less challenging, task.

'A complete change in the centre of gravity of Christianity [has occurred] so that the heartlands of the Church are . . . in Latin America . . . parts of Asia and . . . in Africa.'

Andrew Walls, Emeritus Professor of the University of Edinburgh

In the 20th century, Christianity has faced the challenge of an aggressively atheistic alternative in Communism, lasting in Europe in its Marxist–Leninist form from the Russian revolution of 1917 until the fall of the Berlin Wall in 1989. It has faced also the challenge of neo-pagan Aryan Nazism. The Dutch missionary thinker, Hendrik Kraemer, regarded both as modern 'tribalisms', offering the security of false religions and false absolutes, securities that are also sought by many in the different forms of fundamentalism, religious or otherwise, in the contemporary world. The century has seen much profound reflection on Christian expansion. This was true of the World Missionary Conference at Edinburgh in 1910, even if its optimism would now seem excessive, and of the conferences mounted by the International Missionary Council (which resulted from Edinburgh) and led to analyses of the world scene in Jerusalem in 1928 and Tamabaram, Madras in 1938. It was for this meeting that Kraemer wrote his explosive preparatory volume *The Christian Message in a Non-Christian World*. Since 1950, the documents of the Second Vatican Council have provided highly stimulating reflection on the church's task in *Ad Gentes* (the decree on the Church's Missionary Activity 'to the nations'), *Lumen Gentium* (the dogmatic constitution on the Church as 'the Light of the Nations') and *Nostra Aetate* (the declaration of the relation of the Church to non-Christian religions 'in our age'). Pope John Paul II's recent calls for re-evangelization build on one of his predecessor's reminders of 1975 that evangelization is the church's essential function 'inherent in the very nature of the church', which itself needs to be evangelized before 'carrying forth . . . the good news to every sector of the human race' for its renewal and transformation (Pope Paul VI in *Evangelii Nuntiandi*). Much valuable material for reflection can also be found in the documents of the Lausanne Congress on World Evangelization of 1974, mounted by evangelicals.

> 'The age of missions is at an end; the age of mission has begun.'
>
> **Stephen Neill,** *A History of Christian Missions*

In a changed world and changed context, when, as Paul VI discerned, there is a rift between the gospel and a secularized modern culture, the emphasis on witness remains valid. Luke's words at the beginning of this story 'you will be my witnesses . . . to the ends of the earth' remain as true as ever, even in the light of two millennia of territorial expansion of the Christian faith.

CHRONOLOGY

26–36 Pontius Pilate's governorship in Judea.

c. 30 crucifixion of Jesus of Nazareth.

51 Paul appears before Gallio in Corinth.

64 Nero blames the fire of Rome on Christians. Probable date of Mark's Gospel.

c. 107 Martyrdom of Ignatius, bishop of Antioch, in Rome.

112 Pliny the younger's correspondence with Emperor Trajan about Christians.

312 Constantine's victory at Milvian Bridge.

c. 340 Frumentius in Ethiopia as a Christian.

386 Augustine of Hippo's experience in the garden in Milan.

410 Alaric the Goth sacks Rome.

c. 529 Benedict founds the monastery at Monte Cassino.

563 Columba founds the monastery on Iona.

596 Gregory I (Pope) sends Augustine to Canterbury.

635 Alopen reaches China. Aidan evangelizes Northumbria.

c. 696 Lindisfarne Gospels.

754 Boniface is martyred at Dokkum.

800 Charlemagne is crowned emperor in Rome; possible date of *Book of Kells.*

830 Anskar founds church in Sweden (Stockholm).

910 Monastery at Cluny founded.

c. 988 Vladimir baptized in Kiev.

1098 Cistercian Abbey founded at Citeaux.

1130 Chartres Cathedral begun.

1209 Francis founds order by permission of Innocent III.

1216–8 Dominic founds order.

1415 Jan Hus is burned.

1483 Portuguese in Kongo; African king baptized (1491).

1492 Columbus's voyage of discovery.

1493 Papal bull *Ceteris Partibus* divides world between Spain/Portugal.

1498 Vasco da Gama sails to India.

1520 Cortes destroys Aztec capital and founds Mexico City.

1540 Francis Xavier (Jesuit) to Goa (dies in 1552 off China).

1550 Bartholemew de las Casas debates Indian rights at Valladolid.

1583 Jesuits into China.

1600 East India Company founded.

1614 Jesuits expelled from Japan (entered 1542).

1622 Propaganda Fidei founded in Rome.

1701 Society for the Propagation of the Gospel founded (SPG).

1706 Ziegenbalg and Plütschau to India as first Protestant missionaries.

1739 Moravian community of Genadendal founded in South Africa by G. Schmidt.

1742 David Brainerd begins work among native Americans.

1769 Captain Cook visits Tahiti.

1773 Suppression of the Jesuit Order.

1792 William Carey to India: foundation of the Baptist Missionary Society.

1795 London Missionary Society founded. LMS voyage of *Duff* (1796).

1799 Church Missionary Society (CMS) founded.

1810 American Board of Commissioners for Foreign Missions founded.

1814 Samuel Marsden preaches first Christian sermon in New Zealand.

1815 Basel Missionary Society founded. Society of Mary (Marists) founded (1816).

1839 John Williams martyred on Erromanga, New Hebrides.

1841 Father Chanel martyred on Futuna.

1853–56 David Livingstone's trans-continental journeys in central Africa.

1857 Indian Mutiny (Sepoy rebellion). British Government assumes rule.

1858 Treaty of Tientsin opens interior of China to western influence.

1865 China Inland Mission (CIM) founded by James Hudson Taylor.

1871 John Patteson martyred on Nukapu.

1892 Mangena Mokone founds the 'Ethiopian Church of South Africa'.

1901 James Chalmers is martyred in New Guinea.

1903 Zionist Apostolic Church is founded in Zululand.

1906–09 Azusa Street Revival in Los Angeles: birth of modern Pentecostalism.

1910 Edinburgh World Missionary Conference.

1912 Prophet Harris's campaigns in West Africa.

1921 Simon Kimbangu imprisoned in Belgian Congo.

1952 President Nkrumah head of state in Ghana.

1963–65 Second Vatican Council in Rome.

1974 Lausanne Congress on World Evangelization.

1977 Archbishop Janani Luwum martyred in Uganda.

1990 Nelson Mandela is freed in South Africa.

PART 2

CHRISTIANITY
AND THE CELTS

INTRODUCTION: 'A MAGIC BAG'

The Celts were warriors who sacked the great places of Europe – Rome in 390 BC, and Delphi almost a century later. They were also peace-loving saints, creating some of the first Western laws protecting noncombatants and granting rights to women.

The Celts were some of the most important scholars of history, not only copying countless tomes, but also writing their own works on history, geography, theology, and other subjects. However, Celts were also so secretive about their knowledge that they did not even allow a written language.

Celtic Christians were radically ascetic, submerging themselves in icy waters for hours and using themselves as oxen to pull their monastery's plough. Yet Celtic Christians also thought such radical asceticism was almost sinful – proof not of devotion to God, but of distance from him.

All of these statements were true to varying degrees at various times, and such paradoxes and contradictions make summarizing the Celts and their interaction with Christianity difficult. The problem is compounded by a flood of titles offering everything from *Celtic Spells and Wisdom for Self-Healing, Prosperity, and Great Sex* to *The Celtic Way of Evangelism*.

As J.R.R. Tolkien said, the term 'Celtic' is 'a magic bag, into which anything may be put, and out of which almost anything may come . . . Anything is possible in the fabulous Celtic twilight, which is not so much a twilight of the gods as of the reason.' He lamented this 'lunatic infection' long before Thomas Cahill's *How the Irish Saved Civilization*, *Riverdance* and Enya all became best-sellers.

That so much may be said of the Celtic world, however, does not mean that nothing should be said. Celtic wisdom may be trendy, but there remain important lessons for anyone willing to look. The best way to find them may not be in grand statements that cover all Celts from 700 BC to the modern era, but in stories of Celtic men and women from various eras.

Brennus, the Celtic commander who led the attack on Rome, would hardly have seen himself as kin to Columba, the royal monk who founded a monastery on the Scottish island of Iona in AD 562. The critical Gildas the Wise might have been upset at appearing in the same book as his contemporary David of Wales, whose self-mortification he found abhorrent. Yet all of these people were members of a kind of family, and without any of them the tale of Christianity and the Celts becomes too simple and ultimately incorrect.

An Irish monk, probably writing around the 9th century, understood the need to retell stories that he would rather avoid. Nevertheless, he copied for his contemporaries and future generations the pagan 'Táin Bó Cuailgne', an epic Celtic poem of bloody battles, mystical prophetesses, and cattle raiding. Still, he could not help adding his own postscript: 'I, who copied this history down, or rather this fantasy, do not believe in all the details. Several things in it are devilish lies. Others are the invention of poets. And others again have been thought up for the entertainment of idiots.'

Similarly, scholars have raised doubts about some of the stories retold here. It is not a new complaint; an Irish scholar in the 800s complained of 'the Irish habit of preferring fiction to true history'. But it is not this account's intention to rate the reliability of primary sources or catalogue the most current scholarly debates. (That is done well enough in any number of publications.)

This is less a narrative about 'Celtic Christianity' than it is about Christianity and Celts. Many similar accounts begin with the mission of Patrick to the Irish in the 5th century and end with Viking raids on monasteries in the 8th century. But Christianity touched Celtic lives on a much broader scale, from those living at the time of Jesus himself to today's speakers of Celtic languages in Ireland, Scotland, Wales, the Isle of Man, Brittany, and elsewhere.

Some of these believers were killed for their faith; others killed for it. Some confronted monsters, druids and demons; others fought their own weak flesh. Some travelled across the known world; others stayed cloistered in their monastery.

Around AD 793, Celtic monks began lamenting raids by strange tribes from the north. Nearly twelve centuries earlier, however, it was their Celtic forefathers who were seen as the northern raiders. This is where our stories begin.

CHAPTER 10

'THE WHOLE RACE IS WAR MAD': CELTIC BEGINNINGS

'Their aspect is terrifying,' Greek historian Diodorus Siculus wrote of Celtic warriors in the 1st century BC:

They are very tall in stature, with rippling muscles under clear, white skin. Their hair is blonde, but not naturally so. They bleach it, to this day, artificially, washing it in lime and combing it back on their foreheads . . . The Celtic way of fighting was alarming. They wore . . . bronze helmets with figures picked out on them, even horns, which make them look even taller than they already are . . . while others cover themselves with breast-armour made of chains. But most content themselves with the weapons nature gave them: they go naked into battle.

Alarming indeed. The army of Rome was literally scared to death when it first met a Celtic army from Gaul (an area of Western Europe mainly consisting of modern France and Belgium) at the Allia River on 18 July 390 BC. The Romans were so terrified, wrote the Roman historian Livy some time around the birth of Christ, that 'they fled, whole and unhurt, almost before they had seen their untried foe, without any attempt to fight or even to give back the battle-shout. None were slain while actually fighting; they were cut down from behind whilst hindering one another's flight in a confused, struggling mass.'

The Gauls were so stunned by this easy victory that they were almost certain it was a ruse; a sneak attack would follow at any moment. It did not. They continued the 12 miles southward to Rome, but upon finding the gates wide open, they were even surer of a trap. After a day's partying and resting, the Celtic Gauls continued cautiously into the city. Despite Celts' reputation for being violent barbarians, the actual invasion of Rome was a relatively calm, quiet affair. The residents had retreated to the fortified Capitol,

'This race of men from the plains were all the harder, for hard land had borne them; built on stronger and firmer bones, and endowed with mighty sinew, they were a race undaunted by heat or cold, plague, or strange new foodstuffs.'

Lucretius, *On the Nature of Things*

leaving the city deserted. Now the Gauls were quite sure they were walking into a trap, and were 'appalled by the very desolation of the place'. Those who had scampered off to loot the empty houses quickly returned to seek the safety of numbers.

Finally the Gauls came across some residents. Nine old patricians who had been refused the safety of the Capitol (they were certain to perish anyway, their fellow Romans reasoned) had put on their fanciest clothing and sat motionless, awaiting their fate. In fact, so strange was this encounter that the Gauls wondered if the gentry were really human. A brief stroke of one of the statues' long beards gave the answer. The insulted old Roman, Marcus Papirius, responded by rapping the offending Gaul with his ivory staff. The Gauls were immediately inflamed again with the passions of war, slew the old men, and soon prepared to invade the Capitol.

The Capitol, however, was not as easy a victory as the battlefield of Allia. An initial attack, unwisely made by hastily charging up the Forum's steep hill, was a costly error. A second, sneak attack in the dead of night was unluckily foiled by a skittish flock of sacred geese in the temple of Juno; and a blockade began to go very badly. Seven months after they had entered the city, the Celts found that their greatest enemy was not the sword, but malaria and other diseases. 'They died off like sheep,' Livy recorded. So many died from the pestilence that the Gauls gave up burying their dead. Finally, the Celtic commander, Brennus, convinced the Romans to offer a hefty ransom for their lives: half a ton of gold. But even after the Romans raised the sum, tensions flared between the nations. The Gauls, the Romans complained, were using biased weights. Brennus could not believe his ears. Angry at the hubris but eager to leave, he threw his sword upon the scales. '*Vae Victis!*' he shouted. 'Woe to the vanquished!'

Brennus and his soldiers left the city, concluding the first and only Celtic invasion of Rome. But battles, conquests, and dealings between the Celts and the eternal city would continue for centuries – even long after popes replaced emperors as Rome's most powerful citizens.

Through outsiders' eyes

George Orwell's famous line, 'History is written by the winners,' does not hold true in this case. The Celts left no written record of their siege of Rome or of almost anything else in their long story. Thus it is mainly through Greek and Roman eyes that we first glimpse these far-ranging tribes, called *keltoi* (strangers, or hidden) by the former and *galli* by the latter. They are heavily biased reports, of course, but nearly unified in how they perceived their northern neighbours.

'The whole race is war mad, high spirited, and quick to battle, but otherwise straightforward and not of evil character,' wrote the Greek historian Strabo, a contemporary of Diodorus. Both authors relied heavily on Stoic philosopher Poseidonius, who wrote a century earlier, for their information on the Celts:

At any time or place and on whatever pretext you stir them up, you will have them ready to face danger, even if they have nothing on their side but their own strength and courage. On the other hand, if won over by gentle persuasion they willingly devote their energies to useful pursuits and even take to a literary education . . . To the frankness and high-spiritedness of their character must be added the traits of childish boastfulness and love of decoration. They wear ornaments of gold, torques on their necks, and bracelets on their arms and wrists, while people of high rank wear dyed garments sprinkled with gold. It is this vanity which makes them unbearable in victory and so completely downcast in defeat.

It was not just the warring men who were like this. 'Nearly all the Gauls are of a lofty stature, fair and ruddy complexion: terrible from the sternness of their eyes, very quarrelsome, and of great pride and insolence,' said Ammianus Marcellinus, the last major Roman historian (c. AD 330–95):

A whole troop of foreigners would not be able to withstand a single Celt if he called his wife to his assistance. The wife is even more formidable. She is usually very strong, and with blue eyes; in rage her neck veins swell, she gnashes her teeth, and brandishes

'Slashed with axe or sword, they kept their desperation while they breathed; pierced by arrow or javelin, they did not abate of their passion so long as life remained. Some drew out from their wounds the spears, by which they had been hit, and threw them at the Greeks or used them in close fighting.'

Pausanias, *Description of Greece*

Table manners

Even when blood was not spilled, dinner could be an unsightly mess in the eyes of any Greek or Roman visitor. Diodorus detailed how beards were worn short, but moustaches were grown so long that they covered the Celtic men's mouths. 'Consequently,' he lamented, 'when they are eating, their moustaches become entangled in the food, and when they are drinking, the beverage passes, as it were, through a kind of strainer.' Poseidonius also fussed that though the Celts ate cleanly, they were 'like lions, raising up whole limbs in both hands and biting off the meat'. And always meat – large amounts of animal flesh, boiled in a cauldron or roasted on a spit, served with small portions of bread and gallons upon gallons of alcohol. 'The Gauls are exceedingly addicted to the use of wine,' Diodorus said, 'drinking it unmixed, and since they partake of this drink without moderation by reason of their craving for it, when they become drunk they fall into a stupor or into a maniacal rage.' A wheat-and-honey beer was poured freely among the lower classes. Indeed, the tribes became renowned for liquor – one of the only times Plato ever referred to Celts was to name them among six peoples overly fond of drinking – and Italian wine merchants were happy to take advantage of the situation, sometimes commanding a slave for each libation.

'They also invite strangers to their banquets, and only after the meal do they ask who they are and of what they stand in need.'

Diodorus Siculus, *Historical Library*

her snow-white robust arms. She begins to strike blows mingled with kicks, as if they were so many missiles sent from the string of a catapult.

The Celts were no less animated off the battlefield, if there *was* such a place as off the battlefield. 'It is their custom,' wrote Diodorus, 'even during the course of the meal, to seize upon any trivial matter as an occasion for keen disputation and then to challenge one another to single combat, without any regard for their lives.' Diodorus's source, Poseidonius (whose works are no longer available), was also quoted by Athenaeus:

They gather in arms and engage in mock battles, and fight hand-to-hand, but sometimes wounds are inflicted, and the irritation caused by this may even lead to killing unless the bystanders restrain them. And in former times, when the hindquarters were served up the bravest hero took the thigh piece, and if another man claimed it they stood up and fought in single combat to death.

The Celts were not just brutish, barbarian enemies to the classical world; they were also potential allies. Just a few years after Brennus and his men left Rome, the tyrannical Dionysius of Syracuse hired Celts to aid the Spartans during the Peloponnesian War. A few decades later, in 335 BC, an increasingly cocky Alexander the Great met with some Celtic chieftains who lived near the Adriatic Sea. Fishing for flattery, the Macedonian king asked what they were most afraid of, expecting that they would answer 'You, my lord', or at least give some indication that his fame had spread to their country. 'We fear nothing but that they sky might fall on our heads,' they answered. Despite his disappointment ('They are vainglorious,' he dismissively complained later), Alexander struck a deal with them. The Celtic chiefs would side with Alexander – unless the sky fell on their heads. The oath was apparently a common Celtic vow; centuries later it was still being used in Christian Ireland.

> 'We have no word for the man who is excessively fearless; perhaps one may call such a man mad or bereft of feeling, who fears nothing, neither earthquakes nor waves, as they say of the Celts.'
>
> **Aristotle, *Nicomachean Ethics***

Other Celtic tribes were still on the offensive, sacking the Greek holy places of Delphi in 279 BC, but the tides quickly turned. Slavic tribes began driving Celts out of Eastern Europe, and the Roman military eventually grew far stronger than the frightened bumblers Brennus had met at Allia. The famous military consul Gaius Marius began conquering Celtic territories around 101 BC. His nephew, Julius Caesar, soon followed. The general was interested in more than just the Celts' land, however. Whether for his own legacy or out of a genuine interest in knowledge (likely more of the former than the latter), Caesar attempted to serve as anthropologist as well as conqueror. As he began to claim Gaul for himself, driving the Celts either into subjugation or retreat, he wrote of their lifestyle, their politics and their religion. But neither he nor the other classical writers gave much thought to where the Gauls and other Celts came from, besides the obvious answer 'over the Alps'. A Greek belief held that the Celts were descendants of Hercules. Celtus, the first of the *keltoi,* was the offspring of the strongman and Celtina, daughter of Britannus.

Genesis beyond the Alps

Today, historians and archaeologists are unsure about when and where the Celts emerged as a distinct culture. Many, in fact, argue that any thought of the Celts as a people group should be utterly rejected. Instead, they say, *Celtic* only applies to the family of languages various tribes spoke. Indeed, Celts were unified more by their language than by most cultural categories; they had no common king, no common country, no common creed. Furthermore, that they were unified by tongue is not insignificant or incidental.

> 'They lived in unwalled villages, without any superfluous furniture, for . . . they slept on beds of leaves and fed on meat and were excessively occupied with war and agriculture.'
>
> **Polybius, The Histories**

The Celts placed a high value on their language, so much so, in fact, that they feared the written word. It was not that they did not know their stories could be written down – enough contact with the classical world would have made clear at least some of the value of literacy – it was that they did not *want* them written down. (An illiterate culture was not totally uncommon at the time; historian Peter Ellis argues that Irish became only the third of Europe's written languages.) Much has been made of the history of Celtic languages and how they developed from their Indo-European parent, which also sired the Germanic, Romance, Slavonic and other language families. Linguists also enjoy pointing to how the Celtic tongue forked at some point, splitting the Brythonic (Welsh, Cornish), or P-Celtic, from the Goidelic (Irish, Scottish) Q-Celtic. The Welsh word for 'son', *mab*, is very similar to the Irish *mac*, for example, but 'children' (*plentyn* and *clann*, respectively) and other words are even more divergent.

The language-only historians and linguists have a point, which serves as a counterbalance to the non-scholarly Celtic enthusiasts who would like to believe in a single – and usually utopian – culture wiped out by inconsiderate oppressors. Most Celts, especially those on the continent, likely saw themselves as members of their particular tribal nation rather than as part of 'the Celts'. But they shared more than linguistic similarities, starting from their apparent birth in the Alpine urnfield. Some time after 1000 BC, the people of the Harz mountains in what is now Germany shared a similar culture – the most archaeologically significant aspect of which is their cremation of the dead (hence the urnfield). This culture, also given to much jewellery, bright costumes, partying and fighting, apparently gave birth to a Celtic culture. Within 300 years, the Iron Age had come to the Celts, and they took advantage of it with zeal. They were Europe's first smiths, inventing impressive agricultural tools and weapons – including the important iron-wheeled chariot. But the Celts were not satisfied simply with the *usefulness* of iron ploughshares, reapers, and spears. In 1857, a wealthy would-be archaeologist in La Tène, Switzerland, began unearthing hundreds of weapons, tools, and other objects from the mud beneath Lake Neuchâtel. What they revealed gave evidence to Strabo's remark on the Celts' 'love of decoration' (and evidence against Polybius's comment that 'they had no knowledge whatsoever of any art or science'). From horse harnesses to sword hilts, nearly everything was lavishly decorated with swirls, flowers, and abstract designs. Soon the discovery of several other archaeological sites would demonstrate that such ornamentation was common, but historians still refer to this period of Celtic (if not completely pan-Celtic) culture, which lasted from about 450 BC to 15 BC, as La Tène.

> 'The Gauls, imprisoned as they were by the Alps . . . first found a motive for overflowing into Italy from the circumstance of a Gallic citizen [who] brought with him when he came back some dried figs and grapes and some samples of oil and wine: consequently we may excuse them for having sought to obtain these things even by means of war.'
>
> **Pliny, Natural History**

During this time, the Celts spread throughout Europe and their influence spread even further. Modern maps attempting to illustrate the expansive Celtic areas give the impression of a massive hegemony – an apparent Celtic empire reaching from southern Spain to Turkey, from the Atlantic Ocean to the Black Sea. Add in archaeological digs where Celtic artefacts have been found – an area stretching from Denmark to India – and they seem like some of the most successful conquerors the world has ever seen. But Celtic expansion cannot be seen through the same prism as organized military conquests such as Attila the Hun or Julius Caesar. It was gradual, the result of immigration at least as much as invasion, and most importantly, it was unorganized. As Caesar himself noted, the Celts were 'too much given to faction' to have organized a world conquest. Caesar and other expansionists exploited this propensity for dissension, first using tribal warfare to their advantage, then simply

The Hallstatt graves

Only 11 years before the discovery at La Tène, archaeologists began uncovering an even earlier trove of early Celtic artefacts by Austria's Lake Hallstatt. Over the next 16 years, 980 bodies were discovered, several in elaborate and well-stocked graves. The earliest of these remains dated from around 1200 BC, when the local economy was based on mining rock-salt. But the salt proved even more valuable to the modern archaeologists than it did these prehistoric residents: it preserved clothing, equipment, and even a miner or two. Not all the discoveries at Hallstatt were Celtic, however, especially the earliest ones. But it is likely that most of the Iron Age remains from about 700 BC – including pottery, jewellery, wagons and massive, two-handed, double-edged swords with decorated hilts – were from dominantly Celtic tribes.

paying tribes to assist in battle against their fellow Celtic neighbours. Before they knew it, Europe belonged to the Romans they had once nearly vanquished.

The fall of Celtic Europe

Caesar was by no means the only (or even the greatest) reason the Celts lost dominance in their lands. Fate had turned against them centuries before. But he was certainly responsible for the conquest of Gaul, the land most associated with the continental Celts. Ironically, it began almost by chance: the senatorial nobleman was assigned governorship over Gallia Transalpina (the Celtic area between Roman Italy and the Alps) after the sudden death of another. But Caesar was nothing if not opportunistic. He seized upon a request to drive back the Celtic Helvetti tribe – whose westward migration would potentially destabilize the region – and never looked back. By his own accounts, his conquering of the Helvetti cost more than 250,000 lives. But he was not done yet. Illegally, he continued through Gaul, slaughtering and displacing Celtic tribes that would not subjugate themselves to the man who would become *pontifex maximus*. Gaul was not enough; in 55 BC Caesar led his soldiers across the Channel into Britain. Ostensibly, Caesar was attempting to mete punishment for aid to the Gauls, but he likely had

Vercingetorix's revolt

After Caesar's unsuccessful invasion of Britain, Celts throughout Gaul rose against him in 52 BC. Their leader was Vercingetorix, a young and headstrong nobleman of Arvernia (now central France). 'A man of boundless energy, he terrorized waverers with the rigours of an iron discipline,' Caesar wrote of him. Indeed, even after the Celtic warlord lost his first few battles, the tribal armies did not falter. When Caesar unsuccessfully attacked the Arvernian stronghold of Gergovia, however, it looked like the tide had turned. The Gauls had real hope of defeating the Romans. Even the neighbouring Aedui tribe, long-time Roman

> 'They are wont to change their abode on slight provocation, migrating in bands with all their battle-array, or rather setting out with their households when displaced by a stronger enemy.'
>
> **Strabo, Geography**

allies, defected and cut Caesar off from his supplies. But the Romans quickly rebounded, and Vercingetorix retreated to the hilltop defences at Alesia. It was the wrong move. Caesar surrounded the hill with elaborate siege works, with an inner set trapping Vercingetorix's forces and an outer set defending the Roman army against reinforcements (which came nearly a quarter of a million soldiers strong, but could not budge Caesar's 50,000 men). Caesar records that Vercingetorix summoned a council and told his fellows, 'I did not undertake the war for private ends, but in the cause of national liberty. And since I must now accept my fate, I place myself at your disposal. Make amends to the Romans by killing me or surrender me alive as you think best.' They chose surrender. The Romans imprisoned Vercingetorix for six years, then marched him through the capital to his ritual execution. Vercingetorix's rebellion was not the last revolt the Gauls would make against Caesar, but it was their last real challenge of him.

more conquest in mind. In any case, control of Gaul would be easier to maintain if he did not have to worry about British Celts. But, as historian Norman Davies summarizes, 'He came; he saw; he did not conquer: but he took hostages, withdrew, and claimed a triumph. He headed south for the Alps, and fatefully recrossed the frontier of the Roman Republic on the Rubicon – his point of no return.' The historian Plutarch wrote that 1 million men died during Caesar's conquest of Gaul. A million more had been enslaved.

Early Celtic religion

All this time, Caesar continued to write his *Gallic War,* a propaganda piece intended to justify his conquests of Gaul despite his lack of orders to do so. But advertisement as it was, the work (also known as *Commentaries*) contains fascinating detail about Gallic life, especially Celtic religion. He wrote:

The whole nation of the Gauls is greatly devoted to ritual observances, and for that reason those who are smitten with the more grievous maladies and who are engaged in the perils of battle either sacrifice human victims or vow to do so, employing the druids as ministers for such sacrifices. They believe, in effect, that unless a man's life be paid, the majesty of the immortal gods may not be appeased.

The conqueror detailed such sacrifices in gory detail. One description, which later gained even wider circulation when Victorian-era artists began representing it graphically, explained how dozens of people would be locked into a giant wooden effigy, then burned alive. But this was likely imaginative or speculative. What is more certain – though there are still many historians who contest it – is that some kinds of human sacrifice took place among the Celts. And clearer still is the strong death motif in Celtic religious life. Roman proto-anthropologists and historians may have cribbed each other's notes on such matters, but almost all who wrote about the Celts were fascinated by the stories of human sacrifice. As Strabo wrote:

They used to strike a human being, whom they had devoted to death, in the back with a sword, and then divine from his death-struggle. We are told of still other kinds of human sacrifices; for example, they would shoot victims to death with arrows, or impale them in the temples . . .

Of course, the classical world had its own gruesome traditions, and it may be that what was perceived as religious sacrifice may have been nothing more than ritualized capital punishment. The famous Lindow Man, pulled from the peat of Lindow Moss, 10 miles from Manchester, England, has been cited as proof of sacrifice since his discovery in 1984. When he died, about 2,000 years ago, his killers were eager to make sure he was dead. They hit him on the head three times with an axe, tied a cord around his neck (twisting it with a stick until it acted as a garrotte), broke his neck, then slit his throat and tossed him into a bog. That Lindow Man apparently subjected himself to such treatment without a struggle and ate mistletoe (associated with the druids) before the killing does suggest that he was a kind of willing participant. But historians and archaeologists still disagree about whether he was a religious sacrifice.

Classical writers also confused the basics of pagan Celtic religion. Caesar wrote that their beliefs were 'much like those of other nations', and even assumed that the effigies he saw represented Mercury and other Roman gods. Other early historians assumed that the 'pantheon' of Celtic gods was organized like their own system. But the Celtic religious beliefs were hardly organized at all. A god regarded as extremely important to one Celtic tribe may not have been recognized at all by another, or may have been worshipped under a different name. History has left us with the names of 375 Celtic gods; all but 70 only appear once in extant writings. And even of these little is known. Dagda, the Irish 'Good God' ('good' meaning 'powerful' rather than 'beneficent') carries a club and cauldron, and was apparently venerated – at least in some parts – as the giant father or ruler of the other gods. Cernunnos, 'the horned one', was a Gaulish god of animals. Lugh 'of the long arm', whose importance is reflected in town names such as Lyons, Leiden, and Léon, ruled over arts and skills. The horse goddess Epona, who even became popular in the Roman cavalry in Gaul, may have been associated with fertility, but that seems to be said of almost every female deity.

> 'The Gauls likewise make use of diviners, accounting them worthy of high approbation, and these men foretell the future by means of the flight or cries of birds and of the slaughter of sacred animals, and they have all the multitude subservient to them.'
>
> **Diodorus Siculus, *Historical Library***

These gods had the ability to change shape at will, usually adopting the shape of animals. When appearing in more human form, they often appeared in male and female pairs, but more importantly presented themselves in triples. One god often had two counterparts, might have three names, or might even be depicted with three heads.

But the gods were only one part of Celtic supernatural beliefs. They also venerated sacred animals (especially boars, dogs and birds), sacred places (springs, oddly shaped rocks, old trees), and sacred dates (one of which, the festival of Samhain, still appears on modern calendars as Halloween).

The Celts also found supernatural significance in the human head, which classical writers found abhorrent. 'They cut off the heads of enemies slain in battle and attach them to the necks of their horses,' wrote Diodorus:

The blood-stained spoils they hand over to their attendants and carry off as booty, while striking up a paean and singing a song of victory; and they nail up these first fruits upon their houses just as do those who lay low wild animals in certain kinds of hunting. They embalm in cedar-oil the heads of their most distinguished enemies and preserve them carefully in a chest, and display them with pride to strangers, saying that for this head one of their ancestors, or his father, or the man himself, refused the offer of a large sum of money. They say that some of them boast that they refused the weight of the head in gold.

But these were not headhunters merely seeking trophies. The Celts believed that the essence of a person was in their head – even after death. Thus skulls were even used to adorn temples.

Propagating and unifying all these beliefs were the most famous of the pre-Christian Celts, the druids. Caesar was particularly interested in this brotherhood, noting that its members

. . . are concerned with divine worship, the due performance of sacrifices, public and private, and the interpretation of ritual questions: a great number of young men gather about them for the sake of instruction and hold them in great honour. In fact, it is they who decide in almost all disputes, public and private; and if any crime has been committed, or murder done, or there is any dispute about succession or boundaries, they also decide it, determining awards and penalties.

The druids, then, were not the mere priests so often portrayed in white hooded robes. They were also judges, teachers, healers, politicians and astronomers. Strabo called them 'the most just of men', noting that they were often the ones to broker peace between warring parties. But these men, exempt from military service as well as taxation, could also be responsible for starting battles – elections for chief druid sometimes ended in bloodshed.

'They profess to know the size and shape of the world, the movements of the heavens and the stars, and the will of the gods,' wrote Pomponius Mela, a Spaniard of the 1st century AD. But we will not know the details of these beliefs, because, as Caesar noted, 'The druids think it unlawful to commit this knowledge of theirs to writing.' They certainly knew how to write – Caesar notes their ability to write in Greek – but he attributes their prohibition to a desire for secrecy and a belief that writing weakens the memory.

On this point, Caesar conceded. 'Indeed it does generally happen that those who rely on written documents are less industrious in learning by heart and have a weaker memory,' he wrote. But he could afford to be so generous: he was, after all, driving their society from the continent.

Of course, Celts were not entirely wiped off the face of continental Europe by Caesar and his armies. Although many of the Celts simply chose to become Romanized, pockets of Celtic society still existed, such as Galatia. Rome had long approved of Celtic control in this area (now Turkey) – it helped to destabilize the region, keeping Eastern threats from encroaching on Roman territory. In the early 1st century BC, Rome and Galatia were even allies against Mithridates VI of Pontus. By 25 BC, Galatia was a Roman province, but it maintained much of its Celtic character. Four centuries later, Jerome (considered the most learned of the Latin church fathers) noted in his commentary on Paul's epistle to the Galatians that the area was still very Celtic. 'While the Galatians, in common with the whole East, speak Greek, their own language is almost identical with that of the Treviri [a Celtic tribe of eastern Gaul],' he wrote. And Caesar's observation that the Celts were 'too much given to faction' was still true in Jerome's day: 'Any one who has seen by how many schisms Ancyra [Ankara], the metropolis of Galatia, is rent and torn, and by how many differences and false doctrines the place is debauched, knows this as well as I do . . . The traces of the ancient foolishness remain to this day.'

> 'Not only the Druids, but others as well, say that men's souls, and also the universe, are indestructible, although both fire and water will at some time or other prevail over them.'
>
> **Strabo, Geography**

The first Celtic Christians

Was Paul's letter to the Galatians directed at one of the first Celtic churches? There is some disagreement among New Testament and Celtic scholars, but most believe that Paul's epistle was written to the

Romanized churches in the south (where Paul visited), not the Celtic north. Others, however, note that the apostle addresses his readers as 'Galatians', 'suggesting that they were a people, not just inhabitants of a province'. This was certainly the view of early commentators, including Jerome. Furthermore, the province was under Roman rule but the capital, which Paul may have been addressing, was still a Celtic stronghold.

Perhaps it is best for the legacy of Celtic Christianity that its entry into recorded history does not begin with Paul's chastising, 'You foolish Galatians! Who has bewitched you?' If the epistle was not addressed to a Celtic church, it is of little matter. Celtic Christians appear in reliable records within a century of the apostle's death.

Medieval Christians believed that converting the Celts had been a high priority for the early church: so much so that the major figures of the Gospels had personally taken Christianity into Gaul and beyond. According to legends, no less than Mary, Lazarus, and Mary Magdalene were the first missionaries to Gaul, founding the church in Provence, by the Mediterranean Sea. *The Life of St Martial* tells the story of one of Jesus' original 72 disciples who was present at the resurrection of Lazarus and served the food at the last supper. After baptizing this Martial, Peter reportedly sent him to convert the Gauls. It is nonsense, of course: this account was written in the 11th century to make the 3rd-century – not 1st-century – Martial more popular. (And it worked: Martial's relics in Limoges, France, became among the most venerated in Europe.)

Christianity probably first came to Celts the way it first came to most of the rest of the world: through informal contacts by 'everyday' Christians, most likely traders, whose names are lost. A few names of early Christian Celts, however, do survive.

The first of these comes from the church in Lyons, which enters reliable history in martyrdom. As we have already seen, the city had been founded in honour of the Celtic god Lugh (the original name of the city was Lugdunum, 'Lugh's fort'), but Romans had long since captured the city and made it the capital of Gaul. In AD 12, Lyons became the centre for the worship of Emperor Augustus. As the Christians would later supplant pagan holidays such as Samhain and Saturnalia with observances of All Saints Day and Christmas, so the Romans replaced the

1 August Celtic celebrations of Lugnasadh with the Roman feast of the divine emperor.

How the church in Lyons was founded remains unknown, but when persecution began under Marcus Aurelius in AD 177, it was apparently the only organized church in Gaul (though it had already planted a second congregation in Vienne). Its ethnic make-up is also unclear, but at least one young member was a Celtic Gaul – Vettius Epagathus. According to a letter from the survivors of the pogrom that left 48 Christians dead, Vettius was 'a man filled with love for God and his neighbour . . . zealous for God and fervent in spirit'. He also, despite his youth, had some clout in the community and attempted to defend his fellow Christians when they came under attack. At first, Christians were excluded from the baths, markets and other public places. But mobs soon began pursuing the believers even in their homes. Soon Christians were rounded up, arrested and brought before the governor. It was here that Vettius attempted to come to their defence – but he ended up imprisoned with them. The aged bishop, Pothinus (thought to be originally from Asia Minor), was beaten and died of his wounds two days later. Blandina, the young servant of another martyr, is also considered by reputable historians to have been Celtic. She was, according to the letter, 'filled with such power, that those who tortured her one after the other in every way from morning till evening were wearied and tired . . . Her declaration, "I am a Christian, and there is no evil done amongst us," brought her refreshment, rest, and insensibility to all the sufferings inflicted on her.' Others were tortured to death, roasted in an iron seat, or (like Blandina) fed to wild beasts in the amphitheatre. The bodies of the 48 martyrs were exposed for six days, then burned, and the ashes thrown into the Rhône.

The tragic persecution of the Christians and the death of the 92-year-old Pothinus led to the elevation of Irenaeus, one of the most important Christian writers of the 2nd century and the earliest recorded missionary to the Celts. Having escaped the massacre due to an errand to Rome, Irenaeus (from Asia Minor, like his predecessor) returned to Lyons to write one of the most influential apologetic works of the early church: *Against Heresies*. His five-volume treatise not only refuted such teachings as Gnosticism (the belief that the body and the whole physical world are evil), but also set forth much of the basis of Christian theology. While the Gnostics argued that they had a 'secret knowledge', Irenaeus argued that true belief was found in the teaching of the apostles, continued and guarded by elders and bishops. This argument, in which he listed the succession of Roman bishops as an example, would eventually set the basis for the hierarchy of the church. Irenaeus was also influential in determining the biblical canon, and was first to promote the four Gospels.

But Irenaeus was more than just a theologian – he was also a missionary. Though the bulk of his flock spoke Latin and Greek, the bishop made regular treks into the countryside to preach among the still-Celtic tribes. Indeed, he uses this as an excuse to the readers of *Against Heresies*:

You will not expect from me, a resident among the Celts, and mostly accustomed to a barbarous language, rhetorical skill, which I have never learned, nor power in writing, which I have not acquired, nor beauties of language and style, which I am not acquainted with.

A year or so after the martyrdoms at Lyons, Marcus Aurelius's persecution of Christians was felt by another Celt, Symphorian of Autun. A 5th-century account of his beheading tells how he was encouraged by his Christian mother in her native Gaulish language.

As Christianity continued to spread throughout the Roman world, it also continued to spread through Gaul. Frankish bishop and historian Gregory of Tours (539–94) says that Rome in AD 250 sent seven bishops to establish churches in Gaul. These were likely important additions to an already expanding church. Around this time, Cyprian of Carthage had already been drawn into controversy in the area over whether lapsed Christians could be readmitted to the church, and was pushing for the excommunication of the bishop of Arles.

But with each passing day, the churches in Gaul were less Celtic. Members of the churches may have had tribal blood, and some use of the Celtic languages continued until about AD 500. But it was clear that in almost all areas of culture, Rome had conquered the 'barbarians'. This was especially true in the cities, where Christianity first took root: though far less so in the countryside, where vestiges of Celtic and Greco-Roman paganism continued. Illustrating this difference, a local rhetorician in 395 told a story about a pagan peasant surprised at the power of the cross, 'the sign of that God who alone is worshiped in the large cities'.

In time, however, Rome would also lose control of Gaul, and even the name would disappear, taking instead the name of the Frankish foreigners from the other side of the Rhine. Roman Christianity would continue in the cities, but converting the countryside was a job that went largely unfulfilled. That is, until the Celts returned as Christian missionaries like Columbanus.

CHAPTER 11

CHRISTIANITY IN EARLY BRITAIN

It may seem unbelievable that Mary, Lazarus, and Mary Magdalene personally took the gospel of the resurrected Christ to the Celts of Gaul. Or that a mysterious disciple seemed to appear at every key recorded moment in the Gospels and then set about founding churches through what is now France. But consider the legend England prided itself on for centuries – that the church there was founded by Jesus himself. As ridiculous as it sounds, such a tale was invoked in British disputes with French churches over ascendancy and in Protestant arguments that Rome had

> 'The churches of France and Spain must yield in points of antiquity and precedence to that of Britain, as the latter church was founded by Joseph of Arimathea immediately after the passion of Christ.'
> **Council of Basle, 1434**

nothing to do with the English church. It is unclear how much Christian mystic, artist, and poet William Blake (1757–1827) believed the tale, but his question remains famous (and later became that popular nationalistic hymn, 'Jerusalem'):

And did those feet in ancient time
  walk upon England's mountains green?
And was the holy Lamb of God
  on England's pleasant pastures seen?

According to widespread legends, Joseph of Arimathea, the 'good and just' Jewish leader who petitioned Pilate for Jesus' crucified body, was also Jesus' great-uncle (Mary's uncle). When Mary, Joseph and 12-year-old Jesus went to Jerusalem for Passover, Joseph supposedly housed them – and afterwards took the boy on a tin-trading trip to Glastonbury. Other legends say Jesus returned to the town as an adult to build a home and worked as a ship's carpenter. Older legends – though still unreliable – leave Jesus near the Mediterranean and send Joseph to Britain alone three decades after Jesus' ascension to heaven. Around the year 1240, someone added an introduction to *The Antiquity of the Church of Glastonbury,* written by English historian and monk William of Malmesbury a century before. It tells of how the apostle Philip sent Joseph and 11 others to Britain, where they encountered resistance from 'the barbaric king and his people', but were allowed to establish a church at Glastonbury 'because they came from afar'.

A century after the addition to William's history, John of Glastonbury expanded the Joseph legends, making him into an ancestor of King Arthur and the bearer of 'two cruets, white and silver, filled with the blood and sweat of the prophet Jesus'. This last detail was expanded even further by later legend-makers to make Joseph's prized cargo the Holy Grail itself.

Reliable early historians do not credit Joseph – or anyone else in particular – for bringing Christianity to Britain. They knew only that Christianity somehow made it there. 'In all parts of Spain, among the diverse nations of the Gauls, in regions of the Britons beyond Roman sway but subjected to Christ . . . the name of Christ now reigns,' North African apologist Tertullian wrote in *An Answer to the Jews* some time around AD 200. His contemporary Origen wrote that Christianity had not just come to the northern lands, it had become entirely accepted there. 'When before the coming of Christ,' he asked rhetorically, 'did the land of Britain agree on the worship of one God?' Renowned church historian Eusebius takes note of 'some apostles' who 'passed over the ocean to what are called the British Isles.' Most surprising is a remark by the 6th-century British monk Gildas (whom we shall meet shortly). 'These islands received their beams of light – that is, the holy precepts of Christ – the true Sun, as we know, at the latter part of the reign of Tiberius Caesar,' he claims in *The Ruin and Conquest of Britain* (*De Excidio Britanniae*). Modern scholars dismiss the comment – Tiberius was smothered to death in his bed in AD 37.

> 'The divine goodness of our Lord and Saviour is equally diffused among the Britons, the Africans, and other nations of the world.'
>
> **Origen of Alexandria**

Tiberius was followed by Caligula, then Claudius. In AD 43, two years after Claudius was hailed as emperor of Rome, about 40,000 Roman soldiers finally achieved Julius Caesar's once-thwarted plan to invade Britain. Times had changed; Claudius invaded the island mainly because he could, and he needed the prestige of military victory. Having landed on the coast of Kent, the armies gradually subdued Wales and England, but found themselves overextended after a few victories against the Picts of Scotland.

Hadrian's Wall

By the middle of the 2nd century AD, about one of every eight Roman soldiers was stationed in Britain. But with even 50,000 troops on the island, the Romans could not conquer it all. In the 120s, Emperor Hadrian ordered the building of his great wall, stretching 76 miles down the valleys of the Tyne and Solway rivers. It was more symbolic than defensive, however; any serious attack by the Picts would have found it only a nuisance. Nor was the wall the northernmost extent of the Roman empire: other outposts lay beyond, and a generation later Antoninus Pius built a wall even further north. Hadrian's wall did, however, control the flow of movement and information between cultures, much like the Berlin Wall did in the 20th century.

The British Celts adapted quickly to the lifestyle of their Roman conquerors. Celtic languages were abandoned in favour of Latin, and Celts began bowing to the gods of the Roman pantheon. The antlered Cernunnos still had his devotees, and other Celtic gods were simply Romanized (Apollo Belenos, for example), but the emperor cult became a new addition to Celtic worship.

Britain's first martyr

It was because of this new Romanized British religion that we first learn the name of a British Christian: Alban. It is even impossible to know exactly when he lived – perhaps centuries after Christianity first came to the island. We do know that he was not the first Christian in Britain – his own story precludes it.

Alban enters history a pagan, but a hospitable one. He welcomed into his home a Christian priest who was fleeing persecution. Exactly which persecution is a matter of debate. Anglo-Saxon church historian Bede says it was that of Diocletian (284–305), but the Caesar of Gaul and Britain at that time, Constantius Chlorus, is famous for his toleration of Christians. More likely, the story occurred during the reign of Decius (c. 249–51) or even Septimus Severus (c. 193–211). It would have mattered little to the priest which emperor was responsible for his death warrant. He simply knew that he needed a hiding place.

It did not take long for the priest's religious devotion to influence Alban. Soon, writes Bede, 'Alban renounced the darkness of idolatry and sincerely accepted Christ.' According to another legend, no sooner had Alban knelt in prayer than soldiers appeared at the door, having been informed of the priest's location. Though the legends differ on timing, all agree that the new convert swapped clothes with his spiritual father, donning the priest's hooded cloak. It was not until Alban was brought before the judge (who was then reportedly attending a pagan sacrifice) that his identity was revealed. 'Since you have chosen to conceal a sacrilegious rebel rather than deliver him to the soldiers for his well-deserved punishment for blasphemy,' the judge said angrily, 'you shall undergo all the punishment due to him.' The judge gave one way out – make a sacrifice to the idols. Alban refused. 'What is your family and race?' asked the judge. 'What does that concern you?' Alban responded. 'If you want to know the truth about my religion, know that I am a Christian, and practise Christian rites.' 'I demand to know your name!' 'My parents named me Alban. And I worship and adore the living and true God, who created all things.'

Again the judge ordered Alban to sacrifice to the pagan gods, but again Alban refused, saying whoever did so is 'doomed to the pains of hell'. When beatings and whippings could not change his mind, he was sentenced to death by decapitation.

The tales of the journey to the execution hill and the beheading itself are far more incredible. When Alban and his captors are unable to cross a bridge because of crowds, the saint parted the river like Moses. This miracle led to the conversion of his executioner, who joined Alban in martyrdom. But the substitute executioner, Bede says, was not allowed to rejoice in his duty: 'As the martyr's head fell, [the executioner's] eyes dropped out onto the ground.'

> 'For Christ's sake, [Alban] bore the most horrible torments patiently and gladly, and . . . the judge saw that no torture could break him or make him renounce the worship of Christ . . .'
>
> **Bede, A History of the English Church and People**

Alban became Britain's first recorded martyr, but by no means the only one. Even Bede reports that two Christians from Caerleon-upon-Usk, Aaron and Julius, were martyred during the same persecution.

From division, unity

Not all Christians went so willingly to their deaths. In North Africa, reluctance towards martyrdom led to a permanent split in the church. In 311, 80 North African bishops opposed the ordination of Caecilian as bishop of Carthage. It was not that Caecilian had done anything wrong – but the bishop who ordained him had, in their minds. During Diocletian's Great Persecution, this bishop had handed over sacred Christian works to his oppressors to avoid death. The embittered North African bishops (led by Donatus, and thus called Donatists) appointed someone else for the position. Who, then, was the real bishop of Carthage? And could those who had lapsed under persecution ever again be considered real Christians? 'The servants of God are those who are hated by the world,' claimed the Donatists. Augustine of Hippo spoke for the moderates among the North African church leadership: 'The clouds roll with thunder that the House of the Lord shall be built throughout the earth; and these frogs sit in the marshes and croak, "We are the only Christians!"'

Both sides appealed to Emperor Constantine, credited with establishing religious freedom and promoting Christianity. Under his auspices, in AD 314 bishops came to the southern Gaul city of Arles from around the Christian world to discuss the Carthage controversy. Not only did they declare Caecilian the true bishop of the city, but they pronounced the Donatists heretics. ('What has the emperor to do with the church?' the Donatists huffed, and continued a schism that lasted

The half-converts

Although syncretistic beliefs have been overemphasized by recent writers wanting to show Celtic Christianity as practically pagan, there are several surviving artefacts demonstrating that early conversion could be slow. Pagans and Christians apparently both worshipped in the same building at Lullingstone, Kent. Other early Christian churches in Britain seem to have been built in deliberate imitation of pagan Roman temples and shrines. Meanwhile, a mosaic discovered in Hinton Mary, Dorset, incorporates several pagan and Christian themes. Such is also the case in Ireland, where pagan and Christian statues were found side by side.

until the Muslims invaded North Africa in the 8th century.) Meanwhile, the bishops decided that as long as they were in Arles, they might as well take care of other matters. Gladiators, circus charioteers and theatre workers were excommunicated. Ministers were ordered to stay in the place where they were ordained. Furthermore, in a move that would later become important for the Celtic churches, Pope Sylvester was asked to decide how to determine Easter, 'so that it may be celebrated by us on the same day and at the same time throughout the whole church'.

Among the signatories of these 22 canons were three bishops from Britain: Eborius of York, Restitutus of London and Adelphius of Lincoln. Two others, a presbyter named Sacerdus and a deacon named Arminius, were also from Britain. The numbers may seem small, considering that only five signatories came from the island, but they do not necessarily mean that the British church was tiny. We know that Gaul had 36 bishops at the time, but only 16 attended the Council of Arles. It would have been even more difficult for British bishops to make their way to the city. Nevertheless, British bishops made it not only to Arles in 314, but to the councils of Sardica (Sophia) in 343 and Armininum (Rimini) in 359. At the latter of these, the emperor offered to pay the expenses of all the bishops from Gaul and Britain. Only three British bishops accepted, noting that they were short of cash and did not want to impose on church friends.

That the British church was able to join in so many church councils not only suggests that they were organized relatively early – certainly before Constantine's Edict of Milan granted religious freedom – but also demonstrates that they had extensive contact with the church in North Africa, continental Europe and elsewhere. It was from North Africa that an idea sprang that would resonate through the entire Celtic world – monasticism.

Green deserts

Isolation in the sandy wastelands of the Middle East had always held a special kind of spiritual importance. God spoke to Moses alone on Mount Sinai; Jesus spent 40 days in the Judean wilderness before beginning his public ministry; John the Baptist lived off locusts and honey while residing in the desert. But Antony (251–356), an Egyptian who began a radical existence of poverty and isolation, set the monastic example for centuries. Many disciples sought him out in the Egyptian desert, but thousands more would follow his lead when Athanasius, one of the greatest theologians of the early church, wrote his biography.

The tales of Antony and the other Desert Fathers were promoted heavily by Martin of Tours, a pagan-born ex-soldier from what is now Hungary. Like many other well-known Christian heroes, Martin regularly vacillated between monasticism and church administration, but he was also heavily involved in evangelism. He helped to establish the first monastery in Gaul (at Ligugé), but also made many missionary trips through the countryside, promoting Christianity to the heathen and monasticism to the already converted. One of these Christians who reportedly accepted Martin's call was Ninian, a Briton.

The tale of Ninian, like many characters from church history, is shadowy and unclear. We cannot even be sure of his name: Thomas Clancy of Glasgow University's Celtic department recently made headlines claiming that Bede misspelled Ninian's real name, Uinniau. 'There are quite a lot of stories from the Middle Ages about St Ninia, as he was then called,' Clancy told *The Times* of London. 'But before that time there is nothing written in history to suggest that he existed. There is no mention about cults or churches, which you would expect if he had been so prominent. We do, however, have evidence of St Uinniau, who was in the same area as the so-called St Ninian at the same time. So it appears there has been a mix-up.'

In any case, Ninian (or Uinniau) is credited with being a missionary to Scotland's Picts. He was not necessarily the first to take the gospel north of Hadrian's wall, but he is the first to get credit for it. Martin of Tours reportedly encouraged a few masons to accompany Ninian, and they built a stone church in what is now Whithorn. Bede says it was named Candida Casa, the white house, because the locals had never seen such a structure before.

According to Ninian's unreliable biographer, Aelred (who wrote more to promote Whithorn's authority over other monasteries than to accurately tell the saint's story), the evangelist was so blessed by God in his Christian studies that he did not even need the Candida Casa for shelter. 'When everything around him was soaked, he sat alone with his little book in the downpour, as if protected by the roof of a house,' Aelred wrote. Only once did God's unseen umbrella fail – when 'an unlawful thought stirred in him and desire [was] prompted by the devil'. Drenched and discovered, Ninian 'blushed that he had been overtaken by a vain thought, and in the same moment of time drove away the thought and stayed the shower'.

Ninian's Candida Casa became a monastic centre, eventually drawing students from Ireland and Wales. Ninian, too, made sure to find solitude apart from his administrative tasks and evangelistic work. The cave in which he reportedly took frequent refuge can still be seen today. Its walls have been worn smooth by centuries of waves, but a cross, carved by later disciples, is said to remain.

But as the Picts put pressure on the Roman armies from the north, the heart of the empire itself was facing attack from Germanic tribes. Needing military strength to defend the empire rather than to extend it, Emperor Honorius in 407 recalled the soldiers in Britain to Italy. Within a few years, Roman rule of the island had been obliterated, and within a generation almost all traces of Roman culture – from religion to aqueducts – had vanished. But the withdrawal of Roman troops left the Britons open to invasions from elsewhere. The Picts descended and Scots invaded from Ireland. The real societal change, however, came when Saxons invaded from Germany, followed by Angles, and Jutes from Denmark. The foreign cultures overtook Britain, extinguishing the vestiges of Roman culture; in the eastern parts of the island, Celtic culture disappeared too.

Swords alone did not 'Anglicize' (and Saxonize) the Britons. The British aristocrats who had Romanized themselves probably 'Germanized' themselves to maintain their high social status. Immigration, not just battle deaths, changed the country's demographics. But plenty of Britons still inhabited 5th-century Britain. Without Roman infrastructure, however, life had changed. Communication with the continent contracted. With less contact from Rome, British churches became more insular. Past historians have overemphasized the isolation of the British church, suggesting that it developed in a complete

'Resolute, sometimes impetuous, and often driven to extremes of devotion and self-sacrifice, [early British saints] were great lovers of God and neighbour, at least those who left them in peace.'

Richard J. Woods, The Spirituality of the Celtic Saints

vacuum. This is not true – communication between Britain and the rest of the Western church continued throughout its development. But some modern historians take this too far, denying any detachment. The British church did face isolation; and for the monks following in the steps of St Antony and the Desert Fathers of North Africa, isolation was just fine. Monasticism boomed after the withdrawal of Roman armies. Ironically, these monasteries quickly became the centres of ecclesiastic energy. From the end of the 5th century, nearly every British saint remembered today had been a monk at some point during his life.

Saints of the Round Table

While eastern Britain became strongly Anglo-Saxon, western Britain's character was still dominantly Celtic. Most of the lands now known as Wales had been less Romanized than the east, and many managed to hold the Anglo-Saxons at bay for centuries. The most famous name associated with these battles, of course, is Arthur. 'Arthur fought against them in those days with the kings of the Britons but he himself was leader of battles,' says Nennius's 9th-century *Historia Brittonum* (*History of the Britons*), 'And in all the battles he stood forth as victor.' The most famous king of all legends probably really existed as a Celtic chief, and his fame had spread early. *The Gododin*, written about AD 600, trumpets a military leader who 'gorged black ravens' on the corpses of his fallen adversaries, but cedes 'he was no Arthur'. Likely the real Arthur was no Arthur of legend, either. Nevertheless, he is central to many medieval Celtic tales – and makes appearances in the biographies of many Celtic saints.

One of these Arthurian saints is Dubricus, also known as Dyfrig, who is said to have crowned Arthur and is called by Tennyson's *Idylls of the King* 'chief of the church in Britain'. His colleague, Illtud, supposedly served as a knight in Arthur's army. According to one account, Illtud (450–535) may have even been the famed Galahad. Another says Illtud was Arthur's cousin. But Arthurian legends aside, Dubricus and Illtud were well-known in their own rights. The *Life of Samson*, written in about AD 600, calls Illtud 'the most learned of the Britons in both Testaments and in all kinds of knowledge', from geometry to rhetoric. 'And by birth he was a wise magician, having knowledge of the future,' the biographer adds. Originally from Letavi (which is either in Brittany or central Brednock, England), Illtud is said to have spent his military days a married man – until an angel appeared and urged him to forsake wife and weapons to become a monk. He did so, and around the year 500 founded a church, monastery and school by the Bristol Channel at what is now Llantwit Major in Glamorgan. Its original name came from its founder – Llanilltud Fawr (a *llan* is an enclosure). There he led many disciples in such spiritual devotions as *laus perennis* – unceasing praise. The community's 24 groups were each responsible for an hour of prayer each day. Illtud also kept his mind focused on earth – quite literally. He created new methods of irrigation and cultivation, and even provided other monasteries with his excess seeds. His ex-wife, meanwhile, apparently took the rejection in her stride – who can argue with an angel? – and reportedly founded her own oratory nearby for nuns and widows.

One of Illtud's most famous students was Samson (c. 485–565), a Welshman who had a penchant for wandering – and for succeeding unlucky abbots. After his tutelage under Illtud, Samson went to Ynys Byr (Caldey Island). Not long after his arrival, the *Life of Samson* recounts, tragedy struck:

One dark night, [the abbot] took a solitary stroll into the grounds of the monastery, and what is more serious, so it is said, owing to stupid intoxication, fell headlong into a deep pit. Uttering one piercing cry for help, he was dragged out of the hole by the brothers in a dying condition, and died in the night from his adventure.

Samson was made abbot, and, notes his biographer, 'nobody ever saw him drunk . . . not even in the least degree did any kind of drink injure him in any way'.

Before long, Samson left Ynys Byr to accept an invitation by Irish monks to visit their abbey. Attempting to return to Britain, Samson was stopped by another monk. 'The devil has possessed our abbot,' he explained. Could Samson help? He could, and did. 'While St Samson prayed, the possessed one, in his bed, by God's help, recovered his reason . . . gave his monastery with all its substance to Samson and . . . followed St Samson to this side of the sea and was always his companion,' says the *Life of Samson* (which may be the earliest biography of a British saint). 'Of his good deeds and good conversation after his fall I know full well, but his name I do not know.'

The monk's long résumé continues. Returning to Britain, he set up an oratory, but a synod commanded him to become abbot of Llantwit Major. Not long afterward, an angel told him, 'Thou oughtest to tarry no longer in this country, for thou art ordained to be a pilgrim, and beyond the sea thou wilt be very great in the Church and worthy of the highest priestly dignity.' So off he went to Cornwall, founding four monasteries (installing his father as abbot of one of them). Cornwall could not hold him, either – from there he crossed to Brittany, founding more monasteries. With such an itinerant life, it is hard to place Samson in any 'hometown', but one of these Brittany monasteries managed to make it stick: he is now known as Samson of Dol.

David of Wales

No saint is now more associated with Wales than David (Dewi in his native language). Another reputed student of Illtud, David was reportedly destined for spiritual greatness even before his birth (but then again, the stories of many saints are full of miracles *in utero*). His life had an unfortunate beginning: his mother, a nun named Non, was raped by a local prince. The impregnated Non, however, was honoured, not scorned. As the story goes, when the pregnant Non entered a local church, the priest was immediately struck dumb; because David would surpass all other preachers, God miraculously forbade his inferiors to lecture in his presence.

> 'The whole of his day [David] spent, inflexibly and unweariedly, in teaching, praying, genuflecting, and in care of his brethren. He also fed a multitude of orphans, wards, widows, needy, sick, feeble, and pilgrims. Thus he began; thus he continued; thus he ended his day.'
>
> **Rhigyfarch, Life of David**

David is also credited with founding 12 monasteries, though many of these claims are questionable (including Glastonbury). He is more assuredly associated with the founding of Mynyw, which he named for his hometown and is now called St David's. Here he gained fame as a radical ascetic, with discipline and severity intentionally rivalling Antony's successors in Egypt. 'He imitated the monks of Egypt and lived a life like theirs,' says his biographer. But where the North African monks focused their asceticism on the rocks and sands, David's focus – water – was more suited to his island life. His nickname, Aquaticus (the Waterman), is mostly due to his requiring total abstinence from alcohol. Other aspects of his life were water-oriented as well. The only condoned meat was fish (bread and vegetables were also allowed). And each day, after morning prayers, David 'plunged himself into cold water, remaining in it sufficiently long to subdue all the ardors of the flesh'. David's unreliable hagiographer, Rhigyfarch, even says the saint 'changed the foul water to healthy' at Bath, 'endowing it with a continuous heat that made it suitable for bathing'. David's rule was apparently among the harshest in Britain. No animals were used in ploughing. 'Every man his own ox,' David mandated. Personal property was outlawed. 'Whoever should say "my book" or "my anything else" was immediately subject to a severe penance,' says Rhigyfarch. New candidates for the monastery had to enter 'naked, as though from a shipwreck', and had to wait at the monastery's door for ten days before even being considered. Despite all of this, says Rhigyfarch, 'No complaint was heard; in fact, there was no conversation beyond that which was necessary.'

David's opposition

The foundation of one of David's early monasteries was not appreciated by one of the local men, says the hagiographer Rhigyfarch. But Baia's wife was even more angry, telling her husband 'Rise up . . . and with swords drawn attack these men who have dared to do such a wicked thing and kill them all.' Baia and his men went out to do just that, but changed their minds along the way. Baia's wife then decided to take the situation into her own hands, telling her maids to run around naked in front of the monks, 'using crude words'. They did so, 'imitating sexual intercourse and displaying love's seductive embraces', says Rhigyfarch. 'They drew the minds of some of the monks towards desire, while to others they were an annoyance.' When the monks decided to give up and leave the area, David told them to stay: 'Be strong and invincible in the struggle, in case your enemy should rejoice in your flight.' Rhigyfarch, meanwhile, rejoiced in the destruction of David's enemies. Baia, he says, was 'struck down by an enemy who took him by surprise', while his wife went mad, killed her stepdaughter, and disappeared forever.

All that glitters in the 'golden age of saints' . . .

Such austerity scandalized Gildas (c. 497–570), an angry saint who is credited as one of Britain's first historians. Ploughing without an ox was a likely sign of presumption and pride, he wrote. Where rules like David's penalized indulgences in worldly pleasures, Gildas penalized abstinence without charity. And where extreme ascetics sought isolation, Gildas outlawed leaving a monastic community for a more solitary devotional life. Reclusive monks, however, were only a small part of the problem in the eye of Gildas, born on the banks of the Clyde in Scotland and educated under Illtud at Llantwit Major. For him, the entire country had forsaken God: a case he made in *De excidio et conquestu Britanniae* (*The Ruin and Conquest of Britain*). 'Kings hath Britain, but they are tyrants,' he wrote. 'Judges she hath, but they are impious; priests hath Britain, but they are fools; pastors so-called, but they are wolves alert to slay souls. They do not look to the good of their people, but to the filling of their own bellies.' It was the fault of these temporal and spiritual rulers, Gildas wrote, that the Anglo-Saxon invaders had met with such success. But even the pagan foreigners could not be blamed with filling both church and state with evil – the lax Britons themselves were responsible for such tragedy. 'God's church and his holy law', he lamented, were mocked by those in power.

> 'Holy men used to visit Gildas from distant parts of Britain, and when advised, returned and cherished with delight the encouragements and counsels they had heard from him.'
>
> **Caradoc of Llangarfan, The Life of Gildas, c. 1150**

About a century and a half before Gildas, another British Christian, probably from Wales, similarly ranted against apathy in the Christian church. But this itinerant preacher and former lawyer railed against a sinful church in Rome, not Britain – and became one of the most famous Western heretics in church history. The life story of Pelagius cannot be told accurately. We do know that he was a layman born around 354 somewhere in the British Isles. One of his chief accusers, Jerome, disparagingly says he was 'stuffed with the porridge of the Scots', and he was regularly referred to as Pelagius Brito, Britannus, and other such names that give historical

> 'A man can be without sin and keep the commandments of God, if he wishes; for this ability has been given to him by God.'
>
> **Pelagius, at the Synod of Diospolis**

evidence to his general background, if not hometown. Known as Pelagius to history, he was probably born Morgan (or Morien). In the early 380s he went to Rome to study law, but decided upon his arrival to enter full-time ministry ('The world is saved and inheritance and civil suits are plucked from the abyss because this man, neglecting the law courts, has turned to the Church,' Jerome quipped sarcastically.) He was a huge man, perhaps even larger than the six-foot-plus David of Wales. Another critic, in a letter to Pelagius, wrote of his 'broad shoulders and robust neck, showing your fat even on your forehead'. What angered so many church fathers was Pelagius's claims that humans had absolute free will and an inherent capacity to do good. This was at odds with the doctrines of original sin and divine grace articulated by Augustine of Hippo. Pelagius was particularly upset with Augustine's famous prayer, 'Give what Thou commandest and command what Thou wilt.' To Pelagius, such an emphasis had led to the church's lazy morality: If grace was given freely without any nod to merit, what was the use in doing good at all? Even worse in Pelagius's eyes, Augustine denied that sinless perfection was possible, even after baptism! Had not God himself commanded, 'Be perfect, even as I am perfect?'

Under attack from Augustine, Jerome and others, Pelagius was condemned by two African councils in 416, and was excommunicated by Pope Innocent I in 417. But his ideas lived on, especially in Britain. Bede says that British churches were so overwhelmed with Pelagian teachings that they had to send for help from Gaul. The reply came in the form of two men, Germanus of Auxerre and (probably) Lupus of Troyes. *The Chronicle of Prosper of Aquitaine,* a chronological listing of important events in church history, sees the story slightly differently. Its entry for the year 429 says:

The Pelagian Agricola . . . insidiously corrupted the churches of Britain with his teachings. But, through the negotiation of the deacon Palladius, Pope Ce-lestine sent Germanus, Bishop of Auxerre, to act on his behalf, and he routed the heretics and directed the Britons to the Catholic faith.

In the entry for 431, the deacon appears again: 'Palladius was ordained by Pope Celestine and sent to the Irish believers in Christ as their first bishop.'

CHAPTER 12

PATRICK AND THE CONVERSION OF IRELAND

Palladius's appearance as the bishop of Irish Christians in Prosper's reliable *Chronicle* raises more questions than it answers. Where did these Irish Christians come from? How many were there? How had they been converted? For later writers attempting to support the idea of Patrick as apostle of Ireland, there were even bigger problems. How could Patrick be credited with converting the island if Palladius had got there first? Muirchú moccu Mactheni, who wrote an unreliable hagiography of Patrick around 695, had an answer. 'No one can receive from earth what has not been given by heaven: Palladius was denied success,' he wrote. 'For these wild and obdurate people did not readily accept his doctrine and he himself did not wish to spend a long time in a foreign country, but to return to him who had sent him.'

Palladius's return journey, however, ended on the other side of the Irish Sea – he died almost immediately after leaving Ireland. (Other unreliable accounts say Palladius was martyred by the Irish.) Patrick then swooped in a year later and saved the day – and the island. Why a year later? In the hagiographies, Patrick had to arrive after Palladius, lest Rome's initiative and apostolic authority be deprecated. But Patrick's mission could not seem too long after that of Palladius – others could stake claims as missionaries to at least part of the island. Muirchú wanted Patrick to be apostle of all Ireland – not just some of it. Therefore, because of the hagiographer's efforts, 432 is in the history books as the start of Patrick's mission. (At least that is the current theory. Who knows? Maybe Muirchú actually had information about Palladius's work.) The reality is that we have no idea on the specifics of when Patrick actually went to Ireland, when and where he was born, where he lived and worked, when and where he died, or any of the other important historical reference

> 'When I came to Patrick, I found it impossible to gain any clear conception of the man and his work. The subject was wrapt in obscurity, and this obscurity was encircled in an atmosphere of controversy and conjecture.'
>
> **J.B. Bury, *The Life of St Patrick and His Place in History*, 1905**

points. There are some historical clues that help, however, including language. For example, it is clear by examining the way certain Latin words were integrated into the Irish language that Christianity came from Britain, not continental Europe. In addition to such detective work, we also have historical gold – two works undoubtedly written by Patrick himself – one of them outlining his life story.

While we have a story without specifics for Patrick, in Palladius we have specifics without a story. Unlike Patrick, Palladius has no extant writings describing his motivation, his fears, or his concerns. But while modern historians have rejected the explanations of Muirchú and others, they have come up with their own theories of Palladius's internal life. The picture that emerges is that Pope Celestine – and thus his deacon – had two main priorities in Ireland: countering Pelagianism and extending the Roman church. After Emperor Honorius exiled all Pelagians on 30 April 418, the Pelagians simply retreated beyond the reach of the Roman empire, to Britain. Palladius probably wanted to make sure that if Pelagians were banished from Britain (Germanus's job), they did not simply retreat again to Ireland. Extending the church to the furthest reaches of the known world was also a matter of both spiritual and political significance. As one historian recently wrote:

The activities of Germanus and Palladius, in Britain and in Ireland, demonstrated that a Christian and papal Rome, the Rome of Peter and Paul [as opposed to that of Romulus and Remus], could intervene to safeguard and to spread the Faith in an island which had thrown off imperial authority and also in another island which had never been subject to the sway of the emperor.

Extending its reach not only enhanced the pope's claims to superiority over the church, but also over the state.

So if Palladius was so important to the church, what happened? Where are his hagiographies? Where are his stories? It is very possible they still exist to this day – only now many of the stories of Palladius are attributed to Patrick.

From slave to saint

Today, Patrick is arguably the most famous saint from the 5th century. Each year, when parades in New York, Boston and elsewhere celebrate in his name, a few stories are brought out and passed around again: Patrick drove the snakes out of Ireland; he used the shamrock to explain the Trinity; he single-handedly converted the entire country – without a drop of blood; he offered 'the first de-Romanized Christianity in human history'. Pity that none of these common beliefs about Patrick can be justified by reliable texts.

> 'The Irish gave Patrick more than a home – they gave him a role, a meaning to his life. For only this former slave had the right instincts to impart to the Irish a New Story, one that made new sense of all their old stories and brought them a peace they had never known before.'
>
> **Thomas Cahill, How the Irish Saved Civilization**

Patrick was born into an apparently affluent, religious home. His father, Calpornius, was a deacon, and his grandfather, Potitus, had been a priest. The family was probably part of the local nobility, and owned, in Patrick's words, a 'small estate near the village of Bannavem Taburniae'. (The exact location of this town, which may have been called Banneventa Burniae, is a matter of regular dispute. Because of the uncertainly, dozens of sites along the shores of western Britain claim to be Patrick's hometown.) As noted earlier, being part of the local nobility (*civitas*) in the 400s had its benefits and perils. Wealth and power made life comfortable – but they also made one a target; and there were no more Roman soldiers for protection. Patrick learned this firsthand in a rather unfortunate way – at the age of 16, he was captured by Irish slave-raiders and taken across the sea into captivity.

Patrick says little about his life and the master he served for the next six years of his life, except to say that he 'was made to shepherd the flocks day after day'. The unreliable Tírechán, a 7th-century bishop, says his owner's name was Mílluc moccu Bóin (Milchu), a druid. 'Patrick worked for him in every kind of servitude and heavy labour, and Mílluc placed him as a swineherd in the mountain glens,' he wrote. Herding animals can be a rough and lonely life. Patrick reportedly endured long bouts of hunger, thirst and isolation in the Irish hills. It was during this time that he turned to the Christian God of his family for comfort.

Decades later, writing his *Confessio*, Patrick believed that his slavery was God's punishment for religious apathy. 'I was taken into captivity in Ireland – at that time I was ignorant of the true God – along with many thousand others,' he wrote. 'This was our punishment for departing from God, abandoning his commandments, and ignoring our priests who kept on warning us about our salvation.' The punishment was also grace, and during his captivity Patrick found God:

More and more, the love of God and the fear of him grew in me, and my faith was increased and my spirit enlivened. So much that I prayed up to a hundred times in the day, and almost as often at night. I even remained in the wood and on the mountain to pray. And – come hail, rain, or snow – I was up before dawn to pray, and I sensed no evil nor spiritual laziness within.

'He [Patrick] conquered by steadfastness of faith, by glowing zeal, and by the attractive power of love.'

August Neander, General History of the Christian Religion and Church, 1855

He may have enjoyed making himself a slave to Christ, but Patrick was less inclined to remain a slave to Mílluc. At age 22, he heard a supernatural voice. 'You do well to fast,' the voice said. 'Soon you will return to your homeland.' The voice soon spoke again: 'Behold! Your ship is prepared.' The only problem was that the ship had been prepared on the other end of Ireland, some 200 miles away. Patrick 'felt not the least anxiety' on the journey to the south-eastern harbour, but upon arriving he had another problem. 'Don't even think about travelling with us,' the captain told him disdainfully. The fugitive Patrick did not wish to risk capture by remaining out in the open much longer, so he quickly left the ship and headed for a nearby hut for shelter.

'On the way I began to pray, and before I finished my prayer I heard a crewman shouting loudly to me: "Come quickly! These men are calling you." I turned back at once and they said: "Come on, we are taking you on trust. So show your friendship with us according to whatever custom you choose."' Apparently the custom they wanted him to choose was something called 'sucking their nipples'. Some modern scholars think it was just a figure of speech by Patrick's time – an ancient form of 'kiss and make up'. Others think it was quite literal. In either case, Patrick did not want to enter such an intimate relationship with his pagan shipmates 'on account of the fear of God'. He did, however, want to befriend them in hopes 'that some of them would come to faith in Jesus Christ'.

After a three-day journey, the ship landed. Patrick does not say where, and historians even argue over whether the landing was Britain or Gaul, but the men were forced to wander in a desert for 28 days. (This may simply be Patrick trying to compare himself to the Israelites wandering the desert after their slavery in Egypt, or it may be a historical clue – the ship may have landed in a devastated war zone. Goths and Vandals had devastated northern Gaul between 407 and 410.)

Again the ship's captain became contemptuous. 'What have you to say for yourself, Christian?' he taunted. 'You boast that your God is all-powerful, so why can't you pray for us? We're starving to death, and we may not survive to see another soul.'

Patrick responded confidently: 'Nothing is impossible for God. Turn to him and he will send us food for our journey.' In apparent desperation, the ship's crew obeyed. As they prayed, a herd of pigs suddenly appeared, 'seeming to block our path'. The sated sailors were grateful to Patrick from then on, but still rejected his God. Offering some wild honey to the fugitive slave, one mentioned that it had been offered as a sacrifice. 'Thanks be to God,' Patrick recounted, 'I had tasted none of it.'

A voice cries out in the wilderness

After his sojourn with the sailors, Patrick's *Confessio* has a huge gap – an unfortunate result of the work being a personal defence, not a modern autobiography. 'To narrate in detail wither the whole story of my labours or even parts of it would take a long time,' he explains. When he resumes the story 'after a few years', he is back in Britain with his parents. 'They begged me in good faith after all my adversities to go nowhere else, nor ever leave them again,' he wrote. But he could not keep such a promise for long.

'I had a vision in my dreams of a man who seemed to come from Ireland,' Patrick recalls in the *Confessio*:

His name was Victoricius, and he carried countless letters, one of which he handed over to me. I read aloud where it began: 'The Voice of the Irish'. And as I began to read these words, I seemed to hear the voice of the same men who lived beside the forest of Foclut, which lies near the Western sea where the sun sets. They seemed to shout aloud to me as with one and the same voice: 'Holy broth of a boy, we beg you, come back and walk once more among us.' I was utterly pierced to my heart's core so that I could read no more.

Patrick began preparing to return to the land of his captivity, to Ireland. He did not travel there immediately – first came theological education and official ordination, following the career of his father and grandfather. Muirchú also sends Patrick to Rome 'so that he might learn and understand and fulfil the divine wisdom and the holy mysteries to which God called him'. More likely are reports that Patrick travelled to Gaul, where he studied under Germanus of Auxerre, the anti-Pelagian bishop Pope Celestine sent to Britain. Here Muirchú gets cloudy, which is ironically a sign that he might be more accurate: 'some say he spent forty years there', the hagiographer writes, 'some say thirty'.

Just before Patrick was ordained as a deacon, he confessed a sin to his closest friend. There is no way of knowing what the sin was, but it was probably serious – he had committed it around age 15 (about a year before the Irish raiders captured him) and it still bothered him many years later. Some have supposed that the sin was murder, but it is only a guess. Patrick's *Confessio* tells the story of his confession, but does not repeat it: 'When I was anxious and worried I hinted to my dearest friend about something I had done one day – indeed in one hour – in my youth, for I had not then prevailed over my sinfulness.' His friend did not think it too serious a matter, and forgave him. Certainly he did not think it prohibited him from becoming a deacon. On the contrary, he said, 'Mark my words, you are going to be made bishop.' Patrick said he was unworthy for such a position, but soon attained the rank. His confession to his friend would later come back to haunt him.

While there had to be some Christians in Ireland – who else would have asked Celestine to send a bishop? – Patrick apparently did not encounter them when he returned. 'I dwell among gentiles, in the midst of pagan barbarians, worshippers of idols, and of unclean things,' he wrote. But he maintains he was changing all that. 'In Ireland . . . they never had knowledge of God and celebrated only idols and unclean things,' he wrote. 'Until now.'

In both his surviving works, Patrick portrays himself humbly. 'I am the sinner Patrick,' he begins the *Confessio*. 'I am the most unsophisticated of people, the least of Christians, and for many people I am the most contemptible . . . It is among the people of [Ireland] that my smallness is seen.' Most of this, however, was probably rhetorical humility, like the apostle Paul's statements that he is 'the least of Christians' (Ephesians 3:8) and the 'chief of sinners' (1 Timothy 1:15). Patrick actually saw his work as crucial to the work of the church. Not only was he literally fulfilling Jesus' command to tell people about him 'to the ends of the earth' (Acts 1:8), but by doing so he was hastening Christ's return.

> 'I was like a stone lying in the deepest mire; and then, "he who is mighty" came, and, in his mercy, raised me up. He most truly raised me on high and set me on top of the rampart.'
>
> **Patrick, Confessio**

At the end of the world

Surviving maps by Ptolemy (a 2nd-century astronomer, mathematician and geographer from Alexandria) and from a 13th-century copy of the book of Psalms have significant differences. In the latter, Jerusalem is the centre of the world, and Christ oversees all. But in both maps, Ireland (Hibernia) is practically unseen – it is so far on the margins that it is practically falling off. Such geography was firmly established in Patrick's mind as well. 'Truly, I am greatly in God's debt,' he wrote:

He has given me a great grace, that through me many peoples might be reborn and later brought to completion; and that from among them everywhere clerics should be ordained [to serve] this people – who have but recently come to belief – [and] which the Lord has taken [to himself] 'from the ends of the earth'. He thus fulfilled 'what he once promised through his prophets': 'to you shall the nations come from the ends of the earth and say, "Our fathers have inherited naught but lies, worthless things in which there is no profit" [Jeremiah 16:19]'. And in another place: 'I have set you to be a light for the nations, that you may bring salvation to the uttermost parts of the earth.'

In Patrick's mind, preaching at the end of the world meant bringing about the end of the world. He repeatedly mentions that he is in 'the last days', and regularly quotes Jesus' words in Matthew 24:14: 'All nations will hear the gospel, and then, finally, the end will come.' 'And this is what we see,' Patrick writes. 'It has been fulfilled. Behold! We are [now] witnesses to the fact that the gospel has been preached out to beyond where anyone lives.'

Patrick was not alone in this belief. Christians never gave up the idea that Christ would return when all the nations heard about him; they simply discovered more nations. A millennium after Patrick, Columbus would be driven to America not merely in a quest of fame and riches, but to hasten the Second Coming. 'God made me the messenger of the New Heaven and the New Earth,' he wrote. Columbus even penned his own *Book of Prophesies* to show how his discovery fitted into biblical predictions. In fact, the belief continues today; the major missions push of the late 20th century, with its emphasis on 'unreached people groups', was largely based in the promise of Matthew 24:14.

Rejecting gods of three for the Trinity

Little is known of Patrick's specific conversion methods. The tale about his using a shamrock to explain the Trinity is almost certainly untrue. It would have been unnecessary. A common theme throughout Celtic religion is triune gods – gods with three manifestations, gods who travel in threes, or gods with three heads. We know this about pagan Celtic religion partly through archaeology, but also because later Celtic scribes believed, like Patrick, that pagan religions were pre-Christian rather than anti-Christian. Early and medieval Christians believed Paul's words that 'ever since the creation of the world, God's eternal power and divine nature, invisible though they are, have been understood and are seen through the things he has made' (Romans 1:20). Paul himself exemplified this belief in Athens. He was 'deeply distressed to see that the city was full of idols', but used them in evangelism. 'I see how extremely religious you are in every way,' Paul told the Athenians. 'I found an altar with the inscription, "To an unknown god". What therefore you worship as unknown, this I proclaim to you' (Acts 17:16ff.). Pagan beliefs were therefore part of the 'eternity written on the hearts' of those who never had the chance to hear the full truth.

This is not to say that Patrick and his contemporaries in any way approved of paganism as a distant relative to their religion. On the contrary, they believed that the pagan gods and other supernatural beings likely did exist, but were demons. The old pagan stories did not have to be expelled, they only had to be reinterpreted. Miracles, magic and mysteries probably did occur, the Christians reasoned. Even Pharaoh's magicians had powers – but the God of Moses was more powerful, and more importantly, he was good.

> 'A capacity for worship, a passionate feeling for the supernatural, for the gods, or later, God, is, I believe, the truest and most binding cultural element throughout the entire Celtic world.'
>
> **Anne Ross, *Pagan Celtic Britain***

The druids 'wished to kill holy Patrick', the hagiographies tell us over and over again. These claims cannot be wholly dismissed. Patrick and other missionaries almost certainly faced opposition from the druids – not simply because they were the religious leaders but because they had the most to lose if the culture converted. Indeed, that is what happened – the church replaced the druids as the hub of society. Patrick confirmed that his life was in danger. 'Daily I expect murder, fraud, or captivity,' he wrote. 'But I fear none of these things because of the promises of heaven. I have cast myself into the hands of God almighty who rules everywhere.' (But while he cast himself into the hands of God, he also cast protection money into the hands of his would-be enemies. 'Patrick paid the price of 15 souls in gold and silver so that no evil persons should impede them as they travelled straight across the whole of Ireland,' one hagiographer wrote. In the *Confessio*, Patrick proudly admits paying 15 judges 'so that you might enjoy me and I might always enjoy you in God'.)

Patrick does not record any confrontations with druids, but it is the subject of one of the most famous stories of his life. Since Muirchú is our source, it is likely not a word of it is true. The night before Easter reportedly happened to coincide with a major pagan festival on the Hill of Tara. In defiance of pagan tradition, Patrick lit a bonfire in the distance – but in full view of King Loiguire. 'Who is it who has dared to commit this crime in my kingdom?' the king asked. 'He must die.' The king sent several men – including druids – to seize the missionary. Brought before the king, Patrick was anything but passive. He summoned the power of God to raise one of the druids into the air, then released him. 'Coming down, he smashed his skull on a rock, and died right before them; and the heathen were afraid,' Muirchú says. Then Patrick called down darkness and an earthquake. 'By this disaster, caused by Patrick's curse in the king's presence because of the king's order, seven times seven men fell.'

The next day, Easter Sunday, Patrick entered Loiguire's banquet hall. A druid challenged him to a wonder-working battle. First the druid made snow fall waist-deep. Patrick made it disappear. Then the druid made fog over the land. Patrick cleared it away, too. Then, in a final test, the prayers of Patrick set the druid ablaze. When the enraged king started at Patrick, the missionary stopped him, saying, 'If you do not believe now, you will die on the spot; for the wrath of God descends on your head.'

> 'Hear all ye who love God, the holy merits of the Bishop Patrick, a man blessed in Christ; how, on account of his good actions, he is likened unto the angels, and for his perfect life, is counted equal to the apostles.'
>
> **Hymn of St Patrick, attributed to Secundinus**

'It is better for me to believe than to die,' Loiguire reasoned. Adds Muirchú, 'He believed on that day and turned to the eternal Lord God. Many others also believed on that day.'

Most historians dismiss the tale as a retelling of Moses' encounter with Pharaoh's magicians or Elijah's encounter with the prophets of Baal on Mount Carmel. But to Patrick and his contemporaries, such comparisons would not be evidence of Muirchú's plagiarism. It would have been evidence of God's consistency.

If the hagiographers present Patrick's evangelism methods as unrelenting and deadly, they also present them as gentle and graceful. Tírechán's account of the conversion of Loiguire's daughters is lovely, if implausible in its details. 'Who is God, and where is God, and whose God is he, and where is his house?' one of the women asked Patrick. 'Give us some idea of him: how he may be seen, how loved; how he may be found.'

'Our God is the God of all people,' Patrick replied:

The God of heaven and earth, of the sea and of the rivers, the God of the sun and the moon and of all the stars, the God of the high mountains and of the deep valleys. He is God above heaven and in heaven and under heaven, and has as his dwelling place heaven and earth and the sea and all that are in them. His life is in all things; he makes all things live; he governs all things; he supports all things . . . Truly now, since you are daughters of an earthly king, I wish that you will believe and I wish to wed you to the king of heaven.

They agreed and were baptized. Then they immediately died, their souls ascending to heaven. It is not exactly the modern happy ending, but it apparently suited Tírechán.

There may be a hint of truth behind this story. 'The Irish leaders' sons and daughters are seen to become the monks and virgins of Christ,' Patrick writes in the *Confessio*. And again in his *Letter to Coroticus*: 'Indeed, I could not count how many of the sons and daughters of the rulers of the Irish had become monks and virgins of Christ.' Patrick apparently acted as a foster-parent to many rulers' children. This was an old Irish custom and one of the main societal bonds at the time. In most cases, the natural parents gave the foster-parents an 'after-gift'. In

Prayer of protection

Patrick's most famous work almost certainly was not written by him. The *Lorica* (or Breastplate), also known as 'The Deer's Cry' because it supposedly helped him change into the shape of a deer when Loiguire hunted him, was probably first written in the 7th or 8th century. 'I rise today', it begins, 'in the power's strength, invoking the Trinity, believing in threeness, confessing the oneness, of creation's Creator . . .'

I rise today with the power of God to pilot me, God's strength to sustain me, God's wisdom to guide me, God's eye to look ahead for me, God's ear to hear me, God's word to speak for me, God's hand to protect me, God's way to defend me, God's host to deliver me from snares of devils, from evil temptations, from nature's failings, from all who wish to harm me, far or near, alone and in a crowd . . .

Christ with me, Christ before me, Christ behind me; Christ within me, Christ beneath me, Christ above me; Christ in my lying, Christ in my sitting, Christ in my rising; Christ in the heart of all who think of me, Christ on the tongue of all who speak to me, Christ in the eye of all who see me, Christ in the ear of all who hear me . . . May your salvation, Lord, be with us always.

Patrick's case, money seems to have gone the other direction. No matter for Patrick – the true value lay in bringing more souls to conversion.

Patrick the abolitionist

Patrick was very protective of his converts, and it is because of his defence of them that we have his other document, the *Letter to the Soldiers of Coroticus*. It addresses an intimately familiar enemy – slavery. Its target is Coroticus, a Christian tyrant from Britain who had captured many of Patrick's converts the day after their baptism. 'Still wearing their white baptismal garb [and with] the chrism still on their foreheads,' the young Irish Christians were 'cut down and cruelly put to the sword by these men', Patrick raged. 'Ravenous wolves have gulped down the Lord's own flock which was flourishing in Ireland and the whole church cries out and laments for its sons and daughters.'

The *Letter to the Soldiers of Coroticus* is not just a letter to the soldiers of Coroticus – it is written to 'everyone who fears God'. Patrick's correspondence is designed to excommunicate the slave raiders and their leader. 'The soldiers of Coroticus are strangers to me and to Christ, my God,' he wrote. 'It is not lawful to seek favour from men such as these, nor to eat food or drink with them; nor to accept their alms until they make satisfaction to God with painful penance and the shedding of tears, and free the baptized servants of God.'

Whether Patrick's letter worked or if the slaves were freed is unknown. Muirchú claims Coroticus laughed at the epistle, but Patrick and his God took vengeance. Before the eyes of his closest followers, the tyrant was magically 'transformed into the shape of a little fox' and ran away, never to be seen again.

Patrick had to spend much of his *Letter to the Soldiers of Coroticus* explaining that he was not exceeding his jurisdiction by excommunicating the raiders. If Coroticus was indeed British, then explanation was probably necessary – especially if Patrick was already in trouble with the British church leadership.

Some time after Patrick became bishop, his closest friend betrayed him. The man who had told him, 'Mark my words, you are going to be made bishop', spilled the evangelist's deepest, darkest secret to the church authorities. The disclosure apparently raised quite a scandal – so much so that the church leaders wondered if Patrick could remain a bishop at all. Other charges were added, including one suggesting Patrick had gone to Ireland to financially enrich himself. The church authorities called a synod, and apparently sent a delegation to Ireland to question Patrick. Though Patrick never testified in Britain, his traitorous friend defended him. As the charges circulated on both sides of the Irish Sea, Patrick penned his *Confessio* to refute the charges. All the biographical information he provides serves to defend himself against charges that he had no authority to minister in Ireland, that his conversion tactics were out of order, and that he was enriching himself. God himself had sent him, Patrick asserted, and God was defending him still. 'Indeed he bore me up, though I was trampled underfoot in such a way,' he wrote. 'For although I was put down and shamed, not too much harm came to me.' Though the result is ultimately unclear, Patrick appears to have been successful in his defence.

Beyond the conversion of Ireland

Tradition remembers Patrick as the wandering missionary bishop, converting as much of Ireland as he could before his death. Irish monasticism is more associated with those who came later. But Patrick saw his mission not simply as making Christians – he wanted to make monks and nuns. Like his Christian contemporaries, Patrick saw asceticism as the highest form of the Christian life. He seemed especially proud of a young, beautiful, Irish noblewoman who returned to Patrick a few days after he baptized her, saying 'a divine communication from a messenger of God . . . advised her to become a virgin of Christ' to become closer to Christ. Though her family opposed her action, six days later she took her vows. The young noblewoman would have become a sister to slaves, who apparently formed a large part of Patrick's nunneries. 'Those held in slavery have to work hardest,' Patrick wrote. 'They are continually harassed and even have to suffer being terrorized. But the Lord gives grace to many of his maidservants, and the more they are forbidden to imitate him the more they boldly do this.'

Croagh Patrick

On 'Reek Sunday', the last Sunday of July, 25,000 or so pilgrims climb (many barefoot) to the top of Croagh Patrick, in County Mayo. The legends say this was where Patrick fasted for 40 days during the Lent of 441, and that this is where he drove the snakes from Ireland. Actually, he did no such thing, but as early as the 1100s Giraldus Cambrensis wrote that no snakes could ever live on the island. 'Sometimes for the sake of experiment serpents have been shipped over,' he wrote, 'but were found lifeless and dead as soon as the middle of the Irish Sea was crossed.'

Whether Patrick actually visited the mountain or not, it has been considered a holy site for a very long time. Carbon dating of an oratory at the 2,710-foot summit puts the church somewhere between AD 430 and 890. In the 1100s, when control of the mountain passed from Armagh to Tuam, the former began promoting its own Patrician pilgrimage point: Patrick's Purgatory, an island supposedly housing a cave where the saint entered the underworld during a period of penance.

Nobles, slaves, widows and probably even married people (who took a vow of sexual abstinence) joined Patrick's call to the monastic life. If other monasteries made prospects wait outside the door ten days, Patrick apparently ran out the monastery door and pulled potential recruits in with enthusiasm.

> 'Remember St Patrick. Remember what the fidelity of just one man has meant for Ireland and the world.'
>
> **Pope John Paul II, visiting Ireland in 1979**

Muirchú writes that when Patrick died, 'no night fell; it did not wrap its black wings around the earth; and the evening did not send the darkness which carries the stars. The people of Ulaid say that to the very end of the year in which he departed, the darkness of the nights was never as great as before. There is no doubt that this was testimony to the merit of so great a man.' Muirchú also claims that just before his death, God granted Patrick's demand that he alone shall judge all the Irish, not Christ. In fact, very little can be said with certainty about Patrick's death,

> 'Here is the enigma of Patrick: he looms large on the imaginative horizon of so many people, yet he saw himself as a Christian bishop from the embattled edge of a crumbling empire. As such, he is a man whose world, lifestyle and understanding are in many respects wholly foreign to us.'
>
> **Thomas O'Loughlin, St Patrick: The Man and His Works**

except that it almost certainly occurred on 17 March. The year is less certain, though Irish annals place it at 493. Monasteries all over Ireland – including Armagh, Downpatrick and Saul – claim his remains, but they are probably lost forever. A liturgical calendar from 797 remembers him: 'The flame of a splendid sun, the apostle of virgin Erin [Ireland], may Patrick with many thousands be the shelter of our wickedness.' By then, Ireland had been almost totally Christian for two centuries, thanks largely to Patrick.

CHAPTER 13

IRELAND'S MONKS AND MONASTERIES

About the time of Patrick's death, a Pictish warrior-prince named Énda (c. 450–535) was mourning another death – that of his fiancée. His older sister, a nun, told him to stop mourning. After all, she reasoned, all earthly loves eventually expire; only heavenly love lasts forever. Rather than pine for lost love, she said, Énda should follow her into monastic life. The prince agreed, and set off for Ninian's Candida Casa. Years later, he returned to Ireland and around 484 set up a monastery on rocky Inishmore, one of the Aran Islands off western Ireland. According to tradition, his was the first monastery in Ireland.

There are the inevitable challenges to the claim, including the regular caution that the first *known* person to do something often is not the first to actually do it. As noted earlier, Patrick himself urged converts to become monks and nuns, and he may have lived half a century before Énda. The sea has long claimed any ruins of Inishmore's early foundation. Other early monastic settlements, usually made of daub and wattle, have likewise disappeared with time. But more monks and nuns would follow, building foundations throughout Ireland and creating a culture that would become Celtic Christianity's most notable feature.

Some time in the 800s, an unknown writer tried to chart Irish church history from its inception to 665. His *Catalogue of the Saints of Ireland* tells the tale in three stages. Until 544, 350 non-celibate bishops took their lead from Patrick. In the Second Order (544–98), bishops and presbyters shifted their model from Patrick to the ascetic Antony of Egypt, following practices such as 'avoiding the society of women'. The Third Order became most ascetic of all, with monks 'living on herbs and water and from alms'. But the *Catalogue* writer was unlike many of his contemporaries – he believed the trend was a degeneration, not progress. The First Order was 'most holy', the third was merely 'holy'.

Living martyrdom

Actually, Irish monasticism had no such divisible eras. Énda's monastery, for example, was reportedly one of the more austere and demanding of any time. If there was any division seen by the Christian Celts, it was not one of increasingly ascetic ages but one of degrees of self-sacrifice. As one surviving homily, dating from the late 600s or early 700s, says:

There are in fact three kinds of martyrdom, which we may regard as types of cross in human eyes: namely, white martyrdom, green martyrdom, and red martyrdom. A person undergoes white martyrdom when he leaves all for the sake of Christ, even though this means fasting, hunger, and hard work. Green martyrdom is attributed to someone who through them – that is, fasting and work – is freed of his desires, or undergoes travail in sorrow and penance. Red martyrdom is found in the sufferings of a cross of death for Christ's sake, as was the way of the apostles, because of the persecution of the wicked, and while preaching the truths of God.

White martyrdom we will examine more in later chapters. The era of widespread red martyrdom – as experienced by the church in Lyons, Symphorian of Autun and Alban – had abated centuries before the homily was delivered. Green martyrdom, however, would become not just widespread in Ireland – it would become the dominant manifestation of the Irish church. Celtic Christians no longer had death by persecution to guarantee their entrance into heaven, so a metaphorical death, a 'death of desires', became the next best thing. Such practices may have found rich soil in the area where Pelagianism fought Augustine's doctrines of humanity's depravity and God's divine grace. Pelagius had taught that sinless perfection was possible if someone just tried hard enough. And the Celts certainly tried hard to do it. One monk, writing a poem in the 700s or 800s, summarized his lonely life in pursuit of holiness:

> 'Nowhere in barbarian Europe did monks and their saints so thoroughly dominate the social and spiritual life of the population as in Ireland . . . Their purpose was at once grand and mundane, selfless and self-serving.'
>
> **Lisa Bitel, *Isle of the Saints***

All alone in my little cell, without the company of a single person;
*   precious has been the pilgrimage before going to meet death.*
A hidden secluded little hut, for the forgiveness of my sins:
*   an upright, untroubled conscience towards holy heaven . . .*

A cold and anxious bed, like the lying down of a doomed man:
a brief, apprehensive sleep; invocations frequent and early.
My food as befits my station, precious has been my captivity:
my dinner, without doubt, would not make me full-blooded.
Dry bread weighed out, well we bow the head;
water of the man-coloured hillside, that is the drink I would take.
A bitter meagre dinner; diligently feeding the sick;
keeping off strife and visits; a calm, serene conscience . . .
All alone in my little cell, all alone thus;
alone I came into the world, alone I shall go from it.
If on my own I have sinned through pride of this world,
hear me wail for it all alone, O God!

Kevin of Glendalough

Two centuries before the poem was written, a recently ordained monk named Kevin (or Cóemgen) sought such a holy life in the craggy 'glen of the two lakes' (Glendalough) in the Wicklow mountains. 'There he had no food but the nuts of the forest, the herbs of the earth, and fresh water for drinking,' says his hagiographer. 'For sleeping he had only a stone for a pillow.' He spent most of his days and nights reciting prayers in a tiny cave now called 'Kevin's Bed' (only four feet wide, three feet high, and seven feet deep) or waist-deep in the cold lake waters. After seven years of such austerity, he achieved such a reputation for holiness that he began gaining disciples. For their sake, he moved out of the cave and founded the Glendalough monastery. He was a recluse, but apparently not one who avoided others at all costs – Glendalough was created largely to feed 'companies and strangers and guests and pilgrims . . . No one was refused entertainment.'

Kevin continued his ascetic life even in the community, maintaining his flagstone bed from his days of isolation and regularly escaping his disciples for intense periods of isolation. In a famous story occurring one Lenten season, Kevin was praying with his arms extended when a blackbird hopped into his hand. He maintained his position so she could build her nest, not moving until after the eggs hatched. As if that was not already an extraordinary story, Kevin's hagiographer claims an angel visited,

> 'Let your life be completely detached from the world, and follow the teaching of Christ and the Gospels.'
>
> **The Rule of Columba**

ordering the saint to put his arms down and return to the monastery. 'It is no great thing for me to bear this pain of holding my hand under the blackbird for the sake of heaven's king, for up on the cross of suffering Jesus bore every pain on behalf of Adam's seed,' Kevin eloquently replied. Other animals feature prominently in his story: an otter brought him a daily salmon and rescued his psalter when it sank to the bottom of the lake.

Meanwhile, Glendalough continued to grow. Hundreds of monks came to the monastery, which added huts to live in, a farm to work on, chapels to pray in, and a school to learn in. The size and shape of monasteries varied widely, from a hermit's hut to a massive settlement. Rules from the 700s, however, indicate how many – especially the large and famous – were laid out: 'four boundaries around a sanctuary, the first into which laymen and women enter, the second into which only clerics come. The first is called holy, the second holier, the third most holy. Note that the name of the fourth is lacking.' The monastic centres were usually circular and enclosed by a wall and defensive ditches. By the time a monastery got this big, however, the monk himself was usually long dead and his bones or other relics formed the holy centre. The second focus, of course, was the rectangular church – first made of wood and later stone. Other holy sites were also often found within the monasteries' walls – sacred wells or stones, for example, usually associated with miracles of the monastery's founding saint.

'A melodius bell, pealing out over the glen, such is the will of the fair Lord, that many brothers may be gathered under one discipline.'

The Rule of the Gray Monks

Even the less-holy places were laid out with regard to spiritual importance. Great open courtyards separated the church and other buildings. These mainly consisted of living and working quarters and storage sheds (valuables were later placed in the famous round towers that can still be seen at many monasteries today, but these were not constructed until the 10th century at the earliest). Some monasteries had dormitories, but individual sleeping quarters seem to be more common, housing a monk, two, three, or seven or more. Some of the most magnificent ones remaining can be found on

'If you have withdrawn from the world, remember that you now walk a path of suffering. Do not look to the world, but rather flee from it as you would from a hue and cry.'

The Rule of Comgall

Skellig (meaning 'steep rock of') Michael. The island the monastery sits on, 18 miles off Ireland's southwest coast, is 715 feet high, but only 2,000 feet long. It is not even large enough for the traditional circular enclosure, so the monastery's walls wander all over the rocks. Inside the enclosure was a garden, a graveyard, two chapels, and six rocky 'beehive' cells that still stand. In each of these, one or two monks slept and worked.

Skellig Michael stayed small, its isolation and limited space protecting it from growth. Many other Irish monasteries, however, continued to expand, eventually housing hundreds of clerics and countless more laity. At the turn of the first millennium, the monastery Ard Macha had thousands of residents. (Other monasteries had similar claims – 4,000 at Bangor, 3,000 at Clonmacnoise – but these may be severely inflated.) Ireland had been a fully rural island before Christianity took root. The monasteries became the island's first cities – and only a few of its residents were monks. The rest formed a kind of support structure for the monastery, with metal smiths, farmers, stable keepers, carpenters and others lay workers. Adding to that were the myriad visitors continually entering and exiting. 'Who can count the different crowds and numberless peoples flocking in from all the provinces,' wrote one hagiographer. 'Some for the abundant feasting, others for the healing of their afflictions, others to watch the pageant of the crowds, others with great gifts and offerings.'

The monastic rules and penitentials

Guiding the monastery's life were rules set down by the founder. For centuries these were probably unwritten, but followed nonetheless. It was not until a group of monastic reformers known as the Céli Dé (Clients of God) instituted a widespread revival in the 700s and 800s that the surviving rules were put to paper. The rule attributed to Comgall (c. 517–602), probably written in the late 700s, begins with an overview 'to love Christ, to shun wealth, to remain close to the heavenly king, and to be gentle towards all people'. It also included such directives as ordering monks to prostrate

> 'What a wonderful road it is to remain faithful to self-denial, and to be eager for it. Let the monk daily bear in mind that he will die, and let him be zealous in his concern for every person.'
>
> **The Rule of Comgall**

themselves on the floor 100 times in the morning and again in the evening while chanting psalms. 'If this is done,' the rule says, 'his reward will be great in the kingdom of heaven.' Hundreds more prostrations during the day were also prescribed. Reciting each of the 150 psalms daily was encouraged. During Lent, self-beatings were added. The rule also warns against too much of a good thing: 'Do not practise long, drawn-out devotions, but rather give yourself to prayer at intervals, as you would to food. Pious humbug is an invention of the devil.'

An even more rigorous monastic literature came in the form of penitential books. These apparently rose from a practical theological problem in the church: What do you do with sinning Christians? Believers who had undergone baptism were believed to have been washed free of the guilt of sin – it had all been forgiven. But sins committed after baptism, especially serious sins such as apostasy, murder and fornication could only be undone with penance. For much of the Christian world, though, there was a second problem – you only got one shot at penance. It could not be repeated – second offences meant damnation. So what do you do when someone sins after penance?

For the Celtic monks, penance was not just a one-time attempt at securing entrance into heaven. All offences, from wanting to hit someone to actually murdering him, were slips along a road to sinless perfection. Sins were symptoms of a disease, not a one-time decision for good or evil. Penance therefore was not a ticket; it was therapy. 'A variety of offences make for a variety of penances,' says the *Penitential of Columbanus*. 'And as physicians have to make a variety of medicines, so spiritual doctors must have different cures for the different wounds, ailments, pains, weaknesses of the soul.'

In most cases, especially in the *Penitential of Columbanus,* the medicine fitted the disease in predictable ways: 'The talkative is to be punished with silence, the restless with the practice of gentleness, the gluttonous with fasting, the sleepy with watching, the proud with imprisonment, the deserter with expulsion.' Other sins were spelled out more exactly – stealing meant a year on bread and water. A celibate monk fathering a child deserved seven years on such meagre sustenance. Fornication without fatherhood brought between three and twelve years of the penance, depending on the height of clerical office.

Other penitentials offer different courses, but still see them as remedies. 'If anyone has sinned in his heart through thought,' says the *Penitential of Finnian*, 'and then at once has repented, let him strike his breast, and ask God for pardon, and make satisfaction, and thus he will become well.'

One common penance was work. 'If you labour well you will be content, and if you endure steadily, you will be holy,' says the rule of Molua. The work, however, was not itself holy. Unlike some later continental monks who saw all labour as sacred, or even as a form of prayer, Celtic Christians saw a split between their devotional life and their secular work – and the sacred always won out. One young monk, Mochuda, was supposed to be tending swine when he heard a retinue of monks chanting psalms. He immediately abandoned the swine – the livelihood of his family – to join in. Later he, like many other monks in the hagiographies, found other ways to neglect manual labour. Holy magic or angels would power mills while monks studied and slept. When heaven did not intervene, manual labour was something best left to the professionals. A monk's day was best served in holier service.

What a monk actually did with his day depended on his relative status. A poem from the 11th century listed the job descriptions of one monastic community:

Psalm-singer, beginning student, historian (who is not insignificant), instructor, teacher of ecclesiastical law, head teacher with great knowledge, bishop, priest and deacon, subdeacon (a noble course), lector, porter, swift exorcist . . . vice-abbot, cook (proper and right), counsellor, steward, alternate vice-abbot . . .

Undereducated newcomers might simply be farmers with vows. Those who had grown up at the monastery were highly educated and typically given the duties more associated with Celtic monks – singing, studying, praying and writing.

Prayers of the Celts

Much has been made of Celtic prayers and the way Celtic monks prayed, but for the most part they prayed like the rest of Christian Europe at the time. Surviving manuscripts of prayers used in Mass, baptism and healing are very similar to those used elsewhere, and they are almost always in Latin. The apparent favourite prayer was Psalm 118, known as the *Beati*. 'Give thanks to the Lord for he is good,' the psalm begins. 'His love endures forever.'

'As a man at the foot of the gallows would pour out praise and lamentation to the king, to gain his deliverance,' one monk wrote, 'so we pour forth lamentation to the King of Heaven in the *Beati*, to gain our deliverance.'

Indeed, the *Beati* is not just a psalm of praise; it is also a prayer of protection. 'All the nations surrounded me, but in the name of the Lord I cut them off,' it says. 'They surrounded me on every side, but in the name of the Lord I cut them off. They swarmed around me like bees, but they died out as quickly as burning thorns; in the name of the Lord I cut them off.'

This protective repetition is reflected in many of the vernacular Celtic prayers, especially the *Loricae*. Other protective prayers became more like magical incantations, such as a prayer against headache that went 'Head of Christ, eye of Isaiah, forehead of Noah, lips and tongue of Solomon, throat of Timothy, mind of Benjamin, chest of Paul, joint of John, faith of Abraham: Holy, Holy, Holy, Lord God of Hosts.'

Most prayers, however, focused on prayer, not pragmatism:

Lord, be it thine,
 unfaltering praise of mine!
To thee my whole heart's love be given
 of earth and Heaven Thou King Divine!

Perhaps the best known of the ancient Irish prayers is one from the 700s, which begins: 'Rob tu mo bhoile, a Comdi cride, Ni ni nech aile, acht ri sect nime.' The poem was not translated into English until last century, however. Its 1905 version began, 'Be thou my vision, O Lord of my heart. None other is aught but the King of the seven heavens. Be thou my meditation by day and night; May it be thou that I behold even in my sleep.'

The monks practised beholding God even in their sleep. Each night they would arise at midnight, 3 a.m. and 6 a.m. for liturgical prayers. They even wore their long tunics and hooded cloaks to bed so they would not be detained on their way to pray. 'Do not sleep until it is necessary,' says the rule of Columba. Another rule, listing the characteristics of a holy clerical life, adds 'curtailment of sleep' to the list, between 'perseverance in reading' and 'facility in the reading of history'. Apparently the Celtic monks were no less prone than today's scholars to drift off during their studies.

Saintly scholars

They were also scribblers, writing in the margins of the books they copied. Sometimes they complained about their work. Sometimes they criticized each other's work. At other times, they reacted to what they were copying. 'I am greatly grieved at the aforementioned death,' one wrote after copying the killing of Hector at Troy. Still other times, they daydreamed. 'He is a heart,' wrote one. 'An acorn from the oakwood. He is young. Kiss him!' Another wrote even more scandalously, 'All are keen / To know who'll sleep with the blond Aideen. / All Aideen herself will own / Is that she will not sleep alone.'

> 'The clear-voiced bell /
> On chill wild night God's
> hours doth tell / Rather
> in it I'll put my trust /
> Than in a woman's
> wanton lust.'
>
> **Monastic poem, translated
> by Robin Flower**

One Irish monk described his surroundings as he copied a Latin manuscript by Priscian sometime in the 800s:

A hedge of trees surrounds me, a blackbird's lay sings to me, praise I shall not conceal,
Above my lined book the trilling of the birds sings to me.
A clear-voiced cuckoo sings to me in a grey cloak from the tops of bushes.
May the Lord save me from Judgment; well do I write under the greenwood.

About the time that poem was written, another scribe also described his life – and that of his pet.

I and Pangur Bán, my cat,
'tis a like task we are at;
hunting mice is his delight,
hunting words I sit all night.

'tis a merry thing to see
    at our tasks how glad are we,
when at home we sit and find
    entertainment to our mind.

'Gainst the wall he sets his eye
    full and fierce and sharp and sly;
'gainst the wall of knowledge I
    all my little wisdom try.

So in peace our task we ply,
    Pangur Bán, my cat, and I;
in our arts we find our bliss,
    I have mine and he has his.

> 'In the course of time some of these devoted themselves faithfully to monastic life, while others preferred to travel round to the cells of various teachers and apply themselves to study.'
>
> **Bede, A History of the English Church and People**

They may have been occasionally distracted, but it is clear that most monks had a love for learning. 'Better far than praise of men it is to sit with book and pen,' one wrote. By copying the major works of both the Christian world and the classical world, and by being the first to write down many of the stories of the pre-Christian Celtic world, the monks made a great contribution to history and to learning in general. However, Thomas Cahill's famous declaration that this was 'how the Irish saved civilization' is more than an overstatement (the Irish certainly were not the only ones with old manuscripts), but the monks' scholarly work remains a tremendous legacy.

There were plenty of contemporary benefits for the monasteries' educational work, too. The communities drew support from the clan *Túaths* that formed the local governments. In exchange for the land, the monastery educated the *Túath* children. According to at least one agreement, one out of each seven boys educated would become a monk. The monastery must have had its reasons for the clause, but in retrospect it seems unnecessary – young Irish men flocked to the monasteries at an amazing rate.

Finding a soul friend

One of the most important parts of monastic community life was the practice of *anamchara* or 'soul friend'. The term literally means 'one who shares my cell', as soul friends were often cell mates. But there is more than friendship in the term; more importantly, it has an element of mentoring and discipleship. The idea was not unique to the Celtic Christians; even Solomon repeatedly stresses the need for spiritual teamwork in Proverbs and Ecclesiastes: 'As iron sharpens iron, so one man sharpens another' (Proverbs 27:17). For Celtic Christians, however, it was more than just a good idea. When a young monk's anamchara died, the famous abbess Brigid (whom we will meet in a moment) told him, 'Anyone without a soul friend is a body without a head. Eat no more until you find a soul friend.'

The position may have been of prime importance, but it still had its challenges. 'The office of a spiritual father is a difficult one since, when he prescribes a true remedy, more often than not it is ignored,' says the rule of the Céli Dé. 'But on the other hand, if the spiritual father does not give advice, the culpability is his alone . . . To point out to them where salvation lies is always better, even if they ignore the confessor's advice.'

If a soul friend slackened in his duties, some monastic communities held him responsible for his disciple's sins. Those duties, recounted in the 9th-century rule of Carthage, include 'chanting intercessions at each canonical hour when the bells are rung', '[daily performing] two hundred genuflections while chanting the *Beati* and the recitation of the three fifties (all 150 psalms)', and 'instruct[ing] the unlearned that they may bend to your will'. One of the most important duties tied back into the penitentials: hearing confession. 'If you are a soul friend to a man, do not barter his soul; do not be as the blind leading the blind; do not leave him in neglect,' the rule of Carthage begins its instructions. 'Let penitents confess to you with candour and integrity.' As with penance, confession was medicinal; it did not necessarily clear away the record of sin so the sinner could get into heaven. 'Frequent confession is useless if the transgressions are also frequent,' says the rule of the Céli Dé.

One saint closely associated with the practice of anamchara is Comgall (c. 517–602), an Irish Pict who founded one of the island's most important monasteries at Bangor around 558. When he lost his soul friend, a bishop named Fiacre who worked in Brittany, Comgall echoed the words of Brigid: 'My soul friend has died and I am headless.' Maintaining mentorship was so important to Comgall that he made it a requirement of his monastery. After clerical training, each monk was required to become a 'father of others' and to lead spiritual families. Ironically, Comgall had initially wanted to be out on his own, a wandering missionary like Patrick. When his bishop told him not to do so, Comgall turned to another path – radical austerity. He took several friends to an island to live a life emulating the harshest of desert monks.

'Put in its simplest form, [the] general theology of Celtic Christians thinks of the divine being and act, or better, the divine presence and power, flowing in and through what can only be described as an extended family.'

James Mackey, *Celtic Spirituality*

For many of Comgall's friends, it was too harsh: seven died of starvation after he ordered them to fast for days on end. This severe lifestyle continued after the founding of Bangor, but that did not stop the Celtic youth from joining him. By the time Comgall died, more than 3,000 monks had him as their spiritual father, among them some of the most renowned Celtic monks in the world.

Not all monks lived so severely. Even among the Céli Dé, who fought against growing laziness in the monasteries, some criticized extensive asceticism. 'A time will come to him before his death when he shall not perform a single genuflection,' one leader grumbled after witnessing a monk's passion for prostration.

Brigid, Ireland's un-ascetic patroness

One of Ireland's most famous saints obviously disagreed with many rules against alcohol. 'I should like to have a great pool of ale for the King of Kings; I should like the heavenly host to be drinking it for all eternity,' prayed Brigid (c. 454–524) according to an 8th-century retelling. 'I should like there to be cheerfulness for their sake; I should like Jesus to be there too.'

According to the legends, Brigid would have had little trouble making a great pool of ale for the King of Kings – in a twist on Jesus' ability to turn water into wine, she was able to turn it into beer. Another legend gives credit to Brigid for *wanting* to be ascetic but claims heaven forbade it. After one night of praying in a freezing pond, she returned the next evening to find it dry. The next morning the water was replenished, but each night as she prepared to mortify herself it was empty again.

Brigid's life is full of miracle, myth and legend – perhaps more so than any other Celtic saint. This may be a result of her story becoming enmeshed with that of another Brigid, a Celtic fertility goddess of fire and song. Indeed, many of her stories are that of fertility. She touches a wooden altar and it becomes 'as green as if the sap still flowed from the roots of a flourishing tree'. She touches a cow and it produces an endless stream of milk. She reinvigorates a wife's sexual attraction for her husband. In another story, she has control over fertility in another way – she prays over a pregnant nun shamed by her predicament and the unborn child miraculously disappears.

The goddess Brigid, daughter of 'the good god' Dagda, was apparently beloved by the pagan Irish. The saint Brigid appears even more popular among Celtic Christians. She is patron to scholars and poets (as well

Brigid and the fox

One day, says Cogitosus's *Life of Brigid,* a man saw a fox walking into the royal palace. A crowd had gathered, but no one did anything to save the king from such a nasty animal, so the man took action and killed it. Unfortunately, 'it was a pet, familiar with the king's hall, which entertained the king and his companions with various tricks that it had learned – both requiring intelligence and nimbleness of body'. The king was furious, and sentenced the man to death, along with his wife and sons.

Then Brigid enters the story. Upon hearing the poor man's plight, she jumped into her chariot to go convince the king to change his mind. Along the way, she prayed that God would help her in her pursuit, and he did. Another fox jumped out from its den on the plain and into Brigid's chariot. At the palace, the king refused to hear her pleas for the man's life, so Brigid introduced the fox. 'It went through all the tricks that the other fox had performed, and amused the crowd in exactly the same way,' Cogitosus says. It worked – the prisoner and his family were set free. But that is not the end of the story. 'The same fox, bothered by the crowds, skilfully contrived a safe escape. It was pursued by large numbers of riders and hounds, but made fools of them, fled through the plains, and went into the waste and wooded places and so to its den.' For some reason, Cogitosus records, these events caused everyone to venerate Brigid.

as milkmaids and many other professions), and her name is now on churches around the world – more than even Patrick. She is the patroness of Ireland, 'dove among birds, vine among trees, sun among stars'. She is 'Mary of the Gael'.

Brigid's beginnings are historically unknowable, but there are many wonderful legends. They say she was the daughter of the noble poet Dubhthach and his Christian concubine Brocseach, but was raised by a druid at least until her baptism. Taken back into her father's home, her gifts of charity – in the Robin Hood sense of the term – were first revealed. 'Whatever her hands would find or would get of her father's wealth and food and property she gave to the poor and needy of the Lord,' says her hagiographer. Her infuriated father attempted to sell Brigid into marriage, but the prospective king he tried to sell her to wanted to know why she had given away her father's sword. 'The Virgin Mary's Son knows, if I had your power, with all your wealth, and with all your land, I would give them all to the Lord of the Elements.' The king preferred his status and wealth to Brigid. 'It is not right for us to deal with this young woman, for her merit before God is higher than ours,' he told Dubhthach. Later, even Brigid's monastery would complain that she was giving away too much of their necessities.

With seven other girls Brigid became a nun, but one story has her as the only female bishop in the church. The *Old Life of Brigid* says that Mel of Ardagh, 'through the grace of the Holy Spirit', accidentally read the wrong prayer at her consecration. He had made her a bishop, not a nun. When the error was pointed out, Mel replied, 'I do not have any power in this matter. That dignity has been given by God to Brigid, beyond every other woman.' She certainly seems to have had considerable power for her time, influencing churches around Ireland and joining conferences with abbots and bishops.

Brigid's monastery also apparently had pagan roots. Kildare means 'Church of the Oak'. It may simply have been named for a nearby tree, but oaks were important to the druids and Brigid may have Christianized a pagan site. She would not have been the only one to do so, but she was unique in Ireland in founding Kildare as a double monastery (that is, one for both men and women). A man named Conlaed oversaw the monks while Brigid oversaw the nuns. The nuns, in turn, watched over a sacred fire that may have been originally maintained by pre-Christian virgins. It was kept alight until the Protestant Reformation shut down all Irish monasteries.

Brigid may have been the only woman in Ireland to found a double monastery, but there were many women saints in the country. Some even combated the anti-female mindset that infused much of Celtic Christianity (with women come sin). Patrick's *Lorica,* for example, invokes protection 'against spells cast by women, smiths, and druids'. Kevin avoided the sound of sheep, knowing that sheep led to shepherdesses, which led to temptation. Cannera found this same attitude when she went to Sénán's monastery at Scattery Island. The abbot would not let her, nor any other woman enter the enclosure. 'Christ is no worse than you,' she rebuked him. 'He came to redeem women no less than to redeem men. He suffered for the sake of women as much as for the sake of men. Women as well as men can enter the heavenly kingdom. Why, then should you not allow women to live on this island?'

'You are persistent,' Sénán replied, and relented.

Monenna was the abbess of Cell-Sléibhe-Cuilinn (now known as Killeevy), one of the most prominent women's monasteries of Ireland. She supposedly took her vows from Patrick himself, but one of her more dramatic tales was an encounter with Kevin, the ascetic monk who avoided women by avoiding sheep. Hearing that Monenna had been praying with a thief and raider, Kevin flew into a fury. He was determined to destroy her monastery. Calmly, the abbess exorcised Kevin's jealousy and even drew a hot bath to calm him.

As the story of Kevin and Monenna shows, the Celtic monks were not always the tranquil, peace-loving clergy some books make them seem. Rivalries between monasteries for power, glory and wealth were common. In fact, this is the main reason there are so many hagiographies. The monasteries were eager to showcase the power of their founding saint. In some cases, the hagiographies contain extensive travels and monasteries founded by the saint, arguing that the successor of whatever saint got there first still commanded authority in that region. In other cases, stories were told to literally assert a monastery was 'holier than thou'. Miracle stories would be told to suggest not-so-subtly that 'my saint can beat up your saint'.

It was not just a matter of bragging rights. Powerful monasteries held more political sway with local kings and even commanded tribute and rent from less powerful ones. The *Tripartite Life of Patrick* claimed that every church member in the town of Airtech owed Patrick's 'chief seat' of Armagh one calf each. 'And that this tribute is not given to them causes the community of Patrick to sigh,' the hagiography adds.

Tírechán also wrote his Patrick hagiography and other works to promote Armagh's superiority over other monasteries. In one passage, Patrick tells a monastery's founder, 'Thy seed will be blessed, and from thy seed will come priests of the Lord and worthy leaders owing alms to me and remaining your heirs.' Apparently that monastery was not paying, either. Tírechán described Óno and his family as 'the kindred of dogshit'.

Attacks were not just verbal. In 836, the monks of Armagh attacked the double monastery at Kildare; the followers of Patrick and of Brigid went to battle.

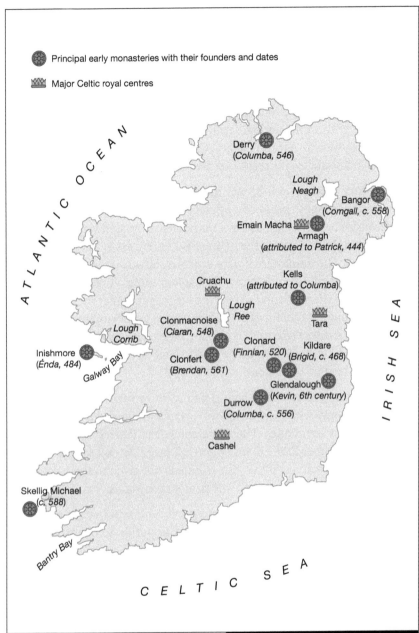

Principal early monasteries with their founders and dates

Major Celtic royal centres

ATLANTIC OCEAN

Derry
(Columba, 546)

Lough Neagh

Bangor
(Comgall, c. 558)

Emain Macha
Armagh
(attributed to Patrick, 444)

Kells
(attributed to Columba)

Cruachu

Lough Ree

Tara

Clonmacnoise
(Ciaran, 548)

Lough Corrib

Clonard
(Finnian, 520)

Kildare
(Brigid, c. 468)

Inishmore
(Énda, 484)

Galway Bay

Clonfert
(Brendan, 561)

Glendalough
(Kevin, 6th century)

Durrow
(Columba, c. 556)

Cashel

Skellig Michael
(c. 588)

Bantry Bay

IRISH SEA

CELTIC SEA

The principal early monasteries of Ireland,
with the names and dates of their founders.

Such behaviour certainly was not condoned by the founding saints. 'If any cleric has committed murder and killed his neighbour, let him do penance for ten years in exile; after these, let him be restored to his native land, if he has performed his penance well on bread and water,' says the *Penitential of Columbanus*. 'But if he does not make satisfaction to [the slain's] relatives, let him never be restored to his native land, but like Cain let him be a wanderer and a fugitive upon the earth.'

Sometimes such wanderings were prescribed for penitence. In other cases (including that of the credited penitential writer himself), leaving one's homeland was done voluntarily.

CHAPTER 14
COLUMBA AND SCOTLAND

'Columba never could spend the space of even one hour without study, or prayer, or writing, or some other holy occupation,' wrote the saint's hagiographer, Adomnán. According to tradition, he loved his studies too much. Studying under Finnian of Moville, Columba came across a beautiful manuscript of the psalms and Gospels, and simply had to have it. So he copied it – without Finnian's permission. When the abbot discovered the duplicate, he was infuriated and demanded that Columba surrender it. The monk refused. Finnian then appealed to Díarmait mac Cerbaill, the high king of Tara and a relative of Columba. But the monk's family ties did him no good. 'To every cow her calf,' the king ruled, 'and to every book its copy.'

About that same time, Díarmait reportedly offended Columba in another way, ordering the execution of one of the monk's young followers – and a prince to boot. Doubly angered, Columba rallied his tribe, the northern Uí Néill, and in the battle of Cúl Dreimne slaughtered 3,000 of Díarmait's men. Recent historians attribute the battle to a dispute over who would succeed Díarmait as king of Tara and say Columba had nothing to do with it. Still, for centuries the 'Cathach' book of Columba would be one of the Celtic world's most famous (and allegedly powerful) relics. More than half of the manuscript is missing, and when in 1813 it was removed from its wooden box, which was enclosed in a silver case, its 58 nine-by-six-inch leaves were stuck together. Still, careful analysis of the psalter suggests that it might actually be from the hand of Columba. Its name, meaning 'battler', comes not from the battle of Cúl Dreimne but from later medieval battles where chiefs paraded it around their army three times to ensure victory.

For Columba, tradition says, victory was short. His soul friend, Molaise of Devenish, assigned him the common penance for causing such carnage – exile. Specifically, Molaise prescribed, Columba should leave Ireland to convert as many souls as had been slain at Cúl Dreimne. A large task indeed, but Columba's legacy would be even bigger.

Royal fox, holy dove

Columba was born for greatness – but all signs indicated that it would be political, not spiritual. He was born on 5 December 521 to Fedilmidh, the great-grandson of one of the most famous Irish political heroes (and one of the earliest undisputed Irish historical figures), Niall Noígiallch, or Niall of the Nine Hostages. His namesake clan, the Uí Néill, invaded Ulster and created a dynasty. Columba may even have been a contender for the throne at Tara. His mother, Ethne, was also reportedly from a powerful family, descending from Leinster king Cathoair Mór. That Columba grew up in the monasteries was simply a matter of course. As noted earlier, many monasteries were given land in exchange for the education of the royal youth. Like Columba, many of these young men never left the life of the church. Columba was reportedly even more eager than many of these, however. His childhood friends waited for him to finish his psalm-reading so often that it was they who nicknamed him 'Colum Cille', meaning 'dove of the church'. (There is some dispute over whether his given name was Colum, meaning 'dove', or Crimthann, meaning 'fox'. In any case, hagiographers and biographers alike have enjoyed using these zoological appellations as a way of characterizing him – crafty and peaceful, sly and holy.)

'The personality of Columcille, which gleams through all his works and all the tales we know of him, convinces us that he is Patrick's spiritual son and worthy successor.'

Thomas Cahill, *How the Irish Saved Civilization*

Growing up, Columba followed several different monastic leaders, including a priest named Cruithnecin, Finnian of Moville (who had studied at Candida Casa), and Finnian of Clonard. He also studied under a Christian bard named Gemmán, whose vocation Columba would later defend to the Irish church. When the monk reached his mid-thirties, Finnian of Clonard pushed to make him a bishop, but Columba's story became the opposite of that of bishopess Brigid. In another ordination mistake, Columba was consecrated as a mere priest. Like the mistake at Brigid's consecration, the error was seen as divine providence. Columba said he would never accept higher rank.

After returning for a time to Clonard, Columba joined Comgall (later of Bangor) in helping another monk, Mobhi, start a monastery at Glasnevin. Unfortunately, an outbreak of the plague crushed the monks' plans and the site was abandoned. Columba then founded his own monastery, at Derry. After that he founded more. One hagiography says he founded a total of 300 before his death. An 1857 study counted more than 40 in Ireland and another 57 in Scotland. But only two sites meet today's strict tests for attribution – Durrow and Kells. The latter is the site of that great illustrated manuscript of the Gospels, the *Book of Kells*, said to be the work 'not of men, but of angels'. Adomnán says Columba himself was similarly angelic:

> 'He was learning's pillar in every stronghold, he was foremost at the book of complex Law. The northern land shone, the western people blazed, he lit up the east with chaste clerics.'
>
> **Memorial after Columba's death**

Devoted from childhood to the Christian novitiate and the study of philosophy, preserving by God's favour integrity of body and purity of soul, he showed himself, though placed on earth, ready for life in heaven; for he was angelic in aspect, refined in speech, holy in work, excellent in ability, great in council.

The founding of Iona

No doubt Columba might have been one of the greatest monastic leaders Ireland has ever known – but it is Scotland he is most associated with. Admonán leaves out the story of the Cathach copyright tiff and any suggestion that Columba's sojourn across the Irish Sea might be a form of penance. But he does mention the battle. 'In the second year following the battle of Cúl Dreimne, when he was 41, Columba sailed away to Britain, choosing to be a pilgrim for Christ.'

'Delightful I think it to be in the bosom of an isle on the crest of a rock, that I may see often the calm of the sea,' Columba wrote. 'That I may see its heavy waves over the glittering ocean as they chant a melody to their Father on their eternal course.' He found that island half a mile west of yet another island, the Island of Mull in the Inner Hebridean islands off Scotland's west coast.

Iona (also called Í, or Hii) is only 3 miles long by a mile and a half wide. Of its 2,000 acres, only 500 are arable. But even before Columba arrived, it had apparently been considered sacred Christian ground. The kings of the Gaelic Dál Riada kingdom were buried here in ground either consecrated by or dedicated to St Oran (d. 549). Columba's hagiography even includes a story of the saint encountering two bishops shortly after landing on the island. 'But God revealed to Columba that they really were not bishops,' the story says. 'They left the island when he told them of their duplicity.' Today Iona is still considered sacred ground, one of the top pilgrimage sites in all Britain. It is not easy to get to, and seems nearly as remote as holy Skellig Michael off the coast of Ireland. Still, when Columba and his 12 disciples landed on Iona's pebbled beach on 12 May 563, they probably did not see it as the isolated centre of 'white martyrdom'. Instead, it was a centre of trade and travel. Sea lanes brought goods from France, the Mediterranean and beyond. The island stood at the northern end of the Dál Riada kingdom, ruled by Columba's cousin, Conall mac Comgaill. It was therefore almost a perfect place for launching an evangelistic mission to convert the Picts, whose territory lay beyond Conall's. (The island may actually have been disputed territory between the Dál Riada and the Picts; the English historian Bede claims it was the Pictish king Brude, not Conall, who gave the island to Columba.) Ireland, only 80 miles away, could provide steady support – and monks – for the monastery. In fact, the Dál Riada had only moved its capital to Scotland from Ireland a generation before Columba's arrival.

Nearby islands would be brought under Iona's watch, serving special monastic purposes. On Tiree, laity served penance. Another island housed old monks living out their lives as green martyrs and anchorites. Iona became the centre for educating and training priests, bishops and scholars. Columba's hut was slightly larger than those of his disciples (which included his uncle Ernan and the son of a king) and placed on top of a slight hill. Iona may have been a hub of activity, but Columba's quarters were still austere. 'For straw mattress', Adomnán wrote, Columba used 'a bare rock, and for pillow a stone'. Historian John T. McNeill counts the other buildings that soon followed: 'a refectory with a kitchen; a scriptorium with a library; a guesthouse for the use of the surprisingly numerous visitors from near and far; a smithy, a kiln, a mill, and two barns; and a small church, later enlarged and strengthened with oak beams brought by sea'.

> 'His monks, the laity, even the animals felt his attraction. He could terrify, he could comfort, he could delight.'
>
> **Kathleen Hughes, The Church in Early Irish Society**

Soon even these buildings were pushed to their limits as recruits came from Scotland, Ireland and Britain. Even Saxons, whose kin were invading Britain from the south, sought peaceful entry into the monastic life at Iona. But the monks of Iona were not just recluses; they were also missionaries. Both the Scots of the Dál Riada and the northern Picts were Columba's evangelistic mission. Exactly how much of the country Columba worked in is some matter of scholarly disagreement, and the historical record is unclear. Unlike many hagiographers, Adomnán did not write his stories to establish his patron's dominion over numerous territories. By his time, Iona was already powerful enough that he did not have to. Instead, Adomnán's task was to keep things that way. Thus he avoided some topics that would have divided his readership, such as Columba's role in the Easter debate (which we shall encounter later). Adomnán's objectives also mean that we do not have long accounts of Columba's travels, though there are a few of these, noting monastic foundations were laid on the islands of Hinba, Tiree and Skye. One of the most important of the saint's trips was to the Pictish king Brude in 564. Adomnán provides no narrative of this meeting, only a series of miracle stories. They begin at the very entrance to Brude's Inverness fortress, where the king, 'elated by the pride of royalty, acted haughtily' and closed the gates. Columba simply made the sign of the cross, then knocked and laid his hand on the gate. It 'instantly flew open of its own accord, the bolts having been driven back with great force', Adomnán says, and Brude and his men forever 'held this holy and reverend man in very great honour, as was due'. They may have continued to give him honour, but according to Adomnán, Columba kept working miracles in front of the king, such as floating a white stone 'like an apple when placed in water'. When some druids tried to stop the monks from singing praises to God, Columba began singing Psalm 44. 'So wonderfully loud, like pealing thunder, did his voice become, that king and people were struck with terror and amazement,' the hagiographer wrote. Unfortunately, Adomnán left no stories about any conversations between the chief and the monk, though Bede suggests the king converted to Christianity.

> 'By virtue of his prayer, and in the name of our Lord Jesus Christ, he healed several persons suffering under various diseases; and . . . expelled from this our island . . . innumerable hosts of malignant spirits, whom he saw with his bodily eyes assailing himself, and beginning to bring deadly distempers on his monastic brotherhood.'
>
> **Adomnán, Life of Columba**

The Loch Ness monster

On this same journey, Columba's sign of the cross became handy in another dangerous encounter – the first recorded sighting of a Loch Ness monster. Columba and his men were attempting to cross the Ness when they encountered a burial party. A local man had been swimming in the waters, the mourners explained, when the monster had savaged him. It was no matter to Columba. He turned to one of his monks, Lugne Mocumin, and told him to swim across the river to fetch a boat from the opposite bank. Lugne disrobed down to his tunic in an instant and jumped in obediently. 'But the monster, which, so far from being satiated, was only roused for more prey, was lying at the bottom of the stream,' Adomnán wrote. 'When it felt the water disturbed above by the man swimming, it suddenly rushed out, and, giving an awful roar, darted after him, with its mouth wide open, as the man swam in the middle of the stream.' The monks and the burial party were terrified, but not Columba. He simply made the sign of the cross again and told the monster, 'Thou shalt go no further, nor touch the man; go back with all speed.' The monster obeyed, fleeing 'more quickly than if it had been pulled back with ropes'. Adomnán then adds the requisite coda about the pagans in the burial party converting to Christianity after witnessing such a miracle.

Modern Nessie fanatics are divided on the story, suggesting that it was not the 'real' Loch Ness monster after all – it is far too violent, and was seen in the wrong part of the lake. But an Italian geologist offers a different opinion, suggesting that something like the incident may have occurred after all, but that the monks only saw waves caused by an earthquake. 'The most seismically active end of the loch is the north end' where Columba had his encounter, Luigi Piccardi told *The Irish Times*. 'In these reports people don't usually describe the beast itself. More often they talk of seeing a lot of commotion in the water, and hearing loud noises, and they assume it to be caused by the monster.'

Integration of church and state

Columba converted the Picts 'to the Faith of Christ by his preaching and example', Bede records. But he maintained his work among the Dál Riada as well. Here, too, the princely monk ministered among kings.

When Conall mac Comgaill died in 574, Columba was on a spiritual retreat on the island of Hinba. Adomnán records that an angel came to him, carrying 'a book of glass, regarding the appointment of kings'. The monk, however, was unwilling to read much of it – he preferred that Gabran ascend to the throne rather than Gabran's brother Aidan, as written in the book. After a beating by the angel, the monk relented and consecrated Aidan at Iona in one of the earliest such ceremonies in British history.

One year after Aidan took the Dál Riada throne, Columba came to his political support again. This time, however, he had to return to Ireland to do it. The trip, which reportedly came near the end of Columba's life, probably was not his only trip back to his homeland, but it was apparently the most important. (A later hagiography, attempting to reconcile Columba's exile and return, records that he always wore a hooded cloak so that he could not see the Irish sky, and always stood on a strip of imported sod from Iona.) One of the main agenda points at the Convention of Druim Cett, or 'conference of kings', was whether the Dál Riada should have to pay tribute to the king of Tara or even become more subservient to the Irish kingdoms. Columba apparently argued persuasively for the independence of Aidan and the kingdom both in Ireland and Scotland. A second agenda item proposed getting rid of the ancient bards. Between their mockery of the powerful, their high fees, and the Christianizing of Ireland, the kings believed it was time to be done with the profession. The saint, who once called Jesus his 'holy druid', saw little harm in the poets' works. On the contrary, he argued, the bards were an important part of Irish society. Yes, sometimes they went too far – and for that they should face discipline and should be forced to be educated at the monasteries – but abolishing their vocation was too harsh an answer. When the kings took the saint's advice, 1,200 bards reportedly burst into the council to sing Columba's praises. Embarrassed, he hid himself inside his cowl.

At the age of 77, back in Iona, an angel again came to Columba and told him he was soon to die. The saint began preparing, making sure that

'Scion of the most powerful family in the north of Ireland, founder of monasteries, and instigator of missions to the Picts and the English, Columba is undoubtedly the most important saint associated with Celtic churches.'

Thomas Owen Clancy, 'Ionas Tough Dove', *Christian History*

there was enough grain stored for the coming year. On his way to return to the monastery, he came across the packhorse that used to carry the monks' milk pails. Instinctively knowing that his master was about to die, the horse laid its head on Columba's breast. Adomnán writes that the horse 'began to neigh plaintively, and, like a human being, to shed copious tears on the saint's chest'. Columba's assistant, Diarmuid, tried to shoo the horse away, but Columba rebuked him and blessed the horse.

Returning to his cell that Saturday, 8 June 597, Columba turned one final time to his lifelong task of copying texts. He ended his psalter at Psalm 34, verse 10: 'The lions may grow weak and hungry, but those who seek the Lord lack no good thing.' 'At the end of the page I must stop. Let Baithene write what follows,' he said. He attended the evening service, then returned to his flagstone bed. There he gave his final instructions to Diarmuid and the other monks:

Be at peace, and have genuine charity among yourselves. If you thus follow the example of the holy fathers, God, the comforter of the good, will be your helper and I, abiding with him, will intercede for you. He will not only give you sufficient to supply the wants of this present life, but will also bestow on you the good and eternal rewards which are laid up for those that keep his commandments.

'There is a grey eye / That will look back upon Erin [Ireland]; / Never again will it see / The men of Erin or women.'

Attributed to Columba

When the bell rang for the midnight hours, Columba raced from his bed ahead of the monks and prostrated himself in front of the altar. As the monks came in with their lights, Columba raised his hand and blessed them with his final breath.

Iona after Columba

For more than a century, Iona remained one of the most influential sites in Celtic Christianity. Monasteries and churches from Britain and Ireland both looked to the small island for leadership, and Columba was as highly honoured as Patrick and Brigid. When controversies rose, the leaders of Iona were key in the consultations. The island also continued to send out missionaries, into Northumbria, Wessex, and even the continent. Still, the historical record remains sketchy about how much the conversion of Scotland (called Alba by the Celts and Caledonia by the Romans) can be attributed to Iona and how much belongs to other monastic settlements, including Candida Casa. Most likely missionaries came from both the west and the south – and they sometimes even worked together.

One of the best-known evangelists who left from Iona was an Irish monk named Aidan. But he began as a substitute. King Oswald of Northumbria had originally sent a request to the holy island for a teacher, and Corman, 'another man of more austere disposition,' was the first volunteer. Bede says he was a failure:

Meeting with no success in his preaching to the English, who refused to listen to him, he returned home and reported to his superiors that he had been unable to teach anything to the nation to whom they had sent him because they were an uncivilized people of an obstinate and barbarous temperament.

As his superiors tried to decide the next step, Aidan challenged his fellow monk. 'It seems to me that you were too severe on your ignorant hearers,' he said. 'You should have followed the practice of the apostles, and begun by giving them the milk of simpler teaching, and gradually instructed them in the Word of God until they were capable of greater perfection and able to follow the sublime precepts of Christ.' The elders then suggested that Aidan try where Corman had failed. He did, and the English welcomed him with open arms. Rather than take up residence in the capital city of Bamburgh, Aidan made his base on another island, Lindisfarne. It became another spiritual metropolis of learning and artistry. One of its most famous creations, the illuminated Lindisfarne Gospels, is now in the British Library as one of the world's great artistic treasures. Aidan, meanwhile, became known by Bede and others as 'the true apostle of England'.

According to Adomnán, Columba foresaw all of the glories of Iona and its monks. 'This place, however small and mean, will have bestowed upon it no small but great honour by the kings and peoples of Ireland, and also by the rulers of even barbarous and foreign nations with their subject tribes,' he said near the end of his life. 'And the saints of other churches too will give it great reverence.'

But Adomnán had his own reasons for pushing Iona's continued glory – he himself was Columba's eighth successor as abbot of Iona. Though he is most famous as Columba's hagiographer, Adomnán (624–704) was a significant leader in his own right. He actually shared more of Columba's characteristics than simply his ecclesiastical position – he was actually an Irish blood relative of the earlier saint. And like Columba, Adomnán was a diplomat, engaged in political and ecclesiastic controversies of his day. Like Columba (and Patrick before him) he too worked hard to free hostages. He was a poet, too. But in his scholarship he may have even surpassed his predecessor.

Adomnán also wrote some very important laws. These include regulations on marriage (a man cannot remarry if his wife becomes a prostitute) and theft (Christians cannot accept stolen cattle as gifts or trade), and several outline dietary and health regulations. 'Sea animals found dead on the shore, and where we do not know how they died, can be eaten in good faith; but may not be eaten if they are putrid,' commands one. Another orders, 'A well in which a carcass (whether human, dog, or other animal) is found is to be emptied, all the mud is to be taken out, and then the well will be found clean.' Several of these rules seem like common sense to modern readers, or may remind historians of Old Testament regulations. But people in Adomnán's day knew little about the spread of disease and germs. These rules kept them safe and alive.

The most famous of Adomnán's edicts was 'The Law of the Innocents'. 'These are the four laws of Ireland,' a document from around the 800s says, 'Patrick's law, not to kill the clergy; and Adomnán's law, not to kill women; Dáire's law, not to kill cattle; and the law of Sunday, not to transgress thereon.' But Adomnán's law was much more than just a prohibition on the killing of women. Enacted in 697 at the Synod of Birr, the law begins with a lengthy introduction about the plight of women and why such a law was needed. Then it describes how an angel came to Adomnán one Pentecost eve and hit him in the side with a staff. 'Go forth into Ireland, and make a law in it that women be not in any manner killed by men, through slaughter or any other death, either by poison, or in water, or in fire, or by any beast, or in a pit, or by dogs, but that they shall die in their lawful bed,' the angel said. The law metes out strict retributions for the slaying of women, including the amputation of the

The Holy Places

Adomnán did not just copy important theological books; he wrote them. One of them, *The Holy Places* (*De Locis Sanctis*) was one of the most important books of his day, and circulated even more than his *Life of Columba,* which was written more for the community at Iona and those interested in it. He supposedly wrote the book after meeting a Gallic bishop named Arculf, who had been shipwrecked on his way back from a pilgrimage to Jerusalem and made his way to Iona. Historian Thomas O'Loughlin argues, however, that the Arculf story only provides a backbone for Adomnán's extensive research into the geography of the Holy Land, which drew from early church writings and other sources. 'The text shows Adomnán as a most competent and searching scriptural scholar, keenly attuned to textual problems and ingenious in his solutions,' O'Loughlin writes. Bede thought so too, calling the abbot 'a wise man, admirably learned in the scriptures'. The English historian even condensed the work for his own *Holy Places* book.

Like Patrick, Adomnán approached his work with a heavy dose of holy humility. 'I have written down these things in what I admit is a poor style,' he writes at the end of *The Holy Places.* 'But I have done so in the face of daily labour coming at me from all sides. The amount of ecclesiastical concerns seems overwhelming. So I wish that you who read these places not neglect to pray for me, the sinner who wrote this, to Christ the judge of the ages.'

left foot and right hand of the killer and the payment of 21 cows from his family (*Cáin Adomnáin* is literally translated 'tax of Adomnán'). The law also protects other non-combatants, such as children and clerics, and includes non-fatal injuries as well: 'If it is a blow with the palm of the hand or with the fist, an ounce of silver [is the fine] for it. If there be a green or red mark, or a swelling, an ounce and six scruples for it.' Rape is of course included in the Law, but also 'seizing women by the hair'. It also guarantees that no 'eye for an eye' justice prevails. 'There shall be no cross-case or balancing of guilt in Adomnán's Law,' it says. 'But each one pays for his crimes for his own hand.'

Adomnán's 'Law of the Innocents' is a landmark in legal history and in the history of human rights. It also demonstrates that by his time, monks were far more than reclusive green martyrs. They often removed themselves for periods of holy solitude, but they were not permanently removed from society. On the contrary, they *were* society. Other monks, however, still desired 'to leave all for the sake of Christ'. These white martyrs, however, would also often find themselves back in public – and thus taking the holy attitudes of their homeland around the known world.

CHAPTER 15

OUT OF, AND BACK INTO, THE WORLD

'Go from your country and your kindred and your father's house to the land that I will show you,' God told Abraham (Genesis 12:1). For many Celtic Christians, it was more than just a historical urging for the father of the Jews; it was a divine command still to be followed. They left their countries and kindred to enter unknown worlds. Some left in search of greater isolation than could be found on their own island. Others left on evangelistic missions, hoping to bring the light of the gospel to people who had not heard it – or who had forgotten it. Still others, like Brendan of Clonfert, followed Abraham's lead and went looking for a literal 'Promised Land'.

Brendan had heard stories of 'the Promised Land of the Saints, where neither night falls nor day ends'. One visitor to his monastery, a grandson of King Niall named Barinthus, had reportedly even been there. 'We saw only flowering plants and trees that bore fruit,' the visitor had recalled, 'and even the stones were precious.'

Brendan wanted to see the island for himself, but would not without God's blessing. Soon enough it came. 'Arise, O Brendan,' an angel told him. 'For God has given you what you sought, the Land of Promise.' Brendan went to a nearby mountain for fasting and spiritual preparation, and the angel appeared again. 'I will . . . teach you how to find the beautiful island of which you have had a vision, and which you desire to attain,' he said. Then, says the 10th-century (or so) *Voyage of Brendan*, the saint

. . . and those with him got iron tools and constructed a light boat ribbed with wood and with a wooden frame, as is usual in those parts. They covered it with ox-hides tanned with the bark of oak and smeared all the joints of the hides on the outside with fat . . . The also placed a mast in the middle of the boat and a sail and the other requirements for steering a boat.

But after 15 days, the wind died and Brendan and his men rowed to exhaustion. Brendan told his men to rest. 'God is our helper,' he

Hell unbound

The sea creature Jasconius was not even the most surprising encounter for Brendan and his crew. One Sunday, the sailors also came upon 'a man, shaggy and unsightly, sitting on a rock'. The waves pounded him mercilessly, but this did not upset the man. For him, it was a beautiful but temporary respite from the fires of hell. 'I am unhappy Judas, the most evil traitor ever,' he explained. 'I am not here in accordance with my deserts but because of the ineffable mercy of Jesus Christ.' Brendan even worked to slightly prolong Judas's relief, keeping at bay the demons who had come to drag the betrayer back to hell. Other characters encountered include a disciple of Patrick, who received a visit from the apostle of Ireland – the day after his death – explaining where to bury his body. Even black-faced leprechauns menaced the crew.

explained. 'He is our navigator and helmsman, and he shall guide us. Pull in the oars and the rudder. Spread the sail and let God do as he wishes with his servants and their boat.' It worked. Every now and then a mysterious wind would blow and change their heading. Likewise, when food ran short, the wind regularly took them to an island. There were several of these, including the Island of Sheep (where the animals grew larger than cows), the Paradise of Birds, and one island that was not quite an island. 'The island was rocky and bare,' the *Voyage* says. 'There were only occasional trees to be seen, and there was no sand on the shoreline at all.' While the rest of the crew went ashore to prepare for Easter Sunday, a discerning Brendan stayed in the boat. After the Easter Mass, the monks had only started to build a cooking fire when 'the island started to heave like a wave'. The monks ran back into the boat and they quickly put 2 miles between themselves and the island. As they turned to look at the still-burning fire – and many of their items left ashore – Brendan explained what he had seen earlier in a vision: 'The island that we were on was nothing other than a sea animal, the foremost of all that swim in the oceans . . . Jasconius is its name.' And for the next several years, Jasconius allowed the monks to return to its back to celebrate Easter.

After five years on the sea without sighting the Land of Promise, Brendan and his men returned to Ireland. A 40-day fast later, they were off again. After another 40 days of sailing, the men finally landed where all the trees bore fruit and night never fell. A young man ran up and greeted them. 'This is the land which you have sought for so long,' he told them. 'You were not able to find it immediately because God wished to show you his many wonders in the great ocean. Return now to the land of your birth, taking with you fruit from this land and as many gems as your boat can carry . . . After the passage of many years, this land will be revealed to your successors when Christians will be suffering persecution.' They did as they were told, returning to the Irish monastery.

> 'St Brendan . . . was a very ascetical man, famed for his miracles and spiritual father to almost three thousand monks.'
>
> **The Voyage of St Brendan**

The rest of Brendan's life story largely consists of the founding of Irish monasteries. One of them, at Clonfert, survived until the Protestant Reformation. There are still more fantastic tales in his hagiography, like his driving a plague of fleas from a town (not quite as fantastic as driving the snakes from Ireland, but miraculous enough to his hagiographer). His life story also includes encounters with almost all of the great Celtic saints. He was a close friend of Comgall of Bangor, with whom he visited Columba at Iona. Íte supposedly advised him on boat-building between his first and second Atlantic voyages. He sought out Brigid after hearing a sea monster invoke her name in a battle with another monster. On a visit to Wales, he stayed with Gildas. He was even reportedly baptized by Erc, one of Patrick's earliest converts. Then there are his encounters with the lesser known saints, including Énda and the 'Twelve Apostles of Ireland' (of which he was one).

Such associations may have done more to enhance the reputations of the other saints than Brendan's. The *Voyage of Brendan* was one of the most popular books of the Middle Ages, translated from Latin into half a dozen or more languages. Whether it was read then as a complex theological allegory, questionable hagiography, or a realistic account of historical events is unknown, but by the end of the 20th century debate was fierce over the story's credibility. Some scholars in the 1960s argued that the islands of sheep and birds were in fact the Faroes; that the Island of Smiths (where 'the sea began to boil as if a volcano were erupting there, with smoke rising from the sea as if from a flaming surface') was volcanic Iceland; that the clear-watered region of fish and whales was near Greenland, and associated other areas with North America. (The arguments themselves were old enough – in 1580, influential mathematician and occultist John Dee made Brendan's voyage a key part of his claim that Britain laid claim to the New World.) The Island of Grapes, one scholar asserted, could have been Jamaica; another postulated that Brendan's episode of the ocean calming 'like a thick curdled mass' must have taken place at the seaweed-heavy Sargasso Sea east of the Bahamas (there are those who say the ancient Phoenicians made it to the Sargasso Sea as well). In 1976, after incredulous historians had reminded Brendan enthusiasts that the story was allegorical – not to mention impossible – British explorer Tim Severin created his own boat just as Brendan's was described. Sailing past the Faroes, Iceland and Greenland – and even encountering friendly whales along the way – Severin's boat was punctured by floating ice. After repairs, he continued on to Newfoundland, suggesting that Brendan *could* have made it to North America in the mid-500s even if he did not. (Of course, returning to Ireland against wind and currents would have been another matter.)

Squeezed out

Whether or not travelling Irish monks made it to America, it is certain they made it at least as far as Iceland in their white martyrdom searches for isolated monasteries. The Norse *Islendingabok* by Ari the Learned says that when the first Norwegian explorers arrived on the island in 874, they found that the monks had been there for about 80 years:

The Christians, whom the Norsemen called Papar, were here. But afterwards they went away because they did not wish to live here together with heathen men, and they left behind Irish books, bells, and crooks. From this it could be seen that they were Irish.

Several centuries earlier, the ethnic relatives of those Irish monks had been forced out of their homes by the distant relatives of the Norsemen – Angles and Saxons from Denmark. By the middle of the 400s, homeless British refugees were swarming Brittany, originally called Armorica by both Celts and Romans (from the Celtic words *ar*, 'on', and *môr*, 'the sea'). Soon there were so many Britons living there they began to call it Britannia Minor (or, by those who lived there, simply Britannia). The

The first Irish-Americans?

Stone carvings in West Virginia appear to be Old Irish writings using the old Ogham alphabet. Christian symbols, such as the chi-rho, are also inscribed. 'It seems possible that the scribes that cut the West Virginia inscriptions may have been Irish missionaries in the wake of Brendan's voyage, for these inscriptions are Christian,' argued the late linguist Barry Fell. 'Early Christian symbols of piety . . . appear at the sites together with the Ogham texts.' Other historians and archaeologists are not as credulous, although at least one respected archaeologist, the University of Calgary's David Kelley, defended Fell's findings. 'I have no personal doubts that some of the inscriptions which have been reported are genuine Celtic Ogham,' he wrote in *Review of Archaeology.*

land was sparsely populated enough that there are no accounts of violence between the Britons and the area's original inhabitants, but there are also no reliable stories of how Christianity first came to the area. We think we know, however, how Celtic Christianity grew in the area. As it was back in Britain and Ireland, monks probably came to the area seeking holy seclusion, but they attracted disciples and laity who needed the services a monastery could provide. Clergy probably led some groups of immigrants from Britain, and other monks probably left their homeland expressly to minister to the displaced throngs. We have already met, for example, Illtud and Samson of Dol, both associated with Brittany monasteries.

> '*A spirit of restless energy possessed them. It was given many names, but its cause must surely be sought in the peculiarly Irish development of Christianity in the early centuries: a seeking curiosity, the desire to expand mental boundaries along with physical, to find new ideas in new settings.*'
> **Katherine Scherman, *The Flowering of Ireland***

One of the earliest remembered monks is an Irishman named Ronán. The son of two of Patrick's converts, he went south around the year 500 and is still actively remembered today, especially at Locronan's *La grande Troménie,* a pilgrim processional remembering one of the saint's most memorable stories. A farmer near Ronán's hermitage lost a sheep to a hungry wolf, who returned it unharmed at the monk's demand. The awed farmer converted to Christianity, but his wife, Keben, sensed evil. Ronán was able to command the wolf, she argued, because he was a werewolf! She set about to prove her point, but was repeatedly rebuffed. When she hid her child in a chest and accused Ronán of eating it, the child died. The saint brought it back to life. Not too long afterwards, Ronán himself died – but his battle with Keben was not over. As four white oxen, carried his body to hermitage without a driver, Keben attacked them, even breaking off one of their horns. God apparently decided Ronán had suffered enough at the woman's hands; the ground opened and swallowed her up. Today's pilgrims now pass the site of the earthquake, 'Keben's Cross', as *La grande Troménie* recreates the oxen's wandering path.

Historian John T. McNeill argues that 'in Celtic Brittany the church never bore great marks of distinction in learning, art, and heroic devotion such as we find in the church of Ireland and Britain'. It does, however, have another distinction. 'The rise of the Breton church', he says, 'was marked by the greatest individualism.' Past scholars of Celtic Christianity have noted that Celtic abbots in some ways took precedence over bishops. This has been overemphasized; bishops still held the power, but abbots usually set the agenda. In Brittany, however, the monastic priest often had neither abbot nor bishop watching over him. The archbishop of Tours occasionally made efforts to bring the churches and monasteries under uniform control, but he was repeatedly rebuffed. Other Frankish church leaders were later agitated by some differences in Celtic and continental practices. Again, the Celtic Christians seem to have disregarded many of these. It was apparently not out of obstinacy, but out of pragmatism. They simply believed that their practices were the way things were done.

> '[For] the Irish people . . . the custom of travelling to foreign lands has now become almost second nature.'
>
> **Walahfrid Strabo, The Life of St Gall**

Columbanus, missionary to Europe

One monk who had several run-ins with the Frankish ecclesiastic rulers is also the monk who most exemplifies the self-exiling peregrini. His name was Columba, which has for centuries frustrated scholars and writers eager to distinguish this 'dove' from the founder of Iona. Some have designated him Columba the Younger, as he was born around 543, about two decades after Iona's Colum Cille (c. 521–97). Others have adopted the Irish name Columbán. The Latin convention of referring to this missionary exile as Columbanus seems most popular.

The peregrini were not mere pilgrims or wanderers. They did not leave their home 'to find themselves' or in search of some mystical place or spiritual relic. Nor were they tourists; when peregrini left home, return would be an unthinkable embarrassment. They were instead missionary monks, driven by both the evangelistic zeal of Patrick and the love of cloistered study. Perhaps no one vocalized their goal as well as Columbanus, who said he sought 'the salvation of many, and a solitary spot of my own'.

Columbanus's first hagiographer, Jonas, wrote a mere 28 years after his subject's death in 613, almost instantaneous when compared to other hagiographies. And before that, Jonas had spent years interviewing Columbanus's many companions. So he was probably not exaggerating much, if at all, when he wrote that Columbanus's 'fine figure, his splendid colour, and his noble manliness made him beloved by all'. And in such beauty lay the problem: 'He aroused . . . the lust of lascivious maidens, especially of those whose fine figure and superficial beauty are wont to enkindle mad desires in the minds of wretched men.' As a young man, he feared he was on the brink of giving in to such vain 'lusts of the world', so he sought the guidance of a local female hermit. 'Away, O youth, away!' she advised. 'Flee from corruption, into which, as you know, many have fallen.' Columbanus left, shaken, to pack his things in preparation for a monastic life. When he told his mother he was leaving, she became so distraught she blocked the doorway. But Columbanus was undeterred, 'leaping over both threshold and mother'.

The exile did not immediately leave the island, but in travelling from Leinster in eastern Ireland to the monastery of Gleenish, in north-western County Fermanagh, home must have seemed far off. He studied under an abbot named Sinell and wrote a commentary on the psalms, but before long continued on to Bangor to study under Sinell's master, Comgall. For almost 25 years, Columbanus studied, prayed, fasted and lived the life of most Irish monks. There is no evidence

'As Saint [Columbanus] pointed out, life itself was a roadway that led to eternity. As long as monks perceived the world beyond the [monastic] enclosure as hostile to survival, they dreamed about taking that roadway through the desert.'

Lisa Bitel, *Isle of the Saints*

that Columbanus was unhappy at Bangor, but by his mid-forties he began to feel that Ireland's north-eastern tip was not a distant enough exile. At first reluctant, Comgall allowed the exile and 12 companions (it was common for monks to deliberately emulate Jesus and his followers in such a manner) to exile themselves to Frankish Gaul.

They founded three monasteries in rapid succession – Annegray, Luxeuil and Fontaine – each one growing so quickly new ones had to be created. 'Modesty and moderation, meekness and mildness adorned them all in equal measure,' wrote Jonas. 'The evils of sloth and dissention were banished. Pride and haughtiness were expiated by severe punishments. Scorn and envy were driven out by faithful diligence. So great was the might of their patience, love and mildness that no one could doubt that the God of mercy dwelt among them.'

Such exemplary living attracted many of the new monks. And, Jonas says, others 'began to crowd about in order that they might recover their health and in order to seek aid in all their infirmities'. But Columbanus's monasteries also probably attracted potential Frankish monks because Irish monastic life, for all its severities, offered opportunities continental monasticism did not. As historian Richard Fletcher notes, 'its emphasis on the supervisory role of the abbot (perhaps a kinsman) of a monastic network – rather than, as previously, the local bishop – was reassuring to families who might be apprehensive, sometimes with justice, of the covetous designs of the nearby bishop of its endowments'.

Indeed, Columbanus had significant run-ins with the local bishops. To them, the Irishman was a schismatic with disregard for church supervision and potentially unorthodox beliefs (these focused especially over the celebration of Easter). To Columbanus, the bishops seemed arrogant and vain. Jonas probably echoes his subject's opinion when he blames 'the carelessness of the bishops' when he notes 'the Christian faith had almost departed from that country'. In 603 the bishops convened a synod at Chalon-sur-Saône to examine Columbanus. Whether he felt the synod was unimportant or whether he feared his often-hot temper would get the better of him in direct confrontation, he did not attend. Instead, he sent a letter that, while superficially friendly, contains some severe underlying criticism: 'I give thanks to my God that for my sake so many holy men have gathered together to treat the truth of faith and good works, and as, befits such, to judge of the matters under dispute with a just judgment, through senses sharpened to the discernment of good and evil,' he begins. Then the jab: 'Would that you did so more often!'

He repeatedly calls for them to be humble, and dismisses their complaints of theological malpractice. 'I am not the author of this difference,' he writes, 'and it is for the sake of Christ the Saviour . . . that I have entered these lands as a pilgrim.' He concludes by asking to continue his life as a stranger among them, and suggests that they love and pray for each other.

Columbanus's apparent disregard for the hierarchical conventions of continental Christianity did not simply apply to the local bishops. It was one thing to begin his letter to them, 'To the holy lords and fathers – or better, brothers – in Christ.' It was quite another to extend that attitude towards a medieval pope.

Nevertheless in a letter to Pope Boniface IV (608–15), Columbanus is not just unceremonious, he is casual, even making light-hearted puns. Of Boniface's predecessor, Vigilus, he riffs, 'Be vigilant, I implore you, pope, be vigilant and again I say be vigilant, since perhaps he who was called Vigilant was not vigilant.' Such a pun echoes an earlier, even more playful letter to Pope Gregory the Great (590–604), in which he used Ecclesiastes 9:4 to make a pun on Pope Leo's name: 'A living dog is better than a dead Leo [lion].'

And he is not unaware of his breaches of protocol. 'What makes me bold, if I may say so,' he wrote to Boniface, 'is partly the freedom of speech which is the custom of my country. For among us it is not the person but the argument that carries weight.'

Perhaps sensing that the bishops' questions over his orthodoxy would not be the last time he and his countrymen would be viewed with suspicion, Columbanus never misses an opportunity to assure Boniface of Ireland's adherence to the gospel. 'For all we Irish, inhabitants of the world's edge, are disciples of Saints Peter and Paul and of all the disciples who, by the Holy Spirit, wrote the divine Scripture,' he wrote to Pope Boniface. 'And we accept nothing outside the evangelical and apostolic teaching. Not one has been a heretic, not one a Judaizer,

> 'Going to Rome is lots of effort, little profit. You won't find the king there unless you take him along.'
>
> **Ancient Irish poem**

not one a schismatic, but the Catholic Faith as it was given to us first by you, that is the successors of the holy apostles, is preserved intact.' Sadly, he suggests, the same cannot necessarily be said of Rome. 'Just as your honour is great because of the dignity of your see, your must take great care not to lose your honour through some untowardness.'

A double exile

But Columbanus's greatest political challenge would come not from Rome, but from his backyard. Brunhilde, a mercenary Visigothic princess, had become ruler of Burgundy after the assassination of her husband. Her son, Theuderic, had visted Luxeuil, but now found himself on the Irish monk's bad side. Theuderic had many concubines, who had borne him four sons. Grandmother Brunhilde was eager to ensure her line. By asking – or rather, demanding – that Columbanus bless the illegitimate heirs, she earned his wrath. He called the children sons of harlots and prophesied that they would never rise to power. It was a costly jeremiad. The monk was arrested and ordered 'to return to the place whence you came to this land'.

This horrified Columbanus. 'I do not think it would be pleasing to my Creator if I should go back to the home which I left because of my love for Christ,' he argued. Nevertheless the voluntary exile became an involuntary exile from Burgundy. He and his fellow Irish monks were rounded up and escorted by military guard from Luxeuil through Besançon, Auexerre, Orleans, and Tours to Nantes, where he was placed aboard a ship bound for Ireland. Perhaps Columbanus was right. Maybe God really was not pleased with the idea of the impertinent Irishman being forced to return home. In any case, the ship bearing Columbanus and his companions ran aground shortly after embarking.

That he escaped was hardly a surprise. As he wrote when the guards came to put him aboard, 'If I escape there is no guard to prevent it; for they seem to desire this, that I should escape.'

Now free but a double exile, Columbanus seemed momentarily directionless. He and his companions travelled east to Metz, and though they met with a friendly reception, decided not to stay long. Instead, they headed up the Rhine to Bregenz, on the shore of Lake Constance in what is now Switzerland. It was likely on this journey that the monk wrote his famous 'Boat Song'. The shanty starts as a tribute to the boat and becomes a metaphor for the Christian life:

Cut in the forests, swept down the two-horned Rhine,
* our keel, tight-caulked, now floats upon the sea.*
Ho, men! Let the echoes resound with our ho!
* But manly strength has force to tame the storm.*
Ho, men! Let the echoes resound with our ho!

Firm faith and holy ardour conquer all.
* The ancient fiend, defeated, breaks his arrows.*
Let your souls, men, remembering Christ, cry ho!

Switzerland was not to hold Columbanus for long, either. Now in his seventies, Columbanus began leading his companions over the Alps into Italy. His aim there was to convert the Arian Lombards, who had come to the country half a century earlier. But on the way, Columbanus's hot temper again flared. Gall, one of his most faithful disciples, became too ill to travel. Unconvinced, the elder demanded that his subordinate rise and walk. When Gall did not, Columbanus took a drastic measure. 'I enjoin on you before I go,' he proclaimed, 'that so long as I live in the body, you do not dare to celebrate Mass.'

While Gall stayed behind, the other Irishmen crossed into Italy. Passing through Milan, they built the first Italo-Irish monastery at Bobbio over the ruins of a church supposedly founded by Peter. Though strong enough to help in the monastery's construction, Columbanus did not last long thereafter. Shortly before his death in November 613, he sent his staff of office north to Gall. Whether it was an act of apology or forgiveness, it was clearly one of reconciliation.

Columbanus's quantifiable legacy is among the most impressive anywhere in church history. He and his disciples founded at least 60 monasteries throughout Europe, and were among the first to bring the passionate Irish Christianity so deeply into the continent.

After Columbanus's death, Gall seems to have somewhat changed in his evangelistic methods. When travelling with his superior, both regularly smashed pagan idols and threw them in the lake. Among the Alemanni around what is now Switzerland, however, Gall's efforts were more akin to those of Patrick two centuries earlier, gently urging conversion. Like those before him, he both befriended the local rulers to assist in his efforts and took the gospel to the homes of the less powerful. Gall was apparently comfortable with those in power (befriending a local duke, for example), but he avoided it for himself. He refused an offer to become abbot of Luxeuil when Columbanus's second successor died, and similarly turned down the bishopric of Constance. Gall believed the bishop of Constance should be a native of the country, so he secured the appointment of one of his students, a German named John. This student had led Gall into the wilds near Lake Constance to find a secluded base. John tried to warn Gall from assuming the area would be as monk-friendly as Ireland, telling tales of ferocious wild animals and even more ferocious weather. Gall turned a deaf ear to the advice, deciding to create a hermitage at the first place he fell. According to Gall's hagiographer, Walahfrid Strabo (who left us the story about the dispute between Gall and Columbanus; Jonas omitted it), John was right about the area's wild beasts. But under God's protection, Gall tamed them. One bear learned how to fetch the monk's firewood in exchange for a loaf of bread.

Gall preached at John's consecration as bishop, and his sermon is the only writing of his that survives (though a German phrase book may also be in his own hand). An even greater legacy, however, remains his monastery, which became one of the greatest of all medieval educational centres. It soon passed from a Celtic rule to the Benedictine Rule, but its library attracted scholars and saints from around the Christian world. By the time of Gall's death in 640, the Alemanni were almost totally Christian.

Fursa the visionary

Brendan's nephew, Fursa, was another famous peregrinus and reportedly one of the most popular preachers in Ireland. He grew up educated in one of his uncle's monasteries, Inchiquin Island, then left to create his own hermitage. Bede raves that Fursa 'was of noble Irish blood, and even more noble in mind than in birth, for from his boyhood he had not only read sacred books and observed monastic discipline, but as is fitting in saints, had also diligently practised all that he had learned'. Fursa, however, was no hermit, travelling around the island to preach. When he 'could no longer endure the crowds that thronged him', says Bede,

Fursa 'made a vow to spend his life as a pilgrim for love of our Lord, and to go wherever God should call him'. The first place God called him was to East Anglia, where Fursa befriended King Sigebert I – one of the most Christian of all monarchs (he had been educated by Columbanus, founded schools, and eventually relinquished his title to become a monk). The king granted the monk an abandoned fort to use as a monastery, but ten years later Fursa decided to give up his administrative tasks to return to a more reclusive life. This too did not last long, as pagans from the Anglo-Saxon region of Mercia launched regular raids on the area. Fursa then decided to cross the southern sea into Normandy. He was well received by the town of Mayoc, which asked him to stay. He is still remembered there, but his stay was brief; he moved on to Neustria, where he founded a monastery near Paris, at Lagny on the Marne. In his mid-seventies, Fursa decided to return to England but died on the way. He was buried at the new church in the northern town of Péronne, where his brother Ultán served as bishop. Until its destruction by Vikings in 880, the church was known as Peronna Scottorum, Péronne of the Irish.

Throughout his life, Fursa experienced ecstatic visions. The first of these seems to have been a near-death experience: after days of praying and fasting in a cross-vigil (with arms extended), the saint had a major fever. Then, says his hagiographer, Fursa's feet went cold, his hands stiffened, and his soul left his body. In fact, several of Fursa's visions came at times of illness. Sometimes, says Bede, God told him 'to continue his diligent preaching of the word, and to maintain his accustomed vigils and prayers with indefatigable zeal'. Other visions were more graphic, and inspired generations of readers. Bede opts not to describe most of these, encouraging his readers to seek out Fursa's hagiography, which

> '[In the tales of peregrini] we do not read of inner crises of decision; rather we get the impression of prompt and unhesitating response to a divine imperative.'
>
> **John T. McNeill, The Celtic Churches**

. . . describes the deceitful cunning with which the devils misrepresented his actions, words, and even thoughts, as though they were recorded in a book; and it tells of the joyful and sorrowful things that he learned both from the angels and from the saints who appeared among the angels.

Having said this, Bede cannot resist retelling one of the stories. Lifted into the heavens by angels, Fursa looks back down at the earth and sees a gloomy valley with four fires in the air. The angels explain that the flames were falsehood, covetousness, discord and cruelty, but all four quickly merged and burst near the saint. Fursa was saved by this attack, but on his return to earth was scorched by a damned soul whose clothing Fursa had worn after the man died. 'You lit this fire, so you were burned,' an angel explained. 'Had you not accepted property from one who died in his sins, you would not have shared in his punishment.' Back in his body and restored to health, Fursa's shoulder and jaw retained the burn marks. This served not only to remind Fursa to maintain his holy separation, but was also evidence for sceptics. Pope Martin I was reportedly one of these doubters, but upon seeing Fursa's scar fell on his knees and apologized. The Christian public, however, was not as sceptical. Fursa's visions circulated and were taken as divine revelations of the afterlife. They even reportedly became one of Dante Alighieri's inspirations for *The Divine Comedy*.

A flood of saints

So many Celtic saints emigrated to Brittany, Gaul and beyond (monastic foundations were established in Spain, Norway and other distant regions) that in 870 Henric of Auxerre wrote in his *Life of Germanus*, 'Almost all of Ireland, despising the sea, is migrating to our shores with a herd of philosophers.' By the mid-600s, Irish peregrini were already creating systems to care for their fellow exiles. One notable example is Fiacra, who set up a hospice near his monastery in Meaux. His legend tells how the local bishop promised the saint as much land as he could mark off with his spade in one day. As Fiacra began to dig, the ground miraculously opened up and marked off the territory for him. (The legend also tells of an angry woman who opposed Fiacra and eventually became both made of stone and the justification for banning women from the monastery.) Today Fiacra is remembered as the patron saint of gardeners. He is also remembered for two less auspicious namesakes: French cabs (four-wheeled cabs premiered in 1620 outside Paris's Hôtel Saint-Fiacre) and St Fiacre's Disease (haemorrhoids).

> 'The new invaders were unarmed white-robed monks with books in their satchels and psalms on their lips, seeking no wealth or comfort but only the opportunity to preach and to pray.'
>
> **John T. McNeill,** *The Celtic Churches*

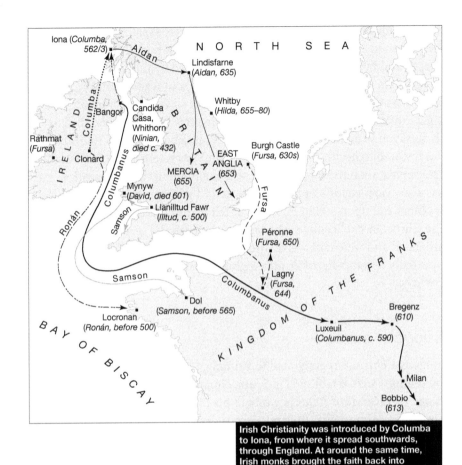

Iona (Columba, 562/3)
Aidan
NORTH SEA
Lindisfarne (Aidan, 635)
Bangor
Candida Casa, Whithorn (Ninian, died c. 432)
Columba
IRELAND
Rathmat (Fursa)
Clonard
Whitby (Hilda, 655–80)
Columbanus
BRITAIN
EAST ANGLIA (653)
Burgh Castle (Fursa, 630s)
MERCIA (655)
Mynyw (David, died 601)
Samson
Llanilltud Fawr (Illtud, c. 500)
Ronán
Fursa
Péronne (Fursa, 650)
Samson
Lagny (Fursa, 644)
Columbanus
KINGDOM OF THE FRANKS
Bregenz (610)
Dol (Samson, before 565)
Locronan (Ronán, before 500)
Luxeuil (Columbanus, c. 590)
BAY OF BISCAY
Milan
Bobbio (613)

Irish Christianity was introduced by Columba to Iona, from where it spread southwards, through England. At around the same time, Irish monks brought the faith back into continental Europe.

One of the Celtic lands' most renowned missionaries was not a Celt at all. Boniface (680–754) was an Anglo-Saxon born in Devonshire (his birthname was Wynfrith or Winfrid). He had spent time as a monk, but his mission to Germany in 719 was not one of peregrini. It was a mission directed by Pope Gregory II, who wanted Boniface not only to convert the heathen (those 'not yet cleansed by the waters of holy Baptism'), but to suppress the heretics (those 'led astray . . . and now serve idols under the guise of the Christian religion'). 'You seem to glow with the salvation-bringing fire which our Lord came to send upon the earth,' Gregory told him. Indeed, Boniface was full of fire, smashing idols, cutting down sacred trees, and demanding that heretical missionaries not only be excommunicated but imprisoned in solitary confinement. Freelance missionary monks had no place in his plan to organize the church. He was not always hostile to Celtic Christians – an Irishman named Abel, for example, was appointed to the See of Rheims – but many were condemned, even those in the Roman hierarchy. The bishop of Salzburg, a Celt named Virgil, was attacked for postulating 'that there are another world and other men under the earth, and another sun and moon'. 'Wandering bishops', meanwhile, were to Boniface's mind some kind of freakish, subhuman creature akin to the mythic centaurs. They were not quite heretical, but they were schismatic. By the time Boniface died, the church around what is now Germany – re-energized largely by the Celtic peregrini – was far more organized and controlled. Peregrini continued to flow in from the north, and were sought out for their knowledge for centuries to come. But the height of their influence over northern Europe was over.

CHAPTER 16

RESURRECTION AND RAIDS

An apocryphal legend says that Pope Gregory the Great, before he became pope, once came upon a merchant selling young slave boys. Having never seen such a fair-haired and fair-skinned race before, Gregory asked where they came from. 'They come from Britain,' he was told, 'where all the people have this appearance.' Not all did. These were not children of Celtic descent but Angles, descendants of the tribes that had migrated to England from southern Jutland (modern Denmark and northern Germany) in the 5th century. Gregory misheard the name of their race. 'That is an appropriate name,' he said,

'From a Celtic perspective, calling Augustine of Canterbury "the Apostle of England" has much in common with naming the New World for Amerigo Vespucci.'

Richard J. Woods, *The Spirituality of the Celtic Saints*

'for they have faces like angels and it is right that they should become fellow-heirs with the angels in heaven.' Gregory reportedly begged the pope to send him to England, but was refused. When he took the papacy, however, he was quick to make sure that England received missionaries.

In 596, Pope Gregory sent Augustine and 40 monks under him to convert England. They had all been trained in Gregory's Roman monastery, and Augustine himself was an expert in theology, monasticism and management. Unfortunately, he was also arrogant. Arriving in Britain, he immediately chastised the local clergy for preferring 'their own customs to those in universal use among Christian churches'. Wondering what to do, seven British bishops and other monks, mainly from Bangor, consulted a 'wise and prudent hermit'.

'If he is a man of God, follow him,' the monk advised. 'If Augustine is meek and lowly of heart, it shows that he bears the yoke of Christ himself, and offers it to you. But if he is haughty and unbending, then he is not of God, and you should not listen to him.'

The troubled clergy wanted more specifics. How would Augustine demonstrate meekness or haughtiness? 'If he rises courteously as you approach, rest assured that he is the servant of Christ and do as he asks,' the hermit answered. 'But if he ignores you and does not rise, then, since you are in the majority, do not comply with his demands.' Augustine did not rise. Instead, he made demands, prophesying that if he was not obeyed, the English would kill the local clerics. 'And, as though by divine judgment, all these things happened as Augustine foretold,' recounts Bede, noting a battle that killed 1,200 monks – most from Bangor.

Actually, everything recounted so far in this chapter comes from Bede, the Anglo-Saxon historian known as the father of English church history. He is a partisan for the Romans and Anglo-Saxons, but he repeatedly praises Celtic Christians for their holiness. 'The Venerable Bede is often portrayed as an apologist for Roman Christianity and as one of the chief architects for the notion of Englishness,' writes modern historian Ian Bradley, 'I firmly believe that he was also largely responsible for initiating the British, and more especially the English, love affair with "Celtic" Christianity.'

The trouble with Easter

Bede's objectivity is brought under the greatest scrutiny when he discusses the differences between the way Celtic and Roman churches calculated Easter. Though this may seem trivial to modern Christians – who may not even know that there is still a difference between Western and Eastern calendars, but for different reasons – to early medieval believers it was terribly important. As early as 314 the Council of Arles, where British bishops were among the delegates, begged Pope Sylvester to 'write immediately to all, giving directions on this observance, so that it may be celebrated by us on the same day and at the same time throughout the world'.

The difference in calculation comes from the difference between a solar year and 12 lunar months (used in determining Jewish festivals like Passover). The earth revolves around the sun every 12.3683 months – so the ancients decided to add an extra lunar month every so often to balance the scales. The Celts threw in 31 months every 84 years (leaving them only 0.0007 of an extra month) while the Roman church added seven months every 19 years (only 0.0001 months over). The controversy was not just astronomical, however. Theology played a much more important role.

Only a few years after the Council of Arles, the Council of Nicea became one of the most important meetings of church history. Foremost among the agenda items was the suppression of the Arians, who believed Jesus was not fully God. But the council also condemned (as schismatics, not heretics) a lesser-known group called the Quartodecimans, a Christian sect that celebrated Easter at the Jewish Passover, whether it fell on a Sunday or not. Another group of Christians had so strongly opposed such ties with Judaism that they did not want to celebrate Easter on Sunday if it *did* coincide with the Passover. Others queried whether Good Friday or Easter Sunday should be associated with the Jewish Passover. Arguments over Easter even hinged on when the day began – at sunrise, sunset, or at some other time? And then there was the issue of the vernal equinox and the symbolism that came with it – at the equinox, day becomes longer than night just as Christ, the Light of the World, conquered the Prince of Darkness in his resurrection.

For early medieval Christians, taking all these matters into account was no game. 'What was at stake was the harmony between human and divine law,' historian Thomas O'Loughlin writes in his book *Celtic Theology*. 'God had created the universe in an orderly and numbered way; everywhere its order was a testimony to the ideas in the mind of God as he created, and to see these patterns in the material creation was to see beyond matter into the divine purposes.' Celtic Christians, Roman Christians, Eastern Christians, and the rest of the early Christian world believed the statement in Wisdom 11:20 that God 'arranged all things in measure, number and weight'. Jesus was clear that the time of his death and resurrection was divinely appointed. 'The hour has come,' he said repeatedly. How wrong it would be, then, to commemorate his resurrection haphazardly.

Many recent historians have downplayed the Easter controversy, saying either that it was simply a manifestation of the battle between Celtic religious autonomy and the hierarchical Roman church, or that it has been greatly exaggerated due to Bede's strong interest in the subject. The controversy, however, appears throughout the history of the Celtic churches. It was apparently a main source of controversy between Columbanus and the provincial religious leaders around Luxeuil, and Columbanus himself worried over the dispute. 'The dangers I mean are the dangers of disagreement,' he wrote to his monastery just before boarding his ill-fated ship back to Ireland. 'I fear lest there be disagreement on account of Easter, lest perhaps, through the devil's tricks, [the community's enemies] wish to divide you, if you do not keep peace with them; for now, without me, you seem to stand less firmly there.'

Were the Celts insubordinate?

Columbanus may have been too informal with popes, even sometimes critical, but he was no Martin Luther. Despite the histories of those trying to draw a line connecting the Celtic churches to Protestantism, Columbanus appears to have bent the knee to Rome. Still, elsewhere Columbanus's letter suggests that he had heard the method Rome used to compute Easter and the reasons for it, but ultimately disagreed. This frustrated Augustine's successor at Canterbury, Laurence, who in 605 questioned Columbanus's claim that he and his fellow Irish preserved the Catholic faith wholly intact. 'When the apostolic see sent us, according to its custom, to preach to pagan peoples in these western lands, and in the whole world, we entered this island which is called Britain,' he said in a letter to Irish Christians. 'Before we learnt the truth, we believed that the Britons and the Irish followed the custom of the universal Church, and so we held both in veneration. When we came to know the Britons, we believed the Irish to be superior. We learnt, however, from . . . the abbot Columbanus in Gaul, that the Irish do not differ at all from the Britons in their way of life.'

Twenty-three years after Laurence's letter to the Irish, another missive came – this time from Pope Honorius himself. 'He earnestly warned them not to imagine that their little community, isolated at the uttermost ends of the earth, had a monopoly of wisdom over all the ancient and new churches throughout the world,' Bede records. 'And he asked them not to keep a different Easter, contrary to the calculations and synodical decrees of all the bishops of the world.'

This argument that the entire world apart from Britain and Ireland celebrated Easter one way may have been more persuasive than the mere fact that the request came from Rome. That question, however, is mired in centuries of arguments between Protestant and Catholic historians.

For Cummian, who was probably the abbot of Darrow, the two issues were inextricably united. 'What can be felt worse for Mother Church than to say, "Rome is mistaken, Jerusalem is mistaken, Alexandria is mistaken, Antioch is mistaken, the Scots and Britons alone have sound wisdom."' Those opposing the change, he said, were 'an insignificant group of Britons and Irish who are almost at the end of the world, and if I may say so, but pimples on the face of the earth'.

In the household of King Oswy of Northumbria, dating differences led to more practical tensions. The king kept to the Celtic date, while his wife, Eanfled, followed the Romans. 'It is said,' Bede writes, 'that

The tonsure

'There was no small argument about this as well,' Bede writes over differences in the tonsure – a sacred shearing of hair when taking clerical vows. The Roman tonsure was a shaved circle on the top of the head. Though it had only been around for about two centuries by Bede's time, the Anglo-Saxon historian believed it dated back to the apostle Peter, who first shaved his head in such a manner to resemble Christ's crown of thorns. 'Therefore we who desire to be saved by Christ's Passion like Peter wear this sign of the Passion on the crown of the head, which is the highest part of the body,' Bede wrote. The tonsure, he believed, gave 'constant protection against the assaults of wicked spirits, and serve[d] as a continual reminder that he must crucify the flesh with all its vices and evil desires'.

Celtic clergy, meanwhile, shaved a line on their head 'from ear to ear' and everything in front of it, allowing their hair to grow in the back (they may have also left a fringe above the forehead). Some historians suggest this may have been a practice of the druids, but Bede and others believed it came from Simon Magus, the Samaritan magician who tried to offer the early apostles money in exchange for the supernatural power of the Holy Spirit. 'I ask what faithful Christian will not instantly detest it, and reject it together with all his magic,' Bede said. But Bede admits that 'the apostles were not all tonsured in the same manner', and Celtic Christians probably associated their tonsure with the apostle John. Much to the consternation of Bede and others, some Celts who accepted the Roman date for Easter still wore the Celtic tonsure, including Adomnán.

the confusion in those days was such that Easter was kept twice in one year, so that when the King had ended Lent and was keeping Easter, the Queen and her attendants were still fasting and keeping Palm Sunday.' Family conflict intensified when Oswy's son, Aldfrith, switched sides and became a vocal supporter of the Roman date.

The Synod of Whitby

With pressure building on all sides, in 664 Oswy called for both parties to meet and settle their differences. They chose to meet at the double monastery of Streanaeshalch, founded by Hilda, 'a woman devoted to God' according to Bede. Though Anglo-Saxon (a member of the Angle royal family, in fact), Hilda was Celtic in practice and spiritual pedigree. A student of Aidan of Lindisfarne, she gained prominence both as spiritual adviser and an administrator of monasteries at Streanaeshalch (now better known by the name later Danes gave it: Whitby) and Hartlepool. 'So great was her prudence that not only ordinary folk, but kings and princes used to come and ask her advice in their difficulties,' writes Bede. Everyone who knew her called her Mother – a designation apparently not universal among abbesses.

> 'Perhaps no one did more to foster this impression of a vanished golden age than the historian through whose eyes all subsequent generations have viewed the Whitby debate. The Venerable Bede . . .'
>
> Ian Bradley, *Celtic Christianity: Making Myths and Chasing Dreams*

Hilda sided with the Celtic Easter date, but she served as host rather than disputant. That role fell to the Irish bishop of Lindisfarne, Colmán. 'The Easter customs which I observe were taught me by my superiors, who sent me here as a bishop,' he began. 'And all our forefathers, men beloved of God, are known to have observed these customs.' Colmán also argued, based on an ancient document known as the *Liber Anatolii,* that the apostle John himself – 'the disciple especially loved by our Lord' – had used their method for Easter dating. (Unfortunately for the Celts, the Quartodecimans had also appealed to John's Easter practices to defend themselves. Even more unfortunately, the *Liber Anatolii* was a forgery and a fraud.)

Scheduled to argue for the Roman date was Agilbert, a Frankish bishop who later became bishop of Paris. He, however, was reluctant to argue through the interpreter, a Celtic bishop named Cedd. Agilbert may have been particularly sensitive to language issues around Anglo-Saxon royalty. Years earlier, Agilbert had served as bishop in Wessex. Unfortunately, Bede records, 'the king, who understood only Saxon, grew tired of the bishop's foreign speech, and invited to the province a bishop of his own tongue'. Perhaps not wishing likewise to bore King Oswy, Agilbert asked that his protégé, a priest named Wilfrid, take his place. It was a smart move. Wilfrid was not just eloquent, he was passionate; he had only recently renounced the Celtic date for the Roman one as a student at Canterbury.

'Our Easter customs are those that we have seen universally observed in Rome,' Wilfrid began, appealing to apostles Peter and Paul over John. 'We have also seen the same customs generally observed throughout Italy and Gaul . . . [and] in Africa, Asia, Egypt, Greece, and throughout the world wherever the church of Christ has spread. The only people who are stupid enough to disagree with the whole world are these Scots and their obstinate adherents the Picts and Britons, who inhabit only a portion of these two islands in the remote ocean.' Furthermore, Wilfrid argued, if the Celts really were following John they would have joined the Quartodecimans in celebrating Easter on whatever day of the week Passover fell on – Sunday or not. 'You conform neither to John nor Peter, the law nor the gospel, in your keeping of our greatest festival,' he concluded.

Again Colmán tried to appeal to his own traditions and forefathers. 'Are we to believe that our most revered Father Columba and his successors, men so dear to God, thought or acted contrary to Holy Scripture when they followed this custom?' he asked rhetorically. 'The holiness of many of them is confirmed by heavenly signs, and their virtues by miracles; and having no doubt that they are saints, I shall never cease to emulate their lives, customs, and discipline.'

At this, Wilfrid became even more acrimonious, quoting Matthew 7:22–23. 'I can only say that when many shall say to our Lord at the day of judgment: "Have we not prophesied in thy name, and cast out devils, and done many wonderful works?" the Lord will reply, "I never knew you."' This is not to say that Columba and all the other Celtic saints were burning in hell, Wilfrid assured his listeners, but they were certainly mistaken. They did not know any better, Wilfrid suggested. Colmán and his ilk, meanwhile, were in danger of damnation by rejecting correction. He asked:

For although your Fathers were holy men, do you imagine that they, a few men in a corner of a remote island, are to be preferred before the universal church of Christ throughout the world? And even if your Columba – or, may I say, yours if he was the servant of Christ – was a saint potent in miracles, can he take precedence before the most blessed Prince of the Apostles, to whom our Lord said: 'Thou art Peter, and upon this rock I will build my church . . . and to thee I will give the keys of the kingdom of heaven'?

When Oswy heard this, the debate was over. Is it true, he asked Colmán, that Jesus gave Peter the keys to heaven, and that Columba had no such authority? The Irish bishop acknowledged this reading of Matthew 16:18. 'Then, I tell you, Peter is the guardian of the gates of heaven, and I shall not contradict him,' Oswy declared. 'Otherwise, when I come to the gates of heaven, he who holds the keys may not be willing to open them.'

Oswy was not alone in his decision. Many leaders of Celtic churches and monasteries began observing Easter with the Romans, including Hilda and Cedd. But not Colmán. He left Lindisfarne and returned (with the relics of Aidan) to Iona, which continued to observe Columba's calendar for another 150 years. After a few years on Iona, Colmán and several of his followers returned to Ireland, settling on the island's western shores.

Through the years, largely as a result of Bede's writing, the so-called Synod of Whitby was seen as the turning point of Celtic church history – the moment that the Romans succeeded in their (depending on your point of view) oppression or correction. It was a pivotal moment, but not on such a grand scale. The meeting marked the end of Iona's ecclesiastic influence over Northumbria (though Northumbrian youth continued to flock to Celtic monasteries), but not the end of Celtic Christianity or the triumph of the Roman church. For one thing, more than half of Ireland had already accepted the Roman Easter dates by the 664 meeting at Streanaeshalch. For another, Oswy was a local king and held little real power over church observances.

Those looking for a more direct confrontation on behalf of Rome can jump ahead another 16 years, to the Synod of Hertford in 672. Wilfrid was there, but the most disdain for the Celtic church seems to have come from Theodore, the archbishop of Canterbury. He believed the Celts to be heretics and schismatics, and the synod's resolutions reflect these beliefs. They not only firmly set down the Roman dating of Easter, but also outlawed monks wandering 'from place to place'. Failure to conform meant excommunication and thus eternal damnation.

Even this decree did not convince everyone. Adomnán, the abbot of Iona and hagiographer of Columba, converted to the Roman reforms around the year 690. This move, Bede records, set him against his disciples. 'On his return home, he tried to lead his own people in Iona and those who were under the jurisdiction of that monastery into the correct ways he had learned and wholeheartedly accepted, but in this he failed.' He had more success during visits to Ireland, reportedly convincing the Irish who were not already using the Roman Easter to accept it, which they did at the Synod of Birr (where they also adopted Adomnán's Law of Innocents). Adomnán returned to Iona and again tried to convince the monks to change their calendar, but again they refused. Before either side could celebrate the next Easter and widen the schism between abbot and monk, Adomnán had died.

The monks of Iona, among the last to accept the Roman reforms, eventually did so around the year 716. It was ultimately not any force from Rome or decree from Canterbury that eventually won them over, but the patient encouragement of a monk named Egbert. 'Being a most persuasive teacher who most faithfully practised all that he taught, he was given a ready hearing by everyone,' Bede says, 'and by his constant and devout exhortations he weaned them from the obsolete traditions of their ancestors.' Egbert himself died on Easter Sunday – the Roman one – 729. Iona was not the last of the hold-outs. Bede laments that even at the time of his writing in 731, the Britons in Wales 'still remain obdurate and crippled by their errors, going about with heads improperly tonsured, and keeping Christ's solemnity without fellowship with the Christian Church'. A few hold-outs also remained at Iona, where they were allowed to maintain their tonsure and calendar until the schism ended quietly in 767.

The fury of the Northmen

Before the end of the century, Iona had a new challenge – the Vikings. They first attacked Columba's island in 795, looting the church, dormitories and other buildings. In 802, they returned, but this time, they were not content to merely rob the buildings of their possessions; they burned the structures themselves to the ground. Four years later, they returned again, murdering 86 monks. The abbot could take no more raids, and the attacks had broken communication between Iona and its daughter monasteries. Oversight was moved from such a precarious island to Kells. With the seat went the

> 'When the Norse first appeared solely as raiders from the sea and were quite external to Irish society, they were regarded as a horror in Ireland, more for their heathenism than for their piracy.'
>
> **Máire and Liam de Paor,** *Early Christian Ireland*

relics of Columba, entombed in a gold and silver shrine. Other monks stayed at Iona. They knew the potential consequences, and some even looked forward to them. One of these was Blathmac, an Irishman who had renounced his royal upbringing and had become an abbot in Ireland. He was not the abbot of Iona, but he knew where Columba's bones were buried. And that was information that the Vikings, who returned on 19 January 825, wanted to know Blathmac refused to reveal the location, and (after celebrating Mass) was slowly hacked to death on the steps of the altar. After this tragedy, Iona's story is less clear. But raids continued against the monastery, even as late as 986.

Iona was an early target, but not the first. In 791, the Scandinavian raiders hit both northern England and northern Scotland. Two years later, the *Anglo-Saxon Chronicle*'s entry is dismal:

In this year dire forewarnings came over the land of the Northumbrians and miserably terrified the people; these were extraordinary whirlwinds and light-nings, and fiery dragons were seen flying in the air. A great famine soon fol-lowed these omens and soon after that, in the same year, the havoc of heathen men miserably destroyed God's church on Lindisfarne.

When word of the raid reached Alcuin in Aachen, he was horrified – even though he had never been to Lindisfarne himself. 'Behold the church of the holy Cuthbert bespattered with the blood of God's priests,

The *Book of Kells*

Sometime around the move from Iona to Kells, work began on the famous *Book of Kells,* one of the Celtic world's most beautiful artworks. Its 12-by-9-inch pages record the biblical Gospels, but more importantly, they illustrate them. 'Here you can look upon the face of the divine majesty drawn in a miraculous way,' historian Giraldus Cambrensis wrote in the late 1100s upon seeing the book.

If you take the trouble to look very closely, and penetrate with your eyes to the secrets of the artistry, you will notice such intricacies, so delicate and subtle, so close together, so well-knitted, so involved and bound together, and so fresh in their colourings, that you will not hesitate to declare that all of these things must have been the result of the work, not of men, but of angels.

The Annals of Ulster call it 'the most precious object in the Western world', but may have been referring to its gold cover and binding rather than the amazing ornamentation inside the book. Sometimes the artwork is holy, portraying a thin, golden-haired Jesus or a long-faced evangelist with a thick beard. At other times, human figures engage in more everyday activities; a man strangles a chicken, two other men wrestle and grab each other's beards. Animals – including Cats, lizards, moths and deer – are also common. Some of the book's most amazing artwork, however, is merely abstract or symbolic, such as its full-page decoration of the chi-rho symbol. Sadly, the book remains unfinished, perhaps due to more Viking raids. Though it escaped direct assault for centuries, in 1007 raiders finally seized the book, tore off its valuable covers, and buried the rest under a sod. Three months later, it was recovered, and it now sits in Dublin's Trinity College.

robbed of all its ornaments, the most venerable place in all Britain given over as prey to the pagans,' he said.

The *Annals of Ulster* are no happier, noting in the same year 'the burning of Rechrann by heathens and Skye was overwhelmed and laid waste'. The story got worse in the following year's entry: 'Devastation of all the islands in Britain by heathens.' By 795, Vikings were raiding both Ireland's east and west coasts.

'From the fury of the Northmen, O Lord, deliver us,' Celtic monks prayed, but the fury continued. At first, the Vikings were content to merely attack from their Scandinavian homelands during an annual raiding season, from May to September. In the margin of a 9th-century manuscript, a monk issues a literary sigh of relief:

Fierce and wild is the wind tonight,
*   it tosses the tresses of the sea to white;*
on such a night as this I take my ease;
*   fierce Northmen only course the quiet seas.*

When raiders had to come over such a distance, the most susceptible targets were outlying islands. Iona was not as dangerous as the Hebrides (once Irish, but renamed 'the islands of the foreigners' within a century of the first Viking raids) and the even more distant Faroes. 'For nearly a hundred years hermits sailing from our country, Ireland, have lived [in the Faroes],' wrote the Irish scholar Dícuil in his 825 work, *Book on the Measurement of the World*. 'But just as they were always deserted from the beginning of the world, so now, because of the Northman pirates, they are emptied of anchorites [religious hermits], and filled with countless sheep and many diverse kinds of seabirds.'

By the 830s, however, the entire year was the raiding season, and just about everywhere was a target. In Ireland, only Connaught escaped the worst of the attacks. By then, the Vikings had apparently taken control of the Isle of Man, allowing them to attack anywhere in the Irish Sea with little warning. The Scandinavian pirates hit Armagh, long seen as the heart of Patrick's legacy, taking the abbot and Patrick's relics. Amazingly, both were returned within a year, after what was surely a huge ransom.

In 839, Vikings established their first winter camp in Ireland, on Lough Neagh. Such settlements allowed them, in the *Annals of Ulster*'s words, to 'plunder the peoples and churches of the north of Ireland', and take 'captive bishops and priests and scholars'. According to later legend-makers, about this same time the raiders became organized under the Viking leader Turgesius, who came with a 'great royal fleet' to northern Ireland and 'assumed the sovereignty of all the foreigners in Ireland'. Turgesius was not just interested in wealth – he sought colonization and total dominion over the islands. According to the legends, he also wanted to replace the

From saint-killers to saints

Historian John T. McNeill argues that the first Viking raid on a Celtic monastery was not in 793, but 617. 'Sea rovers, possibly at the instigation of a local enemy' fell upon Donnan (an Irish friend and disciple of Columba) and his 53 monks on the island of Eigg. The marauders allowed the monks to celebrate the Easter Mass, then slaughtered each of them.

Encounters with Celtic Christians on remote British islands, however, would eventually help to convert the Vikings to Christianity. In the Scilly Isles off Land's End, a young Norwegian named Olaf Trygvesson encountered a Cornish hermit with prophetic gifts. 'Thou wilt become a renowned king and do celebrated deeds,' the hermit told him. 'And that thou not doubt the truth of this answer, listen to this.' He then described how. Olaf's men would attempt to mutiny, and that Olaf would be wounded, carried to his ship on a shield, recover, and become a Christian.

'Many men wilt thou bring to faith and baptism,' the prophet said, 'and both to thy own and others' good.' When everything happened just as the hermit had said, Olaf quickly returned to the island for baptism. Then he set off to convert his homeland by force, saying 'All Norway will be Christian or die.'

islands' Christianity with the worship of Thor, Odin and other Norse gods. He even reportedly took the abbacy of Armagh and put his own wife in charge of the majestic monastery of Clonmacnoise, where she replaced Christian prayers with pagan oracles at the high altar.

While Norwegian invaders continued pillaging from Ireland's north, Danes dominated the south. They were no less ruthless. 'The whole of Munster . . . was plundered by them,' says *The Wars of the Gaedhil and the Gail*:

They made spoil-land, and sword-land and conquered land of her, throughout her land and generally; and they ravaged her chieftainries and her privileged churches and her sanctuaries; and they rent her shrines and her reliquaries and her books . . . In short, until the sand of the sea, or the grass of the field, or the starts of heaven are counted, it will not be easy to recount . . . what the Gaedhill . . . suffered from them.

The chronicler also recalls 'immense floods and countless sea-vomitings of ships and boats and fleets so that there was not a harbour nor a land-port nor a dún nor a fortress nor a fastness . . . without floods of Danes and pirates'. With so many pirates eager for booty, it was inevitable that conflict would arise between parties. The White Heathen and the Black Heathen, as the Norwegians and Danes were respectively called by the Irish, warred among themselves. Perhaps the Irish would have been able to take advantage of this – or unify against the Vikings in some other way – but they too were torn apart by tribal dissention. The Vikings had attacked and demolished monasteries, but they were not the first. The *Annals of Ulster* record 'a battle between the communities of Clonmacnoise and Birr' in 760. Six years later, Clonmacnoise battled again, this time with Durrow – more than 200 died in the raid. In 775, there is 'a skirmish at Clonard between Donnchad [king of Tara] and the community of Clonard'. Some historians even argue that the violence among Irish tribes was already so bad that the Viking raids had little real impact on society.

'When the Vikings were vanquished in the early eleventh century, Irish society recovered, in the sense that the normal business of life sprang back in its expectable patterns. But Ireland would never recover its cultural leadership of European civilization. It had been marginalized once more.'

Thomas Cahill, *How the Irish Saved Civilization*

The legends credit Turgesius and his men with founding Dubh-linn (black pool) and other permanent camps in 841. Raids decreased as the Vikings started demanding tribute and taxes. (The most horrible of which may have been the Danes' nose tax – they demanded an ounce of silver for each Irish nose. Those who did not pay the price lost their nose.) With such settlement, the landscape began to change. The Irish forts became places of international trade – and Ireland's first real cities. No longer were monasteries the dominant demographic landmark. Eventually, the Northmen integrated into Irish society, intermarrying and even accepting Christianity. One prime example is Anlaf Curran, Olaf the Red. The Norwegian ruler controlled Northumbria for 12 years, but was later overthrown, then defeated again as head of Dublin. In 970 Anlaf had raided the monastery at Kells. In 980, he died a monk of Iona, and was given a royal burial there. Seven other Norwegian kings were also buried on the holy island (along with 48 Scottish kings and four Irish ones).

Legend:
- → Norwegian raids
- → Danish raids
- - - → Relics of Columba moved from Iona to Kells, 806
- ● Fortified Viking base (*longphort*)

NORTH SEA

Eigg, possible Viking raid 617

SCOTIA

Iona, raided 795, 802, 806, 825

Dumbarton, sacked from Dublin, 870/1

STRATHCLYDE

Lindisfarne, raided 793

NORTHUMBRIA

Jarrow, raided 794

Lough Neagh, first winter base in Ireland, 839 ●

Annagassan

IRELAND

Isle of Man, under Viking control by 830

LINDSEY

Lough Ree ●

Kells

Dublin founded c. 841

Limerick ●

Arklow

Wexford

Waterford ●

Cork ● ● Youghal

WALES

EAST ANGLIA

MERCIA

London ■
Rochester ■

WESSEX

CORNWALL

Viking raiders initially plundered the monasteries of their treasures and terrorised the local people, but eventually they settled and became integrated into Irish and British society.

The Christianity of the Celts survived. But with Norse, Angles, Saxons, Normans and other foreigners pressing in on the islands from all sides, the image becomes ever more blurred. Irish Christians would still be sought for their learning, knowledge and skills, but the 'golden age' of Celtic Christianity – if there ever was such a thing – was over. This, however, would not stop Christians from trying to recapture its essence over the next millennium.

CHAPTER 17

CELTIC CHRISTIANITY OF THE NON-CELTS

In 1995, Thomas Cahill took Celtic Christians to the American best-seller list. *How the Irish Saved Civilization* spent more than a year as one of the top-selling non-fiction books in the United States. Retelling the tales of Patrick, Columba, Columbanus and other Irish saints, Cahill's book described how holy scholars returned faith and knowledge to the European continent after the invasion of barbarian hordes:

As the Roman empire fell, as all through Europe matted, unwashed barbarians descended on the Roman cities, looting artifacts and burning books, the Irish, who were just learning to read and write, took up the great labour of copying all of Western literature – everything they could get their hands on. These scribes then served as conduits through which the Greco-Roman and Judeo-Christian cultures were transmitted to the tribes of Europe, newly settled amid the rubble and ruined vineyards they had overwhelmed. Without this Service of the Scribes, everything that happened subsequently would have been unthinkable. Without the Mission of the Irish Monks, who single-hand-edly refounded European civilization throughout the continent in the bays and valleys of their exile, the world that came after them would have been an entirely different one – a world without books. And our own world would never have come to be.

Several scholars dismissed Cahill's approach as too enthusiastic, too black-and-white, and bad history. 'This dream has had a pernicious effect on studies of the early Irish church,' wrote Thomas O'Loughlin in his book *Celtic Theology*. 'For it has turned that study into a search for the peculiar, the unique and bizarre: what is common between that culture and the rest of Christendom becomes invisible, and what seems jarring becomes the norm.' Indeed, in his enthralling and descriptive book, Cahill admits he has tipped his journalistic scales in favour of 'many entertainers, persons of substance who have their story to tell, some of whom believe that their story is all there is to tell'. But he does so, he says, because the story of how the Irish saved civilization has gone untold. 'Many historians fail to mention it entirely, and few advert to the breathtaking drama of this cultural cliffhanger,' he writes. The subtitle of his book, in fact, is *The Untold Story of Ireland's Heroic Role from the Fall of Rome to the Rise of Medieval Europe.*

Continuing Celtic curiosity

The story of Celtic Christians and their contributions to the world was not, however, buried during the Viking raids like the *Book of Kells,* only to be dug up and recovered at the end of the last century. Ever since Adomnán and Bede, historians and scholars have been fascinated by the lives of these Celtic Christians and have portrayed them as saintly heroes. Ian Bradley sees at least six different Celtic Christian revivalist movements in the last millennium and a half. However, Bradley writes in *Celtic Christianity: Making Myths and Chasing Dreams,* 'their leading protagonists have generally, although not exclusively, been non-Celts. From the Anglo-Saxon Bede and the Anglo-Norman chroniclers of the 13th century to the predominantly English enthusiasts in the van of the current revival, it has largely been outsiders who have identified a distinctive "Celtic" strain of Christianity and found it particularly attractive.'

The first revival, Bradley says, came from hagiographers, whose emphasis was generally on proving the holiness and power of the specific saints they were writing about. Often, as we have seen, this was for political purposes. The saints, however, were seen as more than excuses for worldly control, they were exemplars. The hagiographers, as well as historians like Bede, saw the Celtic saints of the 400s and 500s as being pure and pious – unlike the decadence, corruption and worldliness they saw in their own day. For example, Bede writes about Aidan of Lindisfarne, 'His life is in marked contrast to the apathy of our own times, for all who accompanied him, whether monks or lay-folk, were required to meditate, that is, either to read the Scriptures or to learn the Psalms.'

'In essence, "Celtic Christianity" is a popular quest for a form of early British and Irish Christianity which is free from the great sins and failures of medieval and modern Christianity in the West.'

Donald E. Meek, 'Surveying the Saints: Reflections on Recent Writings on "Celtic Christianity"', Scottish Bulletin of Evangelical Theology

The second revival began after the Battle of Hastings, as the Norman conquest brought England, Scotland, Wales, and even Ireland under English control. Ironically, the strongest passion for the golden age saints did not come from the conquered desperate to cling to their cultural identity, but from the conquerors. 'Undoubtedly there was a strong element of opportunism and good public relations in this pro-Celtic approach,' Bradley writes. 'It cast the victors of the Norman Conquest in the role of consolidators and continuers of native tradition rather than as unfeeling aliens out to destroy all that they came across.'

Not that they *were* unfeeling aliens, of course. One of these foreigners was Queen Margaret, Scotland's first canonized saint. The descendant of English princes, her father fled to Hungary after the Dane Canute the Great took the throne of England. Her mother was a Bavarian princess whose father, St Stephen, had recently been martyred. When she was about ten, Margaret and her family moved back to England, and she eventually married King Malcolm Gladmore (1058–93). To some, Margaret seems an anti-Celt. She replaced Gaelic with English in the royal court, and sought to eradicate any remaining differences between Christian practices in Scotland and the ones practised by her Benedictine chaplain, Turgot (who later wrote her hagiography). She worked to suppress 'barbarous practices' of the area, including a local liturgy of the Mass and avoidance of the sacraments (some monks so seriously held Paul's warning to the Corinthian church against unworthily partaking of the eucharist that they had apparently stopped taking it altogether). One recent biographical sketch by a respected church historian said she 'succeeded in . . . ridding Scotland of Celtic church practices and bringing the country into the mainstream of Roman Catholicism'. At the same time, however, Margaret was fascinated by the religious history of her new country, especially monasticism. 'At that time very many men, shut up in cells apart, in various places of the Scots, were living in the flesh, but not according to the flesh; for they led the life of angels upon earth,' Turgot wrote. 'The queen endeavoured to venerate and love Christ in them; and to visit them very often with her presence and conversation and to commend herself to their prayers.' Margaret even rebuilt the monastery at Iona. Her reforms may not have been driven by cultural pride, but may have been an attempt to reclaim the spiritual rigour of Celtic Christianity's golden age.

Celtic Christianity also benefited during this period from a major development in Christianity around Europe: the rise of pilgrimage. Tales of monkish travel, especially the *Voyage of Brendan*, became popular around the Christian world. Meanwhile, pilgrimage points – some associated with historical events, others apparently made up during the time – reinforced stories of sanctity and spread them abroad. This was also the time when legends of King Arthur and the Holy Grail began circulating. As England and others in Christendom became enthralled with these tales, their imaginations were inflamed with thoughts of a magical Christian age before theirs.

The third revival period Bradley notes begins around 1250, as nationalist movements, especially those in Scotland, appropriated the saints. The apostle Andrew had grown into the symbol of Scottish independence, but Columba reportedly appeared to several kings, advising on military conquests. Relics of both Columba and the 8th-century monk Fillan were prominently used to rally Scottish troops at the battle of Bannockburn in 1314.

National movements, however, were soon eclipsed by the Protestant Reformation, which shook the British Isles as it had the rest of Europe. At first, the Protestants rigorously opposed any association with the saints of old. Such devotion, they believed, smacked of idolatry. The first Protestant bishop of St David's in Wales, for example, even recommended that his headquarters be moved to another town to end the area's 'ungodly image service, abominable idolatry, and popish pilgrimage'. Relics were destroyed. Monasteries were closed. Someone even attacked Glastonbury's thorn tree, supposedly planted by Joseph of Arimathea himself. The Roman Catholics, meanwhile, begged Mary to 'awake Columba and Patrick' for help.

Protestants and Patrick

Starting with English reformer and Bible translator William Tyndale (c. 1494–1536), however, Protestants too saw their image reflected in the early Christian Celts. Christianity had found its way to the Celtic lands without any help from Rome, they argued. In fact, things only started to go wrong when Augustine showed up, in one reformer's words, 'to prepare Antichrist a seat here in England'. As archbishop of Canterbury Matthew Parker wrote in 1572:

There was a great difference between the Christianity of the Britons and the false Christianity which St Augustine of Canterbury gave the Saxons. The Britons kept their Christianity pure and immaculate, without admixture of human imaginings. Augustine's Christianity veered rather from the matchless purity of the Gospel and was mixed in with much superficiality, human opinions, and vain ceremonies, which did not accord with the nature of the kingdom of Christ.

Few were more adamant in their belief that the Christian Celts were Protestants than Calvinist theologian James Ussher (1581–1656), appointed archbishop of Armagh in 1625. One of his first books, *A Discourse of the Religion anciently professed by the Irish,* sought to prove once and for all that 'the religion professed by the ancient bishops, priests, monks, and other Christians in this land, was for substance the very same' as his own.

Roman Catholics shot back with their own arguments about how they were the continuation of Celtic Christianity. These arguments continued through the centuries (and can still be heard today). But other forces – including patriotism, denominationalism and antiquarianism – joined in the 18th and 19th centuries to form what Ian Bradley sees as Celtic Christianity's fourth revivalist movement. It was also the time of Romanticists, who 'discovered' that Celtic Christianity fitted well with their ideology too. Romanticists were quick to assert that Celtic Christianity had much in common with pre-Christian Celtic beliefs. This belief actually began with the assertion that Celtic pagans 'had a religion so extremely like Christianity that in effect it differed from it only in this: they believed in a Messiah who was to come into this world, as we believe in him that is to come'. Modelled on Christian priests, the druids became described as the white-robed peacemongers so recognizable today.

De-Christianizing Celtic Christianity

By the end of the 1800s, Romanticists had switched the order – Christianity was a mere gloss on Celtic paganism. In a movement that

W.B. Yeats called the 'Celtic Twilight', writers emphasized the Celts' love of nature over their love of Christ. Pantheism, not Christianity, was the true Celtic creed. Bradley notes that when George Russell wrote of Ireland 'long ago known as the sacred isle', he was not referring to the works of Patrick but to the fact that 'the gods lived there'.

'Ever since the early Christian monks of the Celtic Church set themselves the task of recording and adapting the achievements of Celtic paganism, a long line of Celtic antiquaries and scholars have devoted themselves to the same task right to the present day.'

Norman Davies, *The Isles*

Celticism had become more detached from Christianity in the Victorian era. 'Celtic Christianity was now chic [but] secularized and domesticated,' writes Bradley. 'Motifs that properly belonged on liturgical vessels were turning up on dressing tables and in drawing rooms . . . It is from this period that the fashion dates of wearing jewellery based on Celtic designs, and especially of pendants and necklaces in the form of Celtic crosses.'

The Celtic Twilight movement influenced the world's view of Celtic Christianity, but not everyone bought into its pantheistic views. What stuck were notions that the Celts had been ecologically minded, gentle, and at least friendly to the pagans they encountered. Many orthodox Christians, however, believed that this fitted well with their beliefs. One such person was Alexander Carmichael, the son of Scottish farmers from the island of Linsmore. A travelling taxman, Carmichael began befriending the locals he met on his journeys and wrote down thousands of prayers and blessings from their histories and memories. Published in six volumes between 1900 and 1961 (only the first two were edited and published during his lifetime), the *Carmina Gadelica* is still used today as a source for traditional Celtic Christian spirituality. Carmichael even found hymns sung before prayer:

I am bending my knee
in the eye of the Father who created me,
in the eye of the Son who purchased me,
in the eye of the Spirit who cleansed me,
   in friendship and affection.
Through Thine own Anointed One, O God,
bestow upon us fullness in our need,

love towards God,
the affection of God,
the smile of God,
the wisdom of God,
the grace of God,
the fear of God,
and the will of God
to do on the world of the Three,
as angels and saints
do in heaven;
each shade and light,
each day and night,
each time in kindness,
give Thou us Thy Spirit.

Another prayer echoes the *Lorica* falsely attributed to Patrick. Carmichael heard it from Mary Macrae, a 'brave kindly woman with her strong Highland characteristics and her proud Highland spirit', who danced and sang her traditional songs on the Isle of Harris in the face of condemnation.

God with me lying down,
God with me rising up,
God with me in each ray of light,
nor I a ray of joy without Him,
nor one ray without Him.

Christ with me sleeping,
Christ with me waking,
Christ with me watching,
every day and night,
each day and night.

God with me protecting,
the Lord with me directing,
the Spirit with me strengthening,
for ever and for evermore.
Ever and evermore, Amen.
Chief of chiefs, Amen.

Carmichael's *Carmina Gadelica* has formed the backbone of countless recent books on Celtic spirituality, but modern academics complain that he apparently 'improved' them after encountering them in the

Highlands, making fishermen and milkmaids speak with the euphonic, literary style of late Victorian English. One scholar even accuses him of trying to make the prayers sound as ancient as possible when there was no reason for it. In any case, says Bradley:

The notion of a sacred deposit of religious poetry, originally dating from the golden age of Celtic Christianity and still surviving largely unchanged after nearly one a half millennia of oral transmission from generation to generation, however appealing, is difficult to sustain.

While Protestants continued to invoke the names of Columba, Aidan and others in their opposition to Roman Catholicism, a rising ecumenical movement also saw its aims reflected as it gazed into the past. One of the leaders of this movement was a Protestant minister from Glasgow named George MacLeod. He convinced the governors of the island of Iona to let him rebuild the Benedictine abbey on the island, which had been closed since the Reformation. It would be built in 1938 just as it had in Columba's time, by volunteers and those who planned to live and work there in community. It was not the only way that MacLeod attempted to imitate the 6th-century Irish exile. 'The day, organized with military precision, began with reveille at 6.45 a.m., and a swim [naked] in the freezing sea,' wrote MacLeod's biographer. 'He insisted that the Celtic monks bathed in the sea every day of the year and resisted the arguments of faint-hearted ordinands who failed to see why they should slavishly follow masochistic Celtic customs.' Today more than 250,000 pilgrims visit the island annually, seeking what MacLeod called a 'thin place with only a tissue paper separating earth from heaven'.

The recent craze

Bradley dates the launch of the modern revival of Celtic Christianity to the early 1960s. Paperback anthologies began to take prayers of the *Carmina Gadelica* to the masses, writers began emphasizing Celtic theology and spirituality over interchurch rivalries, and marketers realized the potential of Celtic products, from albums of music to jewellery. By the 1980s, the Celtic craze was in full swing.

What happened to Whitby?

If the resurgence of Iona as a place of Celtic Christian revivalism illustrates the appropriation of the past, then Streanaeshalch (Whitby) may illustrate the neglect of it. For years, large pieces of the abbey graveyard have dropped onto the beach 150 feet below the old monastery. The cliffs Streanaeshalch sit on are too dangerous for archaeologists, so the graves of Hilda, Caedmon (the first Anglo-Saxon poet), and artefacts from King Oswy's era risked exposure, damage or irretrievable loss. Fortunately, a new, experimental digger was employed in 2001 to rescue the site. 'We've just got a tiny window of time to retrieve what could be vital clues about our past,' the English Heritage's Peter Busby told *The Guardian*. 'If we had left this dig any longer, an awful lot of history could have fallen into the North Sea and into oblivion.' Sadly, many associate the abbey not with history, but with Bram Stoker's fictional Dracula (who is shipwrecked near the abbey). The area visitors' centre is even emphasizing the vampire in its remodelling of its exhibits. The town of Whitby, meanwhile, has been a relatively prosperous fishing port since the Middle Ages.

The Celtic Twilight movement's pro-pagan and syncretistic attitudes never set. Instead, many of today's books on the Celts – even ones focusing on Celtic spirituality after the cultural acceptance of Christianity – can be found in the neo-pagan, mythology, or New Age sections of bookstores. It is rarely because the books have been wrongly shelved. 'Far from rejecting their old religion, the Christian Celts continued to hold it in the deepest respect, absorbing many of its ideas and attitudes, symbols and rituals, into their new faith,' wrote Anglican priest Robert Van de Weyer in *Celtic Fire*. 'Christianity involved no change in moral belief.' (Patrick, who laments the attitudes of his pagan companions in his *Confessio,* may disagree.)

In her books *The Celtic Year* and *The Celtic Alternative,* Shirley Toulson sees the religion of the golden-age saints as reminiscent of many religions other than orthodox Christianity. After noting 'how much Celtic Christianity was open to the influence of 1st-century Judaism', Toulson asserts:

I am sure that if we want to understand the depths of Celtic spirituality we shall find the nearest parallels in the Buddhist teaching of today as well as in the creation spirituality of such Christian teachers as Matthew Fox [an excommunicated priest].

De-emphasizing the Christianity of Christian Celts has allowed these recent writers, like so many of their past revivalists, to emphasize their own agendas. The 'greenness' of the ancient saints is not a new concept, but it has taken a particular emphasis as environmentalism became more the vogue in the 1980s and 1990s. The point of view of writer John Matthews is clear from the title of one of his books *The Arthurian Tarot.* In another of his books, aimed at a more Christian subject, he writes:

When we read . . . the lives of the Celtic saints, we perceive the same fundamental truths that are present in the lives of the gods and heroes of the past: a love of the earth, of the pattern of the seasons, of the magical presence of animals, of the beauty of the revealed earth.

Theologically conservative Christians began reclaiming the Celtic saints as their own in the early 1990s. Leaders of the Church of England's charismatic movement were among the first to counter the neo-pagan and syncretistic approaches of their contemporaries and to encourage their evangelical comrades in drawing inspiration from the Celtic Christians. 'Evangelism, in Britain at least, has gained a bad name,' Ray Simpson laments in *Exploring Celtic Spirituality: Historic Roots for Our Future.* '[But] one thing that the Celtic churches had in common was a missionary spirit.' As a charismatic, Simpson also found similarities between Celtic Christianity and his movement's emphasis on spiritual warfare, miracles, healing, prophecy, and other spiritual gifts.

> 'It is indeed necessary for the church to address modern concerns, but the solutions lie not in a retreat to a mythical Celtic past, but, as always, in a sensitive Christian engagement with the present and the future.'
>
> **Donald E. Meek, 'Modern Myths of the Medieval Past',** *Christian History*

As interest in Celtic Christianity grew, Christians also began creating works 'in the Celtic tradition'. One of the key creators of this genre has been David Adam, vicar of Lindisfarne. His prayers echo the repetition of the *Carmina Gadelica, Loricae* and other Celtic works: 'Blessed are you, Creator, and giver of peace. Peace be upon us; peace be upon this place; peace be upon this day. The deep, deep peace of God, which the world cannot give, be upon us and remain with us always.' Adam, however, is no Celt, and neither, notes Bradley, are most of the authors writing about Celtic Christianity in the current revival (including this author). Instead, they are:

. . . virtually all English, albeit in some cases with Celtic connections. It is reminiscent of the contribution made by Bede and the Anglo-Norman chroniclers . . . in the first two revivals. There is a similar agenda of romantic idealization, compounded by the certain guilt-induced acknowledgement of the validity of a marginalized tradition and a fascination with the 'outsider' and the 'other.'

This has provoked several modern historians to attack the modern fascination with Celtic Christianity as stuff and nonsense. 'From their southern perspectives, most of our writers reach out to embrace the northern "fringes" of the British Isles, often placing a great deal of emphasis on what might be termed the "purity of the periphery",' writes Donald Meek, chair of Celtic Studies at the University of Aberdeen. 'Those of us who inhabit the fringes find this kind of writing a little patronizing.'

Meek is one of the most vocal critics of the modern revival of Celtic Christianity, saying it has nothing to do with Christianity in the British Isles before 1100 and everything to do with wishful thinking:

'In the context of the current revival, it is tempting to suggest that Celtic Christianity is less an actual phenomenon defined in historical and geographical terms than an artificial construct created out of wishful thinking, romantic nostalgia, and the projection of all kinds of dreams about what should and might be.'

Ian Bradley, Celtic Christianity: Making Myths and Chasing Dreams

'Celtic Christianity' in short, tends to scratch the many itches of our ecclesiastical bodies, public and personal. Given the profusion of our itches, it is hardly surprising that this interpretation of early Christianity in the British Isles crosses denominational, and even religious, boundaries.

Other scholars have gone even farther than Meek, suggesting that any concept of 'Celtic Christianity' past or present is a myth. Still, Meek and others do not see historical Celtic Christianity as untouchable, a practice best left on the shelf. 'There is much that all Christians can appreciate in the hymns, prayers, and stories of the Irish saints, although their message can be fully understood only be diligent scrutiny of the texts in their original forms,' he wrote. To this end, he and other historians are busy debunking myths and promoting areas of similarity, not difference, between Celtic Christians and their religious kindred on the continent.

These scholars are particularly frustrated with the modern revival's emphasis on Christian Celts as nature lovers. Many hagiographies are filled with stories of encounters with animals, but their purpose was rarely to demonstrate the saints' environmental concerns. Adomnán's tale of a crane visiting Iona is one of the most cited evidences of the Celts' 'greenness'. At Columba's order (for he had prophesied the crane's arrival), one of the monks picked the crane up 'gently in its weakness, and carried it to a dwelling that was near, where in its hunger he fed it'. After three days of such care, the bird regained its strength and flew back to where it came from – Northern Ireland. But Adomnán was not demonstrating, as one writer argued, that 'hospitality means welcoming all God's creatures'. Instead, the hagiographer is attempting to show Columba's gift of prophecy. Meek points out another important reason for the story: 'Here Columba is affirming his Irish ancestral roots, and the crane acts as a specific link between the exile and his homeland.' Ignoring the meaning behind the tales is like taking Jesus' words, 'Consider the lilies of the field . . .' as an ecological command.

Modern environmentalists also ignore the past emphasis on dominion over creation. In the *Life of Columba,* the saint opposes nature more often than he indulges in it. 'Partly by mortification, and partly by a bold resistance, he subdued, with the help of Christ, the furious rage of wild beasts,' Adomnán writes in the third sentence of the hagiography. 'The surging waves, also, at times rolling mountains high in a great tempest, became quickly at his prayer quiet and smooth, and his ship, in which he then happened to be, reached the desired haven in a perfect calm.' Animals were used to illustrate God's (and the saints') power and holiness, but this was not unique to the Celts. Even Augustine of Hippo (whom Bradley says 'became the bogeyman for a new breed of pro-Celtic theologians who blamed him for giving Western Christianity its obsession with sin and guilt') revelled in natural splendours. 'With a great voice they cried out, "He made us",' he wrote. 'My question was the attention I gave to them; their response was their beauty.'

While acknowledging that 'wherever and whenever Christians are or have been found there have been differences in the ways they have believed and acted upon those beliefs,' historians are being careful to emphasize that these differences did not mean there was any thing like a 'Celtic church'. 'Far from being different, Celtic Christianity was very much like the faith of the church elsewhere,' says Dominican friar and scholar Gilbert Márkus:

There were differences in detail between the Celtic Christians and their continental neighbours: church architecture, Easter dates, inheritance laws, and local traditions. But almost all the main features of early Celtic Christianity could be found anywhere in Catholic Europe, where every tribe and tongue and nation made the gospel their own. The Celts found their own way of retelling the old story all the while sharing one recognizable faith.

'Even if an authentic Celtic Christian culture is in a certain sense exclusive, and to a large degree a thing of the past, there are still all kinds of ways in which we may learn from this inheritance and make its wisdom our own.'

Oliver Davies and Fiona Bowie, *Celtic Christian Spirituality*

That recognizable faith was not one that looked back at a golden age, even to the time of Jesus and the apostles. Instead, it was forward-looking, to the end of days. As Patrick wrote near the end of his *Confessio*:

For this sun which we now see rises each new day for us at [God's] command, yet it will never reign, nor will its splendour last forever. On the contrary, all who worship it today will be doomed to dreadful punishment. But we who believe and adore the true sun that is Christ, who will never die, nor will those who have done his will but abide forever just as Christ himself will abide for all eternity: who reigns with God the Father almighty, and with the Holy Spirit before time began, and now and through all ages of ages. Amen.

CHRONOLOGY

700 BC Iron Age remains from Celtic tribes, especially near modern Austria's Lake Hallstatt, date from this period.

450 BC La Tène culture begins, as Celtic tribes fashion elaborate metal objects.

390 BC Brennus's Celtic army attacks Rome.

335 BC Alexander the Great meets Celtic chieftains near the Adriatic Sea.

279 BC Celtic tribes sack Delphi, Greece and its shrines.

101 BC Gaius Marius begins conquering Celtic territories.

58–51 BC Julius Caesar conquers Gaul, resulting in one million dead.

55 BC Caesar briefly attacks Britain.

AD 1–50 Legends say Jesus' apostles, family members, or even Christ himself preached to Celts in Gaul and Britain during this time.

AD 43 40,000 Roman soldiers invade Britain.

AD 49 The apostle Paul chastises churches in Galatia in a letter.

AD 122 Hadrian's wall erected.

C. AD 177 Christian Celts among martyrs at Lyons under persecution orders of Marcus Aurelius.

C. AD 178 Irenaeus, one of the leading Christian scholars of the 2nd century, becomes bishop of Lyons and one of the first missionaries to the Celts.

AD 178 Symphorian of Autun, a Christian from Gaul, is beheaded for his religion.

AD 250 Rome sends seven bishops to establish churches in Gaul, likely adding to a growing movement there.

C. AD 250 (contested) Alban is executed for hiding a priest and renouncing Roman paganism, becoming Britain's first recorded Christian martyr.

AD 314 Bishops from Britain and the rest of the growing Christian world meet at the Council of Arles, in Gaul, to settle the Donatist schism, ask Pope Sylvester to set a common date for Easter, and address other issues.

AD 357 Publication of Athanasius's *Life of Antony* inspires monasticism across the Christian world, including the British Isles.

AD 407 Emperor Honorius starts pulling Roman troops out of Britain.

AD 417 Pope Innocent I excommunicates Pelagius, a British Christian who denied the doctrine of original sin.

AD 431 Pope Celestine sends Palladius, an anti-Pelagian deacon, to Ireland. ➡

AD 432 (disputed) Patrick, a British Christian who had earlier been a slave in Ireland, returns to the island as a missionary.

c. AD 432 (contested) Ninian dies. He had founded Candida Casa, a stone church, in what is now Whithorn, Scotland. The site eventually became one of the centres of Celtic monasticism.

c. AD 468 (contested) Brigid, a legendary figure who became Ireland's other patron saint with Patrick, founds a double monastery at Kildare.

c. AD 484 Énda founds a monastery at Inishmore, reportedly Ireland's first.

c. AD 500 Illtud founds Llanilltud Fawr (now Llantwit Major in Glamorgan).

c. AD 500 Ronán leaves Ireland for Brittany.

c. AD 558 Comgall, an Irish Pict, founds a monastery at Bangor, Ireland, after plans to become a travelling missionary fail.

AD 561 Brendan, whose reported sea voyage to the Land of Promise became a favourite medieval tale, founds a monastery at Clúain Ferta Brénaind (Clonfert).

AD 562 Columba founds a monastery on the island of Iona, which would become one of the most powerful in all the British Isles.

c. AD 565 (contested) Samson of Dol, whose monastery in Dol became the centre of the Church in Brittany, dies.

c. AD 570 Gildas, who castigated radical asceticism in *The Ruin and Conquest of Britain,* dies.

AD 596 Pope Gregory sends the Roman bishop Augustine and 40 monks on an evangelistic mission to Britain.

c. AD 601 David of Wales, whose Mynyw (now St David's) became one of the most ascetical monasteries in Britain, reportedly dies at the age of 147.

AD 613 Having left Ireland to establish dozens of monasteries on the European continent, Columbanus dies in Italy.

AD 618 Kevin (Cóemgen) dies, having founded a monastery in the 'glen of the two lakes' (Glendalough) in the Wicklow mountains, where he had initially sought isolation.

AD 644 Fursa, an Irish missionary monk known for his visions, founds a monastery at Lagny, near Paris.

AD 664 At the Synod of Whitby, King Oswy of Northumbria chooses the Roman method of calculating Easter over the Celtic method.

AD 672 Synod of Hertford cracks down on widespread Celtic practices such as wandering monks.

c. AD 695 Muirchú moccu Mactheni writes his *Life of St Patrick.*

AD 697 The Synod of Birr enacts Adomnán's 'Law of the Innocents', a landmark in legal history and human rights.

AD 741 Bede, an Anglo-Saxon historian, completes his *Ecclesiastical History.* It attacks Celtic dates for Easter and other such practices, but praises Celtic saints for their holiness.

AD 767 Iona finally accepts the Roman method of setting Easter.

c. AD 790 Irish monks settle in Iceland.

AD 793 Vikings raid several British monasteries and churches, including Lindisfarne.

AD 795 Vikings raid Iona in the first of several raids.

AD 839 Vikings establish their first winter camp in Ireland.

1093 Queen Margaret of Scotland dies.

1314 Relics of Celtic saints like Columba are used to rally Scottish troops against the English at the battle of Bannockburn.

1623 Calvinist theologian James Ussher, archbishop of Armagh, argues that early Celtic Christians were proto-Protestants in *A Discourse of the Religion anciently professed by the Irish.*

1893 W.B. Yeats begins publishing *The Celtic Twilight,* a series of essays on Irish folklore and mythical creatures.

1900 The first volume of Alexander Carmichael's *Carmina Gadelica,* a collection of old Scottish prayers and blessings, is published.

1938 George MacLeod, a Protestant minister from Glasgow, founds the Iona community in an effort to recapture the beliefs and practices of Columba and other Celtic monks.

1995 Thomas Cahill's *How the Irish Saved Civilization* ignites a wave of interest in Ireland's monastic history.

FURTHER READING

The Expansion of Christianity

General overviews

J. Combey, *How to Understand the History of Christian Mission* (Norwich: SCM Press, 1996).

K.S. Latourette, *A History of the Expansion of Christianity* (7 vols) (New York: Harper and Row, 1971).

Stephen Neill, *A History of Christian Missions* revised edition (London: Penguin, 1986).

Africa

Adrian Hastings, *The Church in Africa 1450–1950* (Oxford: Oxford University Press, 1994).

E. Isichei, *A History of Christianity in Africa* (London: SPCK, 1995).

B.G.M. Sundkler and C. Steed, *A History of the Church in Africa* (Cambridge: Cambridge University Press, 2000).

Asia

S.H. Moffett, *A History of Christianity in Asia: Beginnings to 1500* (Maryknoll: Orbis, 1998).

S. Sundquist (ed.), *A Dictionary of Asian Christianity* (Grand Rapids: Eerdmans, 2001).

Latin America

E. Dussel (ed.), *The Church in Latin America 1492–1992* (New York: Burns and Oates, 1992).

Oceania

I. Breward, *A History of the Churches of Australasia* (Oxford: Oxford University Press, 2001).

C.W. Forman, *The Island Churches of the South Pacific* (Maryknoll: Orbis, 1982).

Special studies

David Bosch, *Transforming Mission* (Maryknoll: Orbis, 1991).

A. Harnack, *The Mission and Expansion of Christianity*, tr. J. Moffatt (New York: Harper, 1904).

Andrew Ross, *A Vision Betrayed: The Jesuits in Japan 1542–1742* (Edinburgh: Edinburgh University Press, 1994).

Andrew Ross, *David Livingstone: Mission and Empire* (Hambledon and London: 2002).

Andrew Walls, *The Missionary Movement in Christian History* (Edinburgh: T & T Clark, 1996).

Timothy Yates, *Christian Mission in the Twentieth Century* (Cambridge: Cambridge University Press, 1994).

Useful reference works

G.H. Anderson (ed.), *Biographical Dictionary of Christian Missions* (New York: Simon & Schuster, 1998).

David Barrett (ed.), *World Christian Encyclopedia* (2 vols) (Oxford: Oxford University Press, 2001).

T. Dowley (ed.), *The Atlas of the Bible and the History of Christianity* (Swindon: British and Foreign Bible Society, 1997).

S.C. Neill, G.H. Anderson and J. Goodwin, *A Concise Dictionary of the Christian World Mission* (London: Lutterworth Press, 1970).

Larger church dictionaries

F.L. Cross and E.A. Livingstone, *The Oxford Dictionary of the Christian Church*, 3rd edition (Oxford: Oxford University Press, 1997).

New Catholic Encyclopedia (15 vols) (New York: McGraw-Hill, 1967).

Christianity and the Celts

As noted in Chapter 17, books on Celtic Christianity and 'spirituality' have been legion for more than a millennium, but the recent flood of titles since the mid-1990s is enough to overwhelm even the fondest enthusiast. One of the best overviews – for both readability and academic credibility – dates from just before this most recent fascination. Some of the information in J.T. McNeill's *The Celtic Churches* (Chicago: University of Chicago, 1974) is now outdated, but I am heavily indebted to his narrative work for this volume.

As ancient documents go, the primary source material for the ancient Celtic saints holds up remarkably well for the modern reader. There are, of course, several excellent translations of Patrick's *Confessio* and *Letter to the Soldiers* of Coroticus (such as John Skinner's, New York: Doubleday, 1998), and some new publications – Máire B. de Paor's *Patrick* (Veritas, 1998) and Thomas O'Loughlin's *Saint Patrick* (London: SPCK, 1999) include fascinating notes.

Celtic Spirituality (Mahwah: Paulist Press, 1999) includes Patrick's works of course, but it is invaluable for its other primary source materials; Oliver Davies's translations of hagiographies, penitentials, poetry, sermons and other works is invaluable. Liam de Paor's *Saint Patrick's World* (Dublin: Four Courts Press, 1993) and Uinseann Ó Maindín's *The Celtic Monk* (Collegeville: Liturgical Press, 1996) also let the Celtic Christians speak for themselves.

Most books on Celtic Christianity concentrate on the lives of a few extraordinary saints and use the daily life of monastic communities only to illustrate the sanctity of their subjects. Lisa Bitel's *Isle of the Saints* (Ithaca: Cornell University Press, 1990) instead focuses on 'ordinary' life at these monasteries, from the role of food to views of labour. Meanwhile, Richard J. Woods's *The Spirituality of the Celtic Saints* (Maryknoll: Orbis, 2000) attempts to draw attention to lesser-known leaders of the faith.

A host of books combine rich illustrations with reliable history to tell the story of the pre-Christian Celts. Among the better ones are Simon James's *The World of the Celts*

(London: Thames and Hudson, 1993) and Barry Cunlifee's *The Celtic World* (New York: St Martin's Press, 1990).

Other helpful books include

Bede, translated by Leo Sherley-Price, *A History of the English Church and People* (London: Penguin, 1955).

Ian Bradley, *Celtic Christianity: Making Myths and Chasing Dreams* (New York: St Martin's Press, 1999).

John B. Bury, *The Life of St Patrick and His Place in History* (New York: Macmillan, 1905).

Thomas Cahill, *How the Irish Saved Civilization* (London: Doubleday, 1995).

T.M. Charles-Edwards, *Early Christian Ireland* (Cambridge: Cambridge University Press, 2000).

Norman Davies, *The Isles: A History* (Oxford: Oxford University Press, 1999).

Oliver Davies and Fiona Bowie, *Celtic Christian Spirituality: An Anthology of Medieval and Modern Sources* (London: Continuum, 1995).

Denise Dersin (ed.), *What Life Was Like Among Druids and High Kings* (Time Life, 1998).

James P. Mackey (ed.), *An Introduction to Celtic Christianity* (Edinburgh: T & T Clark, 1995).

Thomas O'Loughlin, *Journeys on the Edges: The Celtic Tradition* (London: Darton, Longman and Todd, 2000).

Thomas O'Loughlin, *Celtic Theology: Humanity, World and God in Early Irish Writings* (London: Continuum, 2000).

Máire de Paor and Liam de Paor, *Early Christian Ireland* (London: Thames and Hudson, 1958).

Steve Rabey, *In the House of Memory: Ancient Celtic Wisdom for Everyday Life* (Boston: Dutton Press, 1998).

Katherine Scherman, *The Flowering of Ireland: Saints, Scholars and Kings* (London: Little, Brown and Co., 1981).

Edward C. Sellner, *Wisdom of the Celtic Saints* (Notre Dame: Ave Maria Press, 1993).

TEXT ACKNOWLEDGEMENTS

The Expansion of Christianity

Scripture quotations taken from the *New Revised Standard Version Bible*, copyright © 1989, 1995 National Council of the Churches of Christ in the United States of America. Used by permission. All rights reserved worldwide.

Christianity and the Celts

Extracts from Bede are translated by Leo Sherley-Price and are taken from *A History of the English Church and People* (London: Penguin, 1955).

Extracts from Patrick's works are taken from the following sources:

St Patrick: The Man and His Works by Thomas O'Loughlin (London: SPCK, 1999).

The Confession of St Patrick, translated by John Skinner (New York: Image/Doubleday, 1998).

Celtic Spirituality by Oliver Davies (Mahwah: Paulist Press, 1999).

Saint Patrick's World by Liam de Paor (Dublin: Four Courts Press, 1993).

Other extracts:

p. 183: The *Lorica,* translated by Oliver Davies. Text in *Thesaurus Palaeohibernicus,* edited by Whitely Stokes and John Strachan (Cambridge: Cambridge University Press, 1903), 2:296. Taken from *Celtic Christian Spirituality: An Anthology of Medieval and Modern Sources,* edited by Oliver Davies and Fiona Bowie (London: Continuum, 1995), copyright © 1995 Oliver Davies and Fiona Bowie.

pp. 189–90: 'All alone in my little cell . . .' translated by Oliver Davies, from *Kuno Meyer, Eriu* 2, pp. 55–56. Taken from *Celtic Christian Spirituality: An Anthology of Medieval and Modern Sources,* edited by Oliver Davies and Fiona Bowie (London: Continuum, 1995), copyright © 1995 Oliver Davies and Fiona Bowie.

p. 194: 'Psalm-singer, beginning student . . .' translated from *Kuno Meyer, 'Mitteilungen au irischen Handschriften'* (ZCP 5, 1905), pp. 498–99. Taken from *Isle of the Saints,* copyright © 1990 Lisa Bitel. Used by permission of the publisher, Cornell University Press.

p. 195: 'Lord, be it thine . . .' translated by Robin Flower, from *Poems and Translations* (Dublin: The Lilliput Press, 1994). Used by permission.

p. 196: 'The clear-voiced bell . . .' translated by Robin Flower, from *Poems and Translations* (Dublin: The Lilliput Press, 1994). Used by permission.

p. 196: 'A hedge of trees . . .' translated by Gerard Murphy. Taken from *Early*

Irish Lyrics (Dublin: Four Courts Press, 1998). Used by permission.

pp. 196–97: 'Pangur Bán . . .' from 'The Student and His White Cat', translated by Robin Flower, from *Poems and Translations* (Dublin: The Lilliput Press, 1994). Used by permission.

pp. 255–56: 'I am bending my knee . . .' and 'God with me lying down . . .' from *Carmina Gadelica, Hymns and Incantations from the Gaelic*, collected and edited by Alexander Carmichael (Edinburgh: Floris Books, 1992). Used by permission.

INDEX

The Expansion of Christianity

G

Genghis Khan 35, 37, 38
Graul, K. 90, 94
Gregory I (Pope) 43
Gregory VII (Pope) 49
Gregory the Illuminator 26, 80
Guarani 73, 74
Gutzlaff, K. 62, 105

H

Harris, William Wade 67, 125, 127, 128
Henry the Navigator 54, 55, 69
Hilda of Whitby 43
Huddleston, Trevor 130, 131
Hunt, J. 116
Hus, J. 53, 85
Hutu 132

I

Ignatius of Antioch 14
Ignatius of Loyola 95
Ingoli, F. 85, 95
Innocent III (Pope) 50, 51
Innocent IV (Pope) 35
Iroquois 76, 77, 79, 81
Islam 8, 9, 30, 34, 44, 52, 64, 100

J

Jesuits 38, 54, 57, 58, 67, 69, 72, 73–77, 79, 85, 95, 96, 97, 99, 107
Jesus Christ 10, 11, 12, 14, 16, 29
Johnson, W.A.B. 59, 90
Josephus 10, 11

Junod, H. 93
Justin Martyr 17

K

Kemp, J. van der 61, 65, 66, 90
Kikuyu 129
Kimbangu, Simon 127
Kino, E. 75
Kraemer, H. 134, 135
Krapf, J.L. 55, 64, 90
Kublai Khan 35, 36, 37

L

Lavigerie, Cardinal 55, 64, 92
Legge, J. 93, 104
Lenshina, Alice 130
Leopold II of Belgium 63, 127
Limbrock, E. 119, 120
Livingstone, D. 8, 55, 60–63, 80, 89, 126
Llull, R. 52
London Missionary Society 61, 62, 66–67, 89, 90–91, 93, 101, 104–105, 108, 110–11, 114, 117–18
Luke 10, 11–12, 13, 14, 16, 23, 41, 64, 135
Luwum, J. 124, 129

M

Marists 92, 115, 117
Marsden, S. 111, 112
Martyn, H. 99, 100
Maurizius, J. 79
Mayhew, T. 79–80
Mercedarians 74
Methodios 46

Moffatt, R. 8, 61–62, 65, 89, 110
Mokone, M. 67, 124
Moody, D.L. 92
Moravians 55, 61, 80, 83, 85–87, 91, 101, 113
Morrison, R. 89, 104, 105
Moshoeshoe 65, 66
Mutesa 63, 64, 65
Mwanga 64, 65

N

Netherlands Missionary Society 61, 90, 105
Neuendettelsau Missionary Society 90, 119, 120
Nevius, J.L. 108
Nobili, R. de 8, 85, 98

O

Opium Wars 62, 105
Origen 16, 17, 27, 160

P

Padroado 70, 98
Paris Evangelical Mission 65–66, 67, 90, 118
Paton, J.G. 117
Patrick 39, 40
Patteson, J.C. 112, 113, 116
Paul 8, 12–14, 16, 19
Paulinus 43, 44
Peter 8, 10, 11, 12, 14, 23
Philip, J. 55, 61, 84
Picpus Fathers 92, 115
Pietism 85, 86, 87, 88, 89, 90, 91
Pizarro 69, 70

Christianity and the Celts